What students are saying:

"I just completed my first MCAT CARS review with Matthew. To sum it all up, it was a great session. We went over some practice passages, emphasizing how to critically analyze them. His feedback and advice were both very helpful. Even by the end of the session, I felt that I improved. I can't wait to read more passages and critically analyze them using this helpful technique."
– Emmanuel

"I had an amazing session with Jessica today. She was really helpful to point out what I need to work on but also how to work on it. Really professional and patient, Jessica gave me really good feedback throughout the whole session." – Olivier

"Excellent service. They work on each of your weaknesses and guide you on how to overcome your weakness. Highly recommended." – WS

"Charlene was very attentive and went over time to make sure I understood the CARS passage accurately, which I really appreciate. She also gave me tips based on what mistakes I made that I think will be helpful in the future as I continue practicing. Thank you!" – Customer

"I just had a session with Nyasha and it was a great session. She was very patient and detailed and she helped me a lot for my coming test. I felt more confident for the test after the consulting session. Full recommendation!"
– Ruihan

D1361817

"Excellent session I had with Ashley. I thank her for all the help she provided. She was very patient with me and made sure that I was on the same page as her before moving on. I strongly recommend her to other students."
– Christine

"Jillian is such a great advisor to work with. She provides thorough feedback and gently prompts you through realizing any mistakes you have made so you can recognize them and learn. I had a great session with her :) Would definitely recommend. Thanks, Jillian!" – Ali

"I really enjoyed the session. I felt that it was tailored to my needs instead of it just being a scripted session. I also felt more confident about my abilities after the session." – Customer

"This has been such a helpful service! They are very responsive and all advisors are so helpful and professional." – Customer

"Amazing advice. They were extremely good at their job. They know what they are doing!!!" – Niki

"Very insightful session. Learnt a lot about my strengths and weakness and I feel very confident about the real deal now." – Ashir

"My session with Diana was great! She is passionate, funny and professional. I have more confidence than before. So worth it!" – Bonny

"Jillian was an insightful and helpful instructor. She gave me instructive feedback in a calm, collected and friendly manner. I felt like having a session with her was helpful for my overall progress. :-)" – Ian

"Their program allows you to speak 1-on-1 to experts in the field and they really tailor their advice to you." – Customer

"I had a wonderful experience with BeMo's services. Everyone was very kind and encouraging throughout the whole process." – Stefania

"I can't say more positive things about Mustafa! He has been one of my favorite BeMo consultants to work with. he is incredibly genuine, kind, and really cares about all his clients. I am so thankful to him and greatly appreciate the time and effort he put into helping me. I would 11/10 recommend Mustafa." – Pip

"The feedback was very specific, in-depth, and encouraging! I look forward to practicing the structures and strategies we reviewed." – Hannah

BeMo's Ultimate Guide to MCAT®* CARS

**How to Ace the MCAT CARS Using
A Simple 7-Step Process**

BeMo® Academic Consulting Inc.

ISBN 10: B08XG2WDPQ

ISBN 13: 9798711503019

CONTRIBUTING AUTHORS

Dr. Behrouz Moemeni, Ph.D., founder & CEO of BeMo

Dr. Meng Yang, Ph.D., admissions expert & associate lead trainer

Dr. Veena Netrakanti, M.D., admissions expert & lead trainer

Dr. Ashley Grimaldi, Ph.D., admissions expert

Dr. Jillian Kite, Ph.D., admissions expert

Ms. Ashley Witcher, Ph.D. (c), admissions expert

Ms. Ronza Nissan, M.A., admissions expert & lead trainer

Dr. Tatevik Nersisyan, Ph.D., admissions expert

Dr. Braydon Connell, M.D., admissions expert

Dr. Peter Gunderman, M.D., admissions expert

Dr. Monica Hoang, Ph.D. (c), admissions expert

Dr. Charlene Hoi, Ph.D., admissions expert

Ms. Yevgeniya Kramchenkova, M.A., content creator

Ms. Gurmeet Lall, Ph.D. (c), admissions expert

Ms. Ferd Marie Policarpio, B.A., admissions associate

Dr. David Schultz, D.O., admissions expert

Dr. Chen Xiong, Ph.D., admissions expert

Dr. Diana Fernandez, Ph.D., adminissions expert

Would you like us to help you ace the MCAT CARS section?

Go to
BeMoCARS.com

To Schedule Your FREE Initial Consultation Now!

Contents

Acknowledgments

We would like to thank our students and their parents for putting their trust in us and giving us the privilege of being a part of their journey. You have inspired us and taught us lessons we would not have learned on our own. Thank you for your continued support and for investing in our mission. You are the reason we get up in the morning.

We would like to thank the countless number of admissions deans, directors, officers, pre-health advisors and school counselors who have 'unofficially' supported our mission. Thank you for encouraging us and, most importantly, thank you for making us think critically. We appreciate what you do, and we understand the impossible task you face each and every day.

A huge thanks to our team members, both past and present. BeMo wouldn't be what it is today without you.

And, of course, a huge thanks to our family and friends who have been unconditionally supportive, even when we couldn't spend as much time with them because of our obsession with our mission here at BeMo.

Foreword

First, let us take a minute to acknowledge the step that you have decided to take to prepare for your journey ahead. So a BIG congratulations for committing to educate yourself to become a competitive applicant, a better individual, and an effective future professional! The fact that you have purchased this book tells us that you understand the value of continuous learning and self-improvement. The world rewards individuals who continuously seek to educate themselves because *knowledge is power*. Before we dive in, let's get on the same page about the purpose of this book, who this book is for, who it is NOT for, and why you should listen to us. But first, a few words from our founder and CEO, Behrouz Moemeni.

Why I Founded BeMo®: Message from BeMo's Founder and CEO, Dr. Behrouz Moemeni

Sometimes you must do what's necessary, even if the chances of success are slim to none. Students often ask me what gets me up in the morning and what motivated me to found BeMo. The answer for me is simple and has remained the same since day one.

I started BeMo with my cofounder, Dr. Mo Bayegan, in 2013 – see why it's called "BeMo" now? Our partnership began when we first met in high school back in 1996, and later solidified during our undergraduate and graduate years.

We both felt every student deserves access to higher education, whatever his or her social status or cultural background, because education is the best way to introduce positive change in our world.

Sadly, I believe most of the current admissions practices, tools, and procedures are biased, out-dated, and more importantly, scientifically unproven. Therefore, in 2013, as Mo and I were finishing our graduate studies, we decided to create BeMo to make sure no one is treated unfairly due to flawed admissions practices.

At the time, I was finishing my Ph.D. studies in Immunology at the University of Toronto, which was a transformational educational experience. I had the privilege of working with one of the sharpest minds in the field, Dr. Michael Julius. He taught me many things over the years, but two lessons stayed with me: 1) There is tremendous value in having curiosity about scientific or technological innovations to seek the truth rather than confirm one's own opinions, and 2) what you do has to be the reason that gets you up in the morning. Though I wasn't his best student, I was still relatively successful. I won 19 awards, was invited to 7 international conferences, and even had an unsolicited job offer before I had defended my thesis. The job would have given me a secure source of income and I would have been able to start paying my mounting student debt, but I ultimately decided to abandon a career in academia. Instead, I chose to start BeMo. Despite having many well-established competitors and an overall slim chance of success, I felt – and I still do to this day – that the mission was well worth the risk. I truly believe what we do here at BeMo adds more value to each of our students' lives than anything else I could have done in academia, and I would not trade it for the world.

Over the years, our amazing and steadily growing team has helped many students navigate the admissions process. We really couldn't have done it without them, and it's been a privilege to teach with them and learn from them over the years. (Thanks for sticking with us!)

We are aware that our methods are controversial in some circles; innovative ideas often are. However, we are confident in our belief – and the scientific literature supports this – that current admissions practices are rife with bias and must be improved.

This is why, in 2017, I founded another independent company called SortSmart®, which has created what I consider to be the fairest, most scientifically sound, and cost-effective admissions screening tool out there. I invite you to visit SortSmart.io to learn more, and to tell your university admissions office to bring SortSmart to your school.

In the meantime, while SortSmart is gaining momentum, we at BeMo, will continue to support students just like you to make sure no group of students is treated unfairly. You can rest assured that we will not stop until our goals have been achieved.

To your success,

Behrouz Moemeni, Ph.D.

CEO @ BeMo

A Bit About Us: BeMo Academic Consulting (BeMo)

We are an innovative academic consulting firm! This is a team comprised of energetic researchers and professionals, who use a proven evidence-based, and scientific approach to help prospective students with career path development and admissions to undergraduate, graduate, and professional programs such as medicine, law, dentistry, and pharmacy.

We believe your education is one of your most valuable assets, and learning how to become a stellar future professional or scholar doesn't need to be complicated. We also believe that each student deserves access to higher education, regardless of their social status or cultural background. However, most of the current admissions practices, tools, and procedures are biased, outdated, and more importantly, scientifically unproven.

Our goal is to create truly useful (and scientifically sound) programs and tools that work and provide more than just some trivial information like the other admissions consulting companies out there. We want to make sure everyone has a fair chance of admission to highly competitive professional programs despite current biases in admissions practices.

We do whatever it takes to come up with creative solutions and then test them like mad scientists. We are passionate about mentoring our students, we're obsessed with delivering useful educational programs, and we go where others dare not explore.

Why should you listen to us?

We are the leaders in admission preparation for extremely competitive professional schools. Each year, we help thousands of students gain admission to top schools around the world by assisting them with their application documents, CASPer tests, interviews of all styles, and MCAT preparation. We have an exceptional team of practicing professionals, medical doctors, scholars, and scientists who have served as former interview evaluators and admissions committee members. Learn more about our experts at BeMoAcademicConsulting.com.

What we are about to share with you in this book is based on what we learned in our sought-after, paid training programs. What we offer works and it works consistently. In fact, research has shown that our programs can increase applicants' application scores by up to 27% in simulated interviews. Our programs are in high demand and we are certain they will also work for you.

Why did we write this book?

There is so much misinformation surrounding the MCAT, from online forums to university clubs, and even some university guidance counselors and official test administrators. While some of this information is well-intended, the level of inaccuracy is astounding. In particular, the credibility of online forums can be called into question because it is not clear who the authors are or what motivations they have. These forums are frequently filled with fake profiles, some of them official university administrators and test administrators trying to control the flow of information so only their version of 'facts' is distributed. To make matters worse, some of these forums offer sponsorship opportunities to companies, which puts them in a financial conflict of interest. Also be wary of information from most student clubs because, again, these organizations frequently form financial relationships with companies to garner support for their operations and, as a result, receive and distribute one-sided information. Additionally, most books available are incomplete and tend to focus on teaching you 'tricks' about the test without offering a systematic strategy on how to perform well consistently. They do not focus on the big picture that is essential to your success as an applicant, test taker, and future practicing professional.

What is this book about?

This book is about helping you establish a consistent and effective approach to acing the Critical Analysis and Reasoning Skills (CARS) Section of the MCAT. We spend a considerable amount of time walking you through the pitfalls of CARS preparation, how to avoid making those mistakes, and ultimately how to succeed in this section of the test.

Who is this book for and who is it NOT for?

If you are applying to any program that requires you to take the Medical College Admission Test (MCAT), then this book is perfect for you. Regardless of where you are currently with your test preparation; whether you have written the test before and are retaking it, or you are a first-time test taker, this book has something for you, provided that you are willing to put in the hard work and invest in yourself. Getting a competitive CARS score is challenging, as is becoming a practicing professional. In fact, the preparation can be both difficult and very consuming of you time, money, and energy.

We do *not* share any quick 'tricks', 'shortcuts', or 'insider scoops' like some of the other books you may find because:

a) You cannot trick your way to becoming a successful medical professional. Rather, you must put in long hours of self-training. If a professional athlete must train for years – on average ten years, hence the 'ten-year rule' – to get to that level of proficiency, wouldn't it make sense that our future doctors, lawyers, dentists, and pharmacists, who deal with people's lives, would need to put in the effort to learn the necessary skills?

b) Sharing 'tricks' or 'insider scoops' would be highly unethical. You should be immediately alarmed if a book or admissions company claims to be sharing 'insider' information.

c) We have a strict policy at BeMo to only help students who are genuinely interested in becoming a caring future professional who want to serve their communities, not those who may be primarily motivated by financial security, status, or social pressure from their parents and peers, and certainly not those who are looking for an easy, cheap shortcut to get in.

How should you read this book?

We recommend that you first read the book cover to cover and then come back to specific chapters for a detailed read. The more you read the book, the more you will internalize the essential strategies. It is important to note that there is a lot of information in this book, and if you try to do everything at once, it may be overwhelming and lead to discouragement. Therefore, it is best that you first read this book for pleasure from cover to cover, then gradually start to implement our recommendations.

To your success,
Your friends at BeMo

CHAPTER I

What is CARS?

Before we jump into discussing how to ace CARS, let's first understand what the section entails. The Critical Analysis and Reasoning Skills (CARS) section of the MCAT is often the most dreaded portion of the 7.5-hour exam for medical school hopefuls. Students who are proficient at other sections of the MCAT – Biological and Biochemical Foundations of Living Systems, Chemical and Physical Foundations of Biological Systems, and Psychological, Social, and Biological Foundations of Behavior – are often stumped by the unique structure and cognitive demands of CARS. As a test-taker, you may wonder what the point of this section is. Isn't it enough that you have mastered the basic science knowledge you will need as a physician? Why do you also need to be able to critically analyze and reason based on texts in non-medical fields? Even if you don't have these questions, you may feel directionless about the preparation process, which unlike for other sections, does not involve memorizing and understanding a finite amount of information.

This is where we come in to help! Whether you are studying for the MCAT for the first time, or you are retaking it in the hopes of improving your score, we are here to walk you through preparation and practice strategies for CARS, what is often considered the most challenging section of the test for students with a science background. However, before we do that, you need to first understand the history of the MCAT and the purpose of CARS.

History and Rationale Behind the MCAT

From the perspective of medical school admissions committees, the MCAT is a diagnostic tool used to assess the eligibility of applicants. Thus, to understand the rationale behind this standardized test, let's begin with a brief discussion of the history of medical school admissions criteria.

The first medical school, Schola Medica Salernitana, was founded in the 9th century in southern Italy. Their admissions criteria were based entirely on the financial status of the applicants – those who could afford eight years of medical training – rather than previous academic success, critical reasoning, or interpersonal skills. Hundreds of years later, in 1765, the University of Pennsylvania established the Perelman School of Medicine, the first medical school in North America. The Perelman School of Medicine, and other institutions that opened around that time, wanted to train students who already had the foundations necessary the complete their studies, and thus based their admissions criteria on previous academic performance. However, in the early 1920s, rising dropout rates and the publication of the Flexner Report, a book-length critical report of medical education in North America, forced medical colleges to re-evaluate and reconfigure their admissions criteria.

That's why, in 1928, standardized testing was first included in the admissions process in the form of the "Scholastic Aptitude Test for Medical Students" or "Moss Test" created by F. A. Moss and colleagues. This test contained true-or-false and multiple-choice questions on six to eight subtopics testing memory, vocabulary, premedical knowledge, and logical reasoning. Between the 1940's and the 1960's, the test was revamped to include just multiple-choice questions in four subtests –communication, quantitative capabilities, science achievement, and comprehending modern society – and renamed as the Medical College Admissions Test, commonly known as the MCAT. Since then, the test has seen several iterations with changes to scoring method and content, but consistent in each was the inclusion of materials to test applicants' knowledge of broad subject matters and, more importantly, their verbal reasoning skills.

In 2015, the newest and current version of the MCAT was implemented in response to a broad survey soliciting recommendations about the format and content of the MCAT from medical professionals and trainees. Much of the section contents in this version were shifted to emphasize biochemistry, which is regarded as the most important topic to master to ensure student success in their medical curriculum, and psychological and sociological concepts were introduced as they are now considered essential components of healthcare. Importantly for us, the earlier verbal reasoning components was replaced by CARS. Clearly, there is something to be said for why these types of skill – critical analysis and reasoning – are crucial for practicing physicians to have.

Before we dive in to discuss the CARS section specifically, let's look at the overall structure of the MCAT and what you will be assessed on.

The Structure of the MCAT

The current MCAT is divided into four sections: Biological and Biochemical Foundations of Living Systems, Chemical and Physical Foundations of Biological Systems, and Psychological, Social, and Biological Foundations of Behavior, and Critical Analysis and Reasoning Skills. Let's explore each of these in in turn.

Biological and Biochemical Foundations of Living Systems

In this section, you will have 95 minutes to answer 59 multiple choice questions about concepts from introductory biology, organic chemistry, inorganic chemistry, and biochemistry. Here is a breakdown of the proportion of questions that will cover each of these topics:

- Biochemistry: 25%

- Introductory Biology: 65%

- General Chemistry: 5%

- Organic Chemistry: 5%

Chemical and Physical Foundations of Biological Systems

In this section, you will have 95 minutes to answer 59 multiple choice questions about concepts from introductory biology, organic chemistry, inorganic chemistry, physics, and biochemistry. Here is a breakdown of the proportion of questions that will cover each of these topics:

- 1st Semester Biochemistry: 25%

- Introductory Biology: 5%

- General Chemistry: 30%

- Organic Chemistry: 15%

- Introductory Physics: 25%

Psychological, Social, and Biological Foundations of Behavior

In this section, you will have 95 minutes to answer 59 multiple choice questions about how concepts from psychology and sociology inform our understanding of human biology, and how biology in turn influences human perceptions and behaviors. Here is a breakdown of the proportion of questions that will cover each of these topics:

- Introductory Psychology: 65%

- Introductory Sociology: 30%

- Introductory Biology: 5%

In each of the three sections reviewed above, you will be assessed on the follow set of skills, broken down by the proportion of questions targeting the skill in each section:

- Knowledge of Scientific Principles: 35%
- Scientific Reasoning and Problem-Solving: 45%
- Reasoning about the Design and
  Execution of Research: 10%
- Data-based Statistical Reasoning: 10%

Critical Analysis and Reasoning Skills (CARS)

Last but not least, in the CARS section, you will have 90 minutes to answer 53 multiple choice questions about nine passages in the humanities and social sciences. Here is a breakdown of the proportion of questions that will cover each of these topics:

- Humanities: 50%
- Social Sciences: 50%

Just like the other sections, you will be assessed on a set of skills, listed below with the percentage of questions testing each skill:

- Foundations of Comprehension: 30%
- Reasoning Within the Text: 30%
- Reasoning Beyond the Text: 40%

These will be discussed in more depth shortly.

Now that you have gained a better understanding of what the MCAT is composed of, we can begin to delve deeper into the most unique of the four sections: CARS.

The Rationale Behind CARS

As a future physician, you must be able to comprehend large volumes of difficult clinical information and develop effective treatment plans while explaining the reasoning behind your decisions to other

5

colleagues and your patients. You will be doing this every day, and often times, you will need to do it without knowing a lot of information beforehand. For example, you will walk in to see a patient who you may not have met before and they will present with a non-specific complaint like fatigue. From here, you must not jump to conclusions or be influenced by past patients, but rather ask them questions that lead to your critical analysis of the information they presented. From there, you will come to a conclusion of next steps to proceed with. Another example will happen when you collaborate with a colleague about decisions. You must listen to or read their communication to you and reason through the information before deciding what next steps to take.

The Critical Analysis and Reasoning Skills (CARS) section is designed to enable medical schools to evaluate your potential to interpret and utilize new information successfully by testing your ability to comprehend, analyze, and reason about written text in a variety of fields.

CARS Structure

Let's look a little bit more closely at the structure of CARS. CARS is the second of four sections you will encounter on the MCAT. Unlike the other sections, it is composed entirely of questions pertaining to written passages. There are exactly nine passages in total, each between 500 and 600 words in length, with 5 to 7 multiple-choice questions for each passage, totaling 53 questions across the whole section. You are given 90 minutes to complete the section, so on average, you will have about 10 minutes to read each passage and answer the accompanying questions.

About half of the passages will cover humanities subjects like literature, philosophy, ethics, art, history, and so forth, while the other half will cover social sciences, including psychology, sociology, economics, and politics. If you're not familiar with these subject matters, don't worry! CARS questions are not designed to assess your background knowledge in any of these fields. The passages are made to contain all the information you will need to answer the questions, and the questions themselves are designed to focus on the relationships between the ideas rather than your familiarity with them. Therefore, you do not need to be well-versed on the concepts and theories in the humanities or social sciences to do well. In fact, you should avoid referencing outside information as external knowledge may influence your reasoning and cause you to choose the incorrect response.

This is not to say that the passages used in the CARS section are going to be easy to understand and interpret. What makes this section so daunting is precisely the complexity of the writing you will encounter. These passages will be full of advanced vocabulary, sometimes labyrinthine sentence structure, and challenging argumentation. So, although you don't need to (and should not) prepare by simply *learning* humanities or social science concepts, it is paramount that you take the time to understand the kinds of questions you will be asked and train yourself to critically analyze the information presented to you in different texts.

CARS Question Types

There are just three question types in the CARS section, testing you on the following three skills:

1) Foundations of Comprehension

2) Reasoning Within the Text

3) Reasoning Beyond the Text

Let us examine each of these in turn.

1. Foundations of Comprehension

Foundations of Comprehension questions will make up approximately 30% of the 53 questions in the CARS section. These questions are designed to assess your understanding of the passage and will get you rooted in the conceptual building blocks of the passage to enable you to interpret the information effectively. You must learn to tackle this question type to succeed at answering the other two question types because you can't begin to analyze a passage without understanding it first.

There are two sub-types of Foundations of Comprehension: 1) understanding basic text components, and 2) interfering meaning from context. The first and most fundamental comprehension questions in CARS will ask you to identify the overall point of the passage, the author's thesis, the main idea of individual paragraphs, or even the meanings of specific sentences, phrases, and words. The second type of comprehension questions may prove more challenging as they ask you to extract meaning that the author merely implies but doesn't state explicitly. As the name of this type of question suggests, you will have to do so by drawing on contextual cues such as rhetorical devices such as figures of speech and hyperboles, the denotations and connotations of words, the logical relations between sections of the text, and even the tone employed by the author, whether it be serious or humorous, satirical or argumentative.

The following are examples of Foundations of Comprehension Questions:

- Which of the following best captures the main goal of the passage?

- Which of the following best represents the author's conclusion?

- Which approach does the author favor?

- What is the purpose of this phrase in paragraph 2?

2. Reasoning Within the Text

Reasoning Within the Text (RWT) questions make up approximately 30% of the questions in the CARS section. These types of questions will require you to synthesize components of the text to evaluate the author's use of an argument or claim to support his or her intention.

Again, these questions are divided into two subtypes that test a subset of reasoning skills: 1) integrating distant components of the text, and 2) evaluating arguments. The first type is similar to one of the subtypes of comprehension questions in that you need to draw on information presented in other parts of the text. However, these questions may ask you to process and synthesize ideas across paragraphs or the entire passage, rather than rely on immediate context. You may have to do this to infer the author's main thesis if it's not explicitly stated in a sentence in the passage. You will also need to take multiple components into account if you are asked to identify multiple perspectives or any ideas that are incongruent with the rest of the passage. The second type of RWT question will require you to assess the logic and plausibility of the text, how reasonable the author's conclusions are, how sound the arguments are, how appropriate the evidence is, and how credible the author appears to be based on their reasoning, evidence, sources cited, and so forth.

While this may seem like the work of logicians and scholars who have spent their careers studying texts like this, remember most of us perform these tasks daily; we repeatedly analyze information that comes at us from a variety of sources (e.g., the news, advertisements, social media, etc.) and make decisions about whether it is legitimate and how valuable it is to us. Thus, you need only to draw on and refine your ability to understand and analyze information in order to assess the CARS passages you encounter.

The following are examples of Reasoning Within the Text questions:

- Which of the following quotes is presented as evidence of the author's position?

- Which of the following passage assertions are presented as evidence of the author's point?

- Which conclusion does the author use this example to support?

- What is a weakness in the argument that the author makes to support their conclusion?

- What assumption is the author making about [blank]?

- Which of these examples is irrelevant for the claim that the author is making?

- Which of the following statements is an opinion and not a fact?

3. Reasoning Beyond the Text

Reasoning Beyond the Text (RBT) questions make up about 40% of the CARS questions, a slightly larger proportion than the other two question types. These questions will ask you to draw connections between the information within the passage to new or additional information.

The two types of RBT questions are: 1) extrapolating passage ideas to new contexts, and 2) assessing the impact of new information on passage ideas. The first type of RBT question requires you to apply the information in the passage to a novel situation or employ it to solve a problem that is beyond the information given in the passage. The correct answer will be the choice that is the most likely outcome based only on the content provided within the passage and within the question itself. The second type of RBT question asks you to determine how the conclusions of the passage would be altered if additional content or evidence is presented. These are often posed as "what if" questions and require you to re-interpret and re-evaluate the strength or plausibility of the message presented in the passage.

The following are examples of Reasoning Beyond the Text questions:

- Someone who agreed with the author's main point would also be likely to agree with which of the following?

- Which new example is most consistent with the author's definition?

- Which new situation best captures what is described within the text?

- If it were known that [blank], how would this affect the conclusion reached by the author?

- Imagine that [blank], how would this affect the author's argument?

Different students will find different question types harder than others, but your success in the CARS section of the MCAT depends fundamentally on your understanding of and targeted practice with all of these question types.

In this chapter, we have introduced the history of the MCAT and the rationale of the Critical Analysis and Reasoning Skills (CARS) section, and we have outlined what you can expect to encounter in this unique section of the test. In the next chapter, we will dive into another topic about the MCAT and CARS that you are probably keenly interested in – how it is scored.

CHAPTER II

How is the MCAT Scored?

Now that you have an idea of the rationale behind the MCAT and the components of CARS, let's take a closer look at how the MCAT is scored and how your score may be evaluated by medical school admissions committees. Understanding how your score is evaluated will be helpful to you in your preparation as you will gain an appreciation for how that number will be considered by medical schools.

How are your answers totaled?

As you now know, each section of the MCAT, including CARS, is multiple-choice. After a question prompt, you will be given four choices, of which one is the correct answer. Choosing a correct answer will contribute to the total number of correct answers you have per section, while an incorrect or unanswered question simply does not count towards your total number of correct answers. There is no additional penalty for incorrect answers, so there is an advantage of answering every single question, even if you have to make an educated guess.

What are scaled scores?

The total number of correct answers is then converted to a "scaled" score between 118-132 on each section of the MCAT. For example, a total number of correct answers numbering 35 out of the 53 on CARS may result in a scaled score of 123, while a total number of correct answers numbering 47 out of the 53 may result in a scaled score of 128. Your scaled scores on each section of the MCAT are also totalled to give an overall score between 472-528.

In addition to a scaled score, the AAMC will provide percentile scores for each section, and for your overall score. A percentile score indicates the percentage of test-takers that you performed better than. For example, a score in the 65th percentile indicates that your score was better than 65% of those who took the test, while a score in the 90th percentile indicates that your score was better than 90% of those who took the test. Thus, a score in the 90th percentile is higher and more competitive, as you are showing that you performed better than others who took the test. A total score of 500 is considered the "mid-point" or equivalent to a 50th percentile score. Percentile ranks reflect your performance relative to students who have written the MCAT in the last three years and are updated to reflect this timeline every year in May. A score in the 90th percentile on CARS is typically around 129, and a total MCAT score in the 90th percentile is typically around 515.

The AAMC converts the raw number of correct answers you received into the above-mentioned scaled scores. You may be wondering why AAMC does this! Why don't they just report how many questions you got correct out of 53 on CARS and provide that to medical schools? The answer is that the MCAT changes somewhat with each administration of the exam. The MCAT is available to write many times per year, and no two tests are the same; the passages change, the questions change, and so do the topics tested on the science sections. Therefore, it would not be fair to simply compare students' raw scores to each other, as some sittings of the exam may be more difficult than others. The AAMC thus converts the raw score to a scaled score, using data from several previous administrations of the exam going back several years, to provide a score that is "scaled" and thus holds the same value no matter what it is. This means that a score of 128 on CARS can be interpreted consistently by medical schools and compared to other students' CARS scores, as a 128 from one sitting to another means the same thing. On the other hand, a raw score of 50 out of 53 may *not* mean the same thing, as one CARS section may be more difficult than another. The AAMC thus provides a scaled score so your MCAT scores are consistently meaningful.

Please note that scaled scores are not the same as "curved" scores. The MCAT is not graded on a curve. "Grading on a curve" generally applies to exams where students' raw number scores are compared to each other from the same sitting of an exam on the same day. Since the AAMC uses data from many years and many sittings of the exam, the MCAT is not curved.

Unlike many examinations you may have written up to this point, you will have to wait a while to receive your MCAT score. Typically, you will receive your score in AAMC's online portal within 30-35 days of writing the exam. This time period allows AAMC to complete the scaling process.

Every section of the MCAT is scored in the exact same way, so there is no difference between how CARS is scored compared to the other sections.

How will your CARS score be evaluated?

The next thing you may be wondering is how medical schools use your CARS score. Most medical schools consider your entire MCAT score, as well as your score on each section in a balanced way. Therefore, while it is critical to do well on the CARS section, you should aim to do well on every section.

There is no standard way that medical schools use your CARS score. Each school has their own way of assessing your MCAT score, including how they consider each section. Some programs make this information at least somewhat public by stating it on their website, but some programs prefer to keep their admissions processes as opaque as possible and do not share how your score is evaluated anywhere. You should certainly research the schools you are interested in by looking at their websites and contacting their admissions offices in advance of your application. For American medical school applicants, this data is also often found on AAMC's Medical School Admission Requirements (MSAR) online portal.

After doing some research, you may discover that some programs report a strict cut-off score for CARS. What does this mean? Let's say that University X states that your CARS score must be a 125 or higher. Well, that simply means that your application will not be considered for further evaluation unless you scored at least a 125 on CARS. Although a cut-off is useful to know, it simply gives you a floor from which to move upwards. Obtaining a score below the cut-off is a guarantee that you will not be considered, but scoring higher than the cut-off is not a guarantee that you will be granted an admission. The success of your candidacy will depend on a myriad of other factors, including, but not limited to, your written application and interview performance.

Some programs will not have a strict cut-off. Instead, they may report a median or average CARS score of matriculants or successful applicants. For example, University Y states the average CARS score of accepted applicants in their previous cycle was 129. This means that half of their admitted students received a CARS score somewhere below 129 and half received a CARS score somewhere above 129. This is useful information for you to have, as you know what to aim for if you want a competitive CARS score for that school; it should be above that median or average score for you to be a competitive applicant.

Some medical schools, especially in Canada, have moved to putting a greater emphasis on CARS compared to the other MCAT sections. These schools use a different approach than the majority of programs, which still look at your entire MCAT score. Again, this is because CARS is believed to be a stronger reflection of a student's critical thinking skills. This information can usually be readily found through the school's website or admissions office. So, if a school does this, does this mean you should ignore the other sections? Certainly not. Even though a school may put more emphasis on CARS, they may still consider your scores on the other sections. Even for schools that explicitly state they only consider CARS and not the other sections, the AAMC will still report your entire score to every school you apply to, and they will still see your whole score, so it's in your interest to ace every section.

You should keep in mind that the scoring on CARS can be tough. You should be aiming to get every single question correct to receive as high of a scaled score as possible. This can seem daunting when you are first preparing, but rest assured that you can improve with consistent practice! Also, since there are only 53 questions, a good thing to remember is that getting just one or two more questions correct can improve your scaled score! So, every piece of practice counts and will go a long way to improving your performance on this crucial section.

Admission Statistics & Why You Must Ace the MCAT CARS!

Each school uses your MCAT scores in the way they see fit when deciding the ranking of applicants. The best way to find out this information is to consult the official admissions website or contact the admissions office. Regardless, your performance on the CARS section is likely going to be a significant factor in determining how well you rank compared to other candidates.

To give you a more concrete idea of how important the CARS score is in the application process, let's consider some statistics.

At medical schools in the U.S. the average acceptance rate is around 5%, though this varies largely by school (i.e., as high as 39% for the University of Mississippi and as low as 1% for schools like Virginia Tech). For Canadian schools, the acceptance rate is anywhere between 5-10%. This means that in order for you to have a fair chance of being accepted, you need to rank in the 95th, or minimally 90th, percentile! In the 2020-2021 cycle, you needed a total score of 515 and above to be in the top 10 percent of test-takers, and 518 and above to be in the top 5%. For CARS, you would need a section score of 128 to be at the 90th percentile and 129 to be at the 95th percentile.

Many students go into their MCAT thinking they'll compensate for their score in the CARS section with their scores in the other sections because they have a stronger science background. This is a dangerous mentality to have! First, many schools will pay special attention to how students do in the CARS section to ensure that they have the essential analytical skills necessary for success in the medical field. Similarly, schools that look at the breakdown of the MCAT scores also may prefer for the four section scores to be close together. For example, given two candidates with an overall MCAT score of 515, the admissions committee may rank the candidate with section scores of 129/128/129/129 higher than the candidate with section scores 130/124/131/130. Furthermore, some schools, like McMaster University in Canada, *only* look at the CARS score and not at the other three scores!

So, there is absolutely *no* reason to "give up" on a section when what's at stake is so important to your future and *every* reason to buckle down and improve your CARS score. If you can raise your score in this section while also scoring high in the other sections, you would essentially be raising your overall score as well! That is exactly why we wrote this book – to help you overcome the CARS section and get that 90th or 95th percentile score needed to gain admissions into medical school.

In this chapter, we have looked at how the MCAT, including CARS, is scored, how your scores are evaluated by medical schools, and why your score for this section is so important. You are now ready to look at some myths and facts about the CARS section to help you begin preparing.

Are you ready? Let's go!

CHAPTER III

Preparing for CARS – Myths & Facts

B y now you have likely concluded that the CARS section will be a worthy test of your critical analysis and reasoning skills, one that can be a challenge for even the best students. Why is this section of the MCAT so important? This is one of the main ways medical schools assess a student's ability to analyze information and solve problems, key skills aspiring physicians should have. While it is true that CARS can be a challenge, we are going to do everything we can in the next few chapters to equip you with the tools necessary to succeed.

One thing that makes preparing for CARS difficult is the misinformation about how to prepare and what to expect on test day, which can cause you to miss the mark when it comes to your goal of acing the CARS section of the MCAT. For this reason, we have dedicated this chapter to setting the record straight about common CARS myths so you can avoid these pitfalls. We will also discuss key facts that you should have moving forward in your preparation.

Myth #1: You cannot prepare for CARS.

One of the most common myths about the CARS section of the MCAT is that you cannot prepare for it. The CARS section tests your critical analysis and reasoning skills through your ability to make sense of complex written materials; these are skills that nobody is born with, but are instead learned through practice. This means you can absolutely practice for CARS, but you must prepare in the correct way for it to be effective! Of course, you cannot prepare for CARS by memorizing passages or correct answers because each CARS passage is unique; but, just like any other test, there are a number of things you can do in order to prepare in advance.

Myth #2: You must be well-versed in all the content to do well.

The CARS section of the MCAT does not test your background knowledge of content within the passages you will face, but rather tests your ability to decipher the information within the passage to think critically and reason. It is important to note that no background knowledge is needed to answer CARS questions, as all the information you will need is contained within the passages. Referencing external knowledge can even cause you to choose the incorrect answer. For these reasons, you do not need to know all of the possible content areas that could be incorporated into a CARS passage.

   A better approach is to understand the types of questions you will see on test day and how to approach each question type. In *Chapter V: BeMo's Top Strategies & 7 Steps to ACE Any CARS Passage*, you will learn how to identify the common question types and how to answer them correctly. This is the knowledge that you will need to ace CARS because it will equip you to tackle any CARS question that comes your way!

Myth #3: You cannot have fun.

Practice for CARS can be boring, sure; but does it have to be? Absolutely not! For your CARS practice you will need to become accustomed to reading challenging materials. However, the CARS passages that you will face on test day will cover a variety of topics from philosophy to ethics to art, and much more. Look at your CARS practice as an opportunity to read about topics that have always interested you, but that you never had the time to explore. Let's say you have always wanted to learn about personal finances or macroeconomics. Read *The Economist*! Or maybe you have a list of literary classics that you have always wanted to read, but never got around to doing so; this is your chance to dive into those Ernest Hemingway, Oscar Wilde, or Jane Austen books! Tailor some of your CARS practice to your own interests and you will find that your reading is enjoyable in addition to being a productive way to improve your comprehension and reasoning skills as you expand your vocabulary and broaden your perspective. When you encounter texts on topics you've never thought about before, don't reject them; use this as an opportunity to expand your horizons. You may just find yourself gravitating to new and interesting fields.

As you read on, you will learn that the passages and questions in the CARS section are self-contained; the answer to every question in this section can be found within the text given. To add a bit of fun into your CARS practice and your approach on test day, treat each CARS passage as a scavenger hunt for the information that validates the author's thesis, supports a claim, or refutes an argument.

Myth #4: You will feel a time crunch during the test.

The grueling length of the MCAT and the sheer number of questions you will face on test day – 230 total questions over the course of almost eight hours – makes it a challenging test and something that applicants often fear. Yes, the MCAT asks a lot of questions in a short amount of time. For CARS alone, you will need to answer 53 questions relating to nine passages in 90 minutes or less. Often, students struggle to finish the CARS section of the

MCAT, which means their scores are not as high as they could have achieved with more time. However, this time crunch is not inevitable! It is important to begin your CARS practice with ample time to become familiar with the format and how to tackle difficult passages; you need enough time to learn from your mistakes and to hone your strategy. You cannot change the fact that the MCAT is timed, but you can increase your own speed to match it.

Now that we've debunked some myths, let's talk about some facts.

Fact #1: It's like riding a bike (perfect practice makes perfect).

Preparing for CARS is like riding a bike. Practice is key! Perhaps you have heard of the saying "practice makes perfect." Well this is not true, and it is not what we mean by practice. In actuality, practice makes permanent, and only *perfect* practice makes perfect. So, if you continue to practice the *wrong* way, then you will permanently perform the task in the incorrect manner, no matter how much practice you have done.

To ensure that you are practicing in a way that moves you towards success, we have compiled a set of expert strategies, which we will explore in *Chapter V: BeMo's Top Strategies & 7 Steps to ACE Any CARS Passage*.

Fact #2: The best way to practice is realistic simulations.

Your success on the CARS section of the MCAT will require training with materials that closely resemble the difficulty and format of the actual MCAT. When completing CARS practice sections or passages, try to mimic test-day conditions as much as possible. Complete your practice in one sitting and under the appropriate time constraints. This is the best way to learn how to use your time effectively, to understand how test anxiety may affect you, and to determine any weaknesses you need to address. If you complete your MCAT practice in a realistic setting, you will know exactly what to expect on test day.

Fact #3: You need expert feedback.

It is important not only that you are practicing for CARS in the correct way, but that you are getting expert feedback about your performance throughout your practice. Practicing by reading CARS passages over and over again or trying sample questions without any feedback may help to improve your CARS score, but may not be enough to obtain the score you desire. To engage in targeted, effective practice, you need a coach to tell you what you are doing well, what you are doing poorly, and how to do better. Ideally, you would receive this kind of expert feedback at consistent intervals throughout your preparation to track your progress. That is the BeMo difference!

Fact #4: Books, guides, and crash courses/boot camps are ineffective.

If you are preparing for CARS, books and guides alone, or last-minute crash courses, are not very helpful. You must practice reading passages critically and strategize for answering questions. You cannot just read about how to do so; you must get hands-on practice to see if you are able to successfully implement the strategies that you read about. Instead of crash courses, use CARS passages to pinpoint your weaknesses, then focus your practice in these areas so you are ensuring maximum improvement. Cramming practice in the nights or weeks before your MCAT, or reading about CARS strategies in a book or guide with little time to practice, is not effective. Aim to take the evening before your MCAT off to relax and get a good night's sleep. This is not the time to try to cram and pull an all-nighter as that will simply impact your performance on test day.

Fact #5: You must have a strategy for each CARS question type.

It is critical to have a strategy in place to tackle each CARS question type. The first step is understanding the question types, but beyond this you will need a fool-proof plan to help you correctly answer each type of question. Different types of questions will require their own answer strategies. Of course, you cannot predict the actual passages or questions that you will be asked on test day, but having solid answer strategies for each question type guarantees that when you read any CARS question you will be able to identify the question type, approach the passage accordingly, and keep your cool as you determine the correct answer.

Fact #6: You must have a strategy to manage stress.

Preparing to ace CARS will be stressful, so you would be remiss not to build a stress management plan into your MCAT preparations. You will need both long-term stress management techniques for your months of MCAT preparation as well as short-term stress management techniques for the days before the test, the morning of, and during the MCAT. Check out *Chapter VII: Long-term and Short-term Stress Management Strategies* for more detailed information about stress management for CARS. Avoid dealing with stress in unhealthy ways, such as eating junk food and skipping exercise or time spent with family and friends. Studies have shown that both exercise and proper sleep are essential in mitigating and managing stress. Do not overlook the importance of positive thinking, a healthy diet, and taking time to exercise and relax!

Fact #7: There is no magic pill.

Remember, CARS preparation takes months of hard work. There is no quick way to ensure you will ace this section of the MCAT. Not dedicating enough time to practicing and preparing for CARS, or trying to take shortcuts, will result in disappointment. You need to dedicate several months to CARS preparation – there is no magic pill! You need enough time to build your critical thinking and analysis skills, learn strategies for each question type, overcome the time crunch, and get expert feedback on your progress. If you give yourself ample time and follow our advice, you will be on the road to success.

Now, it is up to you how you want to move forward. You can choose to believe the myths you have heard about CARS and do nothing to prepare for this section of your upcoming MCAT...OR you can reject these myths, accept the facts, and get to work preparing for CARS! We hope you have chosen the latter because we are eager to continue sharing what we know with you to help you succeed. In the next chapter, we will be discussing the most common mistakes applicants make on CARS to help you avoid making the same errors.

CHAPTER IV

Top 8 Reasons Applicants Score Low on CARS

In the previous chapter we debunked the myths and established the facts about CARS preparation. Now, let's take a look at the common mistakes applicants make when they prepare for this section of the MCAT and during the test itself. It is important that you understand why these errors may hurt your performance and what you can do to avoid making them yourself.

In this chapter, we focus on eight errors: insufficient preparation, only practicing with test materials, not practicing with realistic passages, not practicing in a realistic setting, not actively reading during practice, not identifying the question types, importing outside knowledge when answering questions, and not getting expert feedback. As we discuss each one, evaluate your own CARS preparation thus far and think about whether you have made these mistakes yourself.

1. Insufficient Preparation

As we have hopefully convinced you, preparation can definitely improve your CARS performance. Yet, applicants still often neglect to prepare sufficiently in advance. This mistake is commonly made by those who feel confident about their test-taking skills, whether this confidence is well-grounded or not. Others may assume that they already possess sufficient critical thinking and reasoning skills to do well on CARS, or that it is impossible to improve one's critical thinking and reasoning skills. In reality, it is both possible and crucial to work on improving the skills necessary to do well on this section of the MCAT.

Unlike many similar critical thinking exams you may have encountered up to this point in your academic career, the MCAT CARS requires sophisticated, higher-level analytical skills. Avoid making the mistake of thinking that CARS is simply assessing your reading comprehension abilities. While you may encounter some more traditional reading comprehension questions in CARS, you will also be asked questions that assess the logic of an author's argument, questions that have you analyze the validity of an abstract idea, or questions that ask you to reason beyond the text by using or even challenging ideas articulated within the text. Since the ability to analyze texts and ideas is not something that can be memorized, it must be nurtured through consistent practice and application.

Furthermore, sufficient preparation for CARS in addition to the other sections of the MCAT can serve to reduce test-taking nerves. If you have taken the proper steps to be fully prepared for the CARS and have verified your readiness through appropriate practice, there will be much less cause for stress or worry going into the exam. Even if you have strong critical thinking and reasoning skills to begin with, they can always improve. Like exercising a muscle to increase strength, frequent practice will help you develop your critical thinking and reasoning talents. Moreover, it is worth investing the time and energy to increase your efficiency in exercising these skills to make for a smoother test-taking experience.

To fully prepare for the MCAT CARS section, strive for long-term and frequent preparation. Last minute cramming is an imprudent strategy for any section of the MCAT, but particularly so for CARS. Students who perform very well on this section of the exam have developed their active reading skills over years and become accustomed to a variety of forms of written argumentation. Of course, not everyone has years to devote to their MCAT preparation, but the earlier you get started, the better! If you're wondering how quickly you will run out of CARS test materials, there's no need to worry. Some of the best preparation available comes in the form of classic literature, journal articles, and other readily available texts, and as you will see below, neglecting these kinds of materials is a mistake.

2. Only Practicing with Test Materials

The CARS section borrows texts from humanities and social science disciplines, which can vary widely in tone, content, and style and tend to be quite different from traditional science texts. Many of you preparing for the MCAT are accustomed to basic science texts or other, more technical texts utilized in STEM fields. These kinds of texts are typically fairly straightforward and lack the literary flourish you might encounter in a piece of literature or a humanities academic journal article. Often, these stylistic flourishes can be distracting from the author's argument, so more critical thinking is required to sift through the text to discern its true message.

Thus, if you are only briefly exposed to such humanities and social science texts through CARS preparation, you are far less likely to do well on CARS. Only practicing with test materials limits your ability to become comfortable with CARS texts, whereas extending your practice to other, similar written materials allows for additional growth in your critical thinking and reasoning skills.

Isolating your exposure to humanities and social science texts to practice with CARS test materials limits the development of your ability to discern which parts of a text are vital to the overall argument in a complex text, and which parts are less valuable. Learning to dismantle an author's argument and assess their logic takes preparation, which cannot be adequately gained through fragmented practice. Further, writing styles within the humanities and social sciences disciplines are diverse and require frequent exposure to them in order to increase your analytical competence. The more kinds of texts you utilize in your test preparation, the better equipped you will be to succeed when taking the real CARS. Using CARS test materials is necessary to prepare for the exam, but it is insufficient. Considering the myriad content genres, purposes, tones, and styles, limiting yourself to test materials will stunt your potential growth in both breadth and depth of textual analysis. Failing to seek out diverse texts and analyze their arguments will curb your ability to develop your active reading skills, which are vital to CARS success. True active reading skills are only developed over the long-term, through extended and extensive engagement with new and challenging reading material.

Students who only practice with test materials also limit the expansion of their vocabulary, which is a crucial part of enhancing their understanding of complex texts. Broadening your exposure to materials beyond the text will help to broaden your vocabulary as well. Having a large vocabulary and some recognition of humanities and social sciences jargon will facilitate more thorough and quicker understanding of the text at hand. In addition to simply refining your ability to read actively and recognize sophisticated vocabulary, it is imperative that you work on doing so quickly and efficiently. Check out *Chapter V: BeMo's Top Strategies & 7 Steps to ACE Any CARS Passage* for tips on what to read and where to find it!

3. Not Practicing with Realistic Passages

While practice with materials outside of CARS passages is important, you cannot ace CARS without also practicing with CARS passages. You must do *both*.

Selecting practice texts that don't realistically reflect the difficulty of CARS material is a crucial test preparation mistake. Since CARS assesses your ability to critically analyze new material, what you read will likely be about topics that are unfamiliar to you. Not only is the content complex, but the style can be too. Sometimes evaluating an author's argument can be difficult because it is highly embedded within the text, asking the reader to make inferences in a way that is less common in STEM fields. When you're reading materials on subjects you're familiar with, you can get away with skimming and just picking out a few key words. Chances are, you'll still be able to piece together the overall message. You will not be able to do this with challenging texts outside of the fields you're comfortable with. Given these variations in expression and argumentation as well as the overall difficulty of the exam, CARS success requires practice with realistic passages.

If the passages you use to practice aren't as complicated or challenging to read as those found on the actual exam, you will be developing your critical analysis and reasoning skills at a lower level, which will ultimately be detrimental to your MCAT score. Underdevelopment of your critical analysis and reasoning skills leads to overall under-preparation for CARS, and we all know that there's nothing worse than being underprepared for an important test. It's like the common academic anxiety dream in which you show up to a final exam and suddenly remember you completely neglected to study for it. Avoid that sinking feeling in your stomach and don't make the common mistake of not practicing with realistic passages!

In fact, texts selected for inclusion in CARS are altered to increase their level of difficulty by removing transitional words or phrases and eliminating traditional thesis statements in order to make you put in even more effort to determine the meaning of the passage. Including other passages in the humanities and social sciences disciplines that are equally difficult to comprehend in your CARS preparation will help you understand how diverse arguments are constructed and conveyed through the texts. Thus, when presented with novel CARS prep materials, you may be able to draw upon argument structures and rhetorical techniques you've worked with in outside texts to help you identify relevant information. So, where do you get this kind of practice material? We'll discuss this in *Chapter V: BeMo's Top Strategies & 7 Steps to ACE Any CARS Passage*.

4. Not Practicing in a Realistic Setting

Although initially it may seem inconsequential, not practicing in a realistic setting can be detrimental to your CARS performance. As you prepare for the exam, failing to establish a realistic practice setting can lead to the development of inadequate time management skills, insufficient test-taking endurance, and overall poorer performance. A large part of the challenge of taking an exam like the MCAT is developing endurance. Just because you may be able to do very well in 10-minute bursts by practicing with one passage at a time does not mean you will necessarily do well on CARS or the MCAT as a whole. Most people can maintain intense focus for a short period of time, but it gets more difficult to concentrate on analyzing complex passages the longer the time you spend doing it.

Think about an athlete preparing for a marathon. When training, they wouldn't train in short bursts of time, or run just a mile per day. Such brief and sporadic moments of practice would never add up to enough practice to do well in a marathon, particularly because marathons test perseverance and endurance. On the other hand, an athlete preparing for a marathon wouldn't run a full marathon regularly for practice either, because that kind of unrealistic training would probably lead to burnout or injury. Rather, an athlete preparing for a marathon would train through substantial practice sessions of several miles at a time, just as you should prepare for the MCAT CARS through practice sessions of 90 minutes. In this way, you're neither practicing for short periods of time that won't culminate in sufficient practice nor "running the full marathon" by writing a full MCAT every time you practice, but dividing your preparation into substantial, yet manageable chunks to achieve the maximum possible impact.

Similarly, you need to be sure you are developing time management skills to enable your success on CARS. Time management is important not only because of the demands of answering 53 questions in 90 minutes, but also because you may have to allocate more time to analyzing a particularly difficult passage than you do for the rest. Understanding and getting comfortable with what 90 minutes is truly like when tackling nine difficult passages and their accompanying questions is vital to doing well on CARS, so don't make the mistake of not practicing in a realistic setting for a full 90 minutes. To truly understand what you can accomplish in 90 minutes of a test-taking scenario, it would be a mistake to fail to make sure your environment reflects testing conditions. Sitting anywhere besides a desk in a quiet, private area will give you an unrealistic idea of what taking the MCAT CARS will be like. If you aren't practicing in timed, 90-minute blocks in a quiet environment, you aren't preparing yourself for a realistic testing scenario.

Relatedly, another mistake you could be making is only practicing one section at a time. While you may be doing well on each section, your scores will be inflated because i) you will not be practicing test-taking endurance for the full length of the MCAT, and ii) you will not be practicing the mental flexibility required to switch from section to section. Remember that you will be doing CARS as part of a larger exam following the Chemical and Physical Foundations of Living Systems section, so it is crucial to get used to switching your mindset from the problem-solving and scientific inquiry mindset used in previous sections to a critical analysis and reasoning mindset for humanities and social science texts. Other sections require some knowledge in the relevant fields, but as you will see, you will need to ignore any prior knowledge you may have about the topics you read about in CARS passages to do well in this section. Given this need to adapt quickly to each section, not practicing CARS in conjunction with other sessions is a mistake that must be avoided if you want to achieve a high score.

5. Not Actively Reading During Practice

In this chapter, we have already touched on the different kinds of texts you may encounter in CARS, all coming from different subfields in the humanities and social sciences disciplines. No matter the genre, you can rest assured that the passages will be complex and challenging. Even if you've been successful on exams in the past by skimming reading passages, don't make the serious mistake of not actively reading the passages in the CARS portion of the MCAT! Failing to read CARS passages actively will likely lead to you missing key information that you need to answer the corresponding questions correctly.

Active reading differs from passive reading in that it, unsurprisingly, requires active processing and engagement with the material. Passive reading requires no interaction with the text, no interrogation of its purpose, no assessment of the author's tone, argument, or purpose. When you read a passage actively, you examine all aspects of the text and read with the active goal of understanding the text so that you can analyze it. Finishing a passage doesn't mean you are finished actively reading it; rather, active reading is a process that extends before and after the literal reading of a text because it requires making predictions, critically assessing the text as you read, and reflecting upon it afterwards. Quite the opposite, passive reading results in the barest form of comprehension possible, as it is simply the understanding of words and sentences put together to create meaning.

Strategies like active reading are just as important to hone during practice with outside materials as they are with CARS passages. Without actively reading all passages, you may miss the arguments of the texts, since they are not always presented in a straightforward manner. If you fail to identify the central themes of the piece and its explicit or implicit thesis through active reading, there is no way you will be able to adequately assess the logic of the author's argument. Active reading requires sifting through extraneous details in the text to determine the most important points the author is attempting to make so that you can ultimately determine if the premises expressed throughout the body of the passage logically add up to the author's conclusion. So, if you neglect active reading strategies like making a summary of the message of each paragraph and assessing how each sentence contributes to the meaning of the paragraph and how each paragraph contributes to the meaning of the overall argument or thesis of the passage, it will be very difficult to attack exam questions efficiently and with all of the relevant information you need to answer those questions.

6. Not Identifying the Question Types

It can be tempting to think that if you put in the necessary practice to prepare for CARS and practice active reading strategies, that identifying question types is unwarranted. After all, the CARS section examines your ability to critically analyze and reason through texts, which must include simple test questions, right? Not exactly. Even if you can analyze questions well, you would be ignoring the fact that each of the three different question types in CARS calls for a different approach to arrive at the answer. The process of matching each question type to its appropriate approach brings to mind the toy many toddlers play with that presents a flat surface full of different shaped holes, each with a corresponding peg that mirrors the shape of its matching hole. Through much trial and error, the toddlers playing with the toy learn that a square peg can't fit into a round hole, and as much annoyance as it brings, the circular peg will never fit into the triangle-shaped hole. Clearly, CARS question types and approaches are the different shaped holes and pegs in this example. Avoid the frustration of trying to use a Reasoning within the Text question approach to respond to a Foundations of Comprehension question.

In other words, even if you do everything else right by actively reading, practicing consistently for 90-minute periods, and so on, if you are unable to identify the question type and its corresponding strategy to arrive at the answer, you are much more likely to select the wrong approach and arrive at the incorrect answer. Check out *Chapter I: What is CARS?* for a list of question types and examples.

7. Importing Outside Knowledge When Answering Questions

Quite different from the other three sections of the MCAT, CARS does not require extensive knowledge of outside material in order to perform well and earn a high score. Since CARS evaluates widely applicable skills like your ability to critically analyze a complicated text, the texts will likely be unfamiliar to you, especially if you have primarily studied common pre-medical fields like basic sciences prior to applying to medical school. You may be thinking that someone with a lot of additional knowledge in the humanities and/or social sciences would perform well on this section, but that isn't necessarily the case. In fact, importing outside knowledge when answering questions is a big mistake when tackling CARS, even if your outside knowledge is related to the topic of the passage. Why would knowing more about CARS passage topics not always be beneficial to someone taking the MCAT? CARS questions require you to use *only what is within the passages and the questions themselves.* Even when Reasoning Beyond the Text questions present additional information, still refrain from considering any outside information you may possess about the topic.

Even if you know a significant amount about the passage topic, refrain from mistakenly importing outside knowledge when answering questions. Even if the outside knowledge you employ to tackle a CARS question is entirely correct, you must remain cognizant of the fact that some of these passages can be quite subjective, and as a result they may not portray the information in an objective way that reflects your knowledge of the topic in question. In this sense, using outside knowledge to assess a very specific, potentially subjective passage can be quite misleading. Accordingly, importing outside knowledge to address questions about particular passages may cause you to select incorrect answers. This tendency to use additional knowledge about passage subjects becomes especially dangerous when your understanding of a specific topic differs from that of the author. Don't forget that your task in this section is not to demonstrate knowledge on any of these topics, but to analyze the passages and their arguments in isolation. Many times, your ability to answer a CARS question correctly hinges upon your ability to interpret information within and beyond the text *from the author's perspective*, so using outside knowledge would actually be a hindrance in many cases.

8. Not Getting Expert Feedback

By now you know to avoid: insufficient preparation, only practicing with test materials, not practicing with realistic passages, not practicing in a realistic setting, not actively reading during practice, not identifying the question types, and importing outside knowledge when answering questions. You've read a lot about the MCAT CARS, feel like you know what to expect, and have created a thorough study plan, complete with test prep materials that guide you through the right answers in their answer keys. What else could you possibly need? Don't forget the last reason applicants score low on CARS – not getting expert feedback!

Even the most well-developed test prep materials with thorough explanations of the rationale behind each right answer pale in comparison to the substantial insights you can gain by seeking expert feedback on your CARS preparation and performance. Though test prep materials may help you realize where you went wrong on individual questions and model the correct way of thinking about challenging questions, they can't recognize patterns of error nor cater improvement strategies to your particular needs. Experts can help you identify the certain question types or genres of texts that pose the biggest obstacles to you and walk you through how to eliminate your patterns of error in response to those specific types of questions or texts.

For instance, you may consistently be getting Reasoning Beyond the Text questions incorrect on practice passages, but you know what the strategy is to tackle those sorts of test questions. Test prep materials may help you recognize that you tend to miss Reasoning Beyond the Text questions and explain the logic behind each correct answer, but you wouldn't be able to talk through your thought process or application of the strategy provided in order to identify the erroneous thinking patterns that consistently led you to choose the incorrect answer for Reasoning Beyond the Text questions. Not only can experts help you identify these flawed thought patterns, but they can provide strategies to mitigate these errors and formulate a game plan to make sure you are able to do so in a timely manner so that you stay on track during your test prep schedule. Make the most of your preparation and don't make the mistake of forgetting to seek expert feedback.

Deciding how to tackle preparation for the MCAT CARS can be daunting, a task made all the more intimidating if you're coming from a strictly scientific background. You may not be accustomed to the kinds of humanities and social sciences texts that CARS will ask you to analyze. However, with some careful planning and adherence to the advice set forth in this book, you will have all of the tools you need to successfully prepare for this section of the MCAT. Sometimes half of the battle is knowing precisely what *not to do*, which is why we've provided you with this list of 8 reasons applicants don't score well on CARS.

Now that we have discussed the most common errors applicants make during their CARS preparation and test, we are excited to share with you the strategies that will enable you to excel in this section. Let's take a look at them together in the next chapter!

CHAPTER V

BeMo's Top Strategies & 7 Steps to ACE Any CARS Passage

Great work—you have taken another step towards acing CARS by understanding all of the reasons applicants can score poorly. You are now well-positioned to begin learning and adopting expert strategies that will help you to get that dream score. By implementing these seven steps to approaching each question, you will be able to practice *perfectly*, which, as you know, is the only way to achieve *perfect* performance.

But wait! Before we get there, we want to first share with you five important preparation strategies that will help you to build the basic skills you need to ace CARS. As you will see, preparation for this very challenging section of the MCAT will require planning, persistence, and a lot of patience. At the end of this chapter, we will also answer one of the most frequently asked questions as students begin the preparation process: When is a good time to take the MCAT?

Are you ready? Let's do this!

Top 5 Preparation Strategies

1. Start Practice Early by Reading

This may seem like a no-brainer, but it's a piece of sound advice that is often neglected, so we feel the need to spend time emphasizing it. If you are an avid reader and have always had a great appetite for a variety of literary material, then you've already been laying the groundwork for acing CARS. Most of us, however, are not that person, so we must proactively make the choice to improve our reading ability. Whether you are planning to take the test in two years or in six months, the best time to start practicing for the CARS section is *today*.

In the other sections of the MCAT, you will be tested on your knowledge and understanding of a large but finite set of concepts that are covered in college courses you are likely already taking and textbooks which you've read. In contrast, the CARS section tests you on a particular skillset: critical analysis and reasoning. These skills cannot be acquired or improved by cramming or by reading sporadically. It is the fruit of long-term, dedicated practice, accumulated through frequent and repeated engagement in the activity.

Establishing good reading habits does not mean you need to blow through a 500-page novel every week. If you aim to read too much in one go, you will exhaust yourself and likely drop the activity all together. If you are not a habitual reader, start small. Begin with an amount that suits your reading appetite and allows you to balance all of your other responsibilities without overstretching yourself.

We recommend starting with 30 minutes a day, *every day*. Most of us are able to carve out half an hour a day for this activity. Likely, you would simply be reducing the time you spend reading emails, texts, and social media posts and spending it on reading the types of material that will actually sharpen your analytical skills. So really, it's not a change in activity at all, but rather a change in reading material. Unlike reading texts and emails, however, you will need to do your

30 minutes of intentional reading in one continuous chunk, free from other distractions. This will ensure that you are focused enough to engage with the text actively.

To ensure that you are reading consistently, you must think of this as a planned activity. Unlike reading other, more casual texts, you should not just pick up the New Yorker or a journal article on a whim and decide to spend 30 minutes on it. Instead, schedule the 30 minutes into your day. Ideally, this would be at a time when you are mostly likely to be mentally alert and least likely to be pulled away from the task by other responsibilities. For example, you could do this before your workday begins or during your break time. You may not find the right time right away, but as soon as you notice a time is not working for you, change it to another time until you find a schedule that can be maintained.

Part of your planning should also be deciding what you will read *before* your scheduled 30 minutes. Not doing this would not only cause you to waste time deciding on your reading material at the beginning of your reading time, it would also make it easier for you to skip the activity all together. If you schedule your reading time for the morning or during the day, then spend 5 minutes the evening before picking the article or book you're going to read so that the next day, you can hit the ground running.

It's never too early to begin sharpening the skills critical to your success on this section of the MCAT and as a future physician. This is why the first preparation strategy to acing CARS is to *start reading now*.

2. Read Diverse and Challenging Materials

Now, you may be thinking, "I've been reading for as long as I can remember," or, "As a student, haven't I been practicing critical analysis and reasoning all my life?" Yes, that's likely the case. Most of us read every day, throughout the day. We are constantly engrossed in text messages, social media posts, emails, and so forth. Many of us also spend a considerable amount of time reading technical materials such as course textbooks, reports, and journal articles, which we inevitably have to think about critically and analyze to some extent. So, what more must we do?

Well, keep in mind that even though we may read a lot in terms of sheer volume, most of us tend to read the same *types* of materials. Our exposure to text is thus limited in both subject matter and writing style. Someone who only reads novels, even if the novels are demanding literary classics, may struggle to connect the ideas in a scientific paper. Conversely, someone who is only accustomed to reading scientific literature may find it difficult to analyze works by Orwell or Kierkegaard. The best way to improve on our ability to process unfamiliar writing styles is simply to get familiar with them.

The same idea applies to CARS. Remember that this is a section in which passages are drawn from a breadth of topics in the humanities and social sciences. These passages will therefore not only cover unfamiliar topics, but will also be written using unfamiliar styles of prose. So, to get yourself familiar with different types of writing, you must expose yourself to a variety of texts.

While you are getting comfortable with a variety of texts, it's important to also start increasing the level of difficulty in the materials you read. You may gravitate towards easily digestible reads, but if you're not being challenged by the text, you are not adequately preparing for CARS. If you were an athlete preparing for a weightlifting competition, you would want to be gradually increasing the weight of the plates during practice until you could consistently lift the target weight. The same applies for CARS training. Remember, passages in the CARS section are notoriously difficult to interpret, so you need to be reading materials that approximate that level of difficulty. The following is a list of sources to get you started.

1) Newspapers and Magazines

   - The New Yorker

   - The Economist

   - The New York Times

   - The New York Review of Books

2) Humanities and Social Science Journal Articles

   - Journal of Personality and Social Psychology

   - Journal of Applied Social Psychology

- Journal of Organizational Behavior
- American Journal of Sociology
- American Sociological Review
- American Journal of Political Science
- Political Analysis
- Journal of Politics
- World Politics
- The Philosophical Review
- Philosophy and Phenomenological Research
- Philosophical Quarterly

3) Literary Classics:

- Ernest Hemingway
- Oscar Wilde
- George Orwell
- Margaret Atwood

4) Other ideas for literature:

- Nobel Prize for Literature winners
- Pulitzer Prize winners (fiction and nonfiction)
- National Book Award winners (fiction and nonfiction)

If you're enrolled in a university, you can check your university library to see if they carry these books or have subscriptions to these magazines, newspapers, and journals. If that's not an option for you, you may have to purchase them yourself, but we promise you that the small investment is worth it!

One of the biggest reasons people give up on reading different and challenging material is that the amount of new vocabulary in the work makes the ideas very difficult to access and therefore impossible to appreciate. How do you overcome this? There is just one simple solution: look up the words you don't know and create a vocabulary bank.

"Isn't there a shortcut?" you may ask. Afterall, for other standardized tests like the Scholastic Assessment Test (SAT) or the Graduate Record Examination (GRE), you can access numerous free resources with lists of vocabulary you may be tested on as well as their definitions. Many of these resources are even conveniently organized into online flashcards, ready for you to use for all your test prep needs. Can you find something similar for CARS? The answer is: **no**. The vocabulary you encounter in CARS depends on the exact passages you get on the test, so it doesn't make sense to study a finite list of words. Also, while memorizing the definitions of a set of words may give you a boost when you're reading CARS passages, the difference will be marginal at best. This is because it's more important to understand the word in context (i.e., how it relates to other ideas, how it expresses logical relations between ideas, and so forth), rather than in isolation. Furthermore, authors may use words in unconventional ways. A word that typically means one thing in most other contexts may take on new or additional meaning depending on how the author uses it. Afterall, an author is a creative agent who can exercise their artistic license at any time. Therefore, the best way to build vocabulary in preparation for CARS is *organically* – by exposing yourself to new words through reading new texts, and intentionally taking the time to understand the meaning of these words in relation to the rest of the text in which they are embedded.

If you find yourself looking up a new word every few sentences, you may feel discouraged and want to stop all together. Don't give up! As with most new tasks we engage in, there is going to be a learning curve, so rather than letting it get to you, just embrace it! Take the time to look up words you've never seen before. Sometimes, it's even worthwhile to look up words you have seen before to be extra sure you know exactly what it means and how it fits in the given context. You may be surprised to find that your prior understanding of some words differs from their actual meaning! It may be a slow and painful exercise at first, but overtime, you will be stopping less frequently, and you will be more confident in your understanding of the text.

The exercise of reading diverse, challenging material and building your vocabulary will not only prepare you to ace CARS, it will make you a stronger reader overall!

3. Work on Speed

Equally important to building vocabulary is increasing your reading speed. As you know, you will have 90 minutes answer 53 multiple choice questions pertaining to nine different passages in CARS. This means you will have no more than 10 minutes to read and process each of the 500-600-word passages and answer five to seven questions about each of them! It is therefore imperative that you learn to read both actively and quickly.

Up until this point, it may seem like everything we've been telling you to do actually *slows down* your reading speed. Not only have we advised you to read challenging material, we've also asked you to stop every time you encounter a word you're not familiar with to look it up and understand how it fits within the text. How do you read faster if there are so many things slowing you down? It's as if we're asking you to sprint through a marsh!

Well, sprint through a marsh of passages and questions is exactly what you have to do to ace CARS, and you have to do it with extreme accuracy as well. The more challenging the material you read early on, the easier you will find it to digest new and equally challenging materials later on. The more vocabulary you have, the less you will have to stop to look up new words. When reading and understanding difficult text becomes *effortless*, you can begin to add resistance to your mental training by reducing the amount of time you have to read and analyze a block of text. Do this until you can actively read about 500-600 words in approximately five minutes. Notice that as you increase your reading speed, you will be able to get through more text in your designated 30 minutes of daily practice. Therefore, you will be able to get more practice without necessarily having to increase the amount of time you spend on the activity.

Remember: Speed cannot come at the expense of accuracy. You must maintain the same level of comprehension and correct interpretation whilst increasing speed. It's meaningless to scan through a passage of text without actually processing what it says. Only by advancing both speed and accuracy in comprehension will you be able to succeed with CARS.

4. Practice with Realistic Passages in a Realistic Setting

Thus far, our discussion has been focused what you can do to improve your reading skills with passages from diverse sources. Make no mistake, this is absolutely necessary for expanding your repertoire, but it's still not enough. In addition to just improving your overall reading comprehension and speed, you'll want to make sure you can successfully transfer these meticulously honed skills to the actual test. Though you may be able to quickly read and analyze a wide variety of texts, you will need to learn to answer multiple choice questions that will undoubtedly challenge your understanding of what you just read. Therefore, at some point in your preparation, you will need to spend additional time outside of your planned reading time for reading passages and answering multiple choice questions that are similar to the ones you will encounter on the test. Note, you should not be *substituting* your more general active reading exercises for practicing CARS passages. In order to prepare adequately for CARS, it's imperative that you do *both*.

While many test prep companies offer practice material that is like the CARS section in format, even the most reputable companies have failed to match the official test materials in terms of difficulty. As we explained earlier, it's important that you select practice materials that approximate the level of difficulty of the actual test. There is thus no better source for test prep materials than the organization that administers the test, the Association of American Medical Colleges (AAMC). The AAMC offers question packs for each section of the MCAT, including two volumes for the CARS section, each containing 120 passages and questions. Practicing with these materials will allow you to gauge your true performance level and work to improve it before your test.

A few months before you intend to take the MCAT, start practicing with these passages. Begin with just one passage and the associated questions each day and gradually increase the number of passages you complete in one sitting. Don't worry about timing yourself at first as there will be an adjustment process. You will need to eventually work to increase your speed, but again, not at the expense of accuracy. You must first ensure that you can correctly answer all the questions for a given passage almost 100% of the time.

Then, you can begin to work on decreasing the amount of time you spend on each passage.

Once you can complete each passage within 10 minutes, you can begin to practice doing CARS questions in a more realistic setting. This means mimicking the setting of the actual test in the following way:

1. *Length:* Read and complete questions for nine passages in a row. Reserve up to 10 sets of these (i.e., 90 passages) from the AAMC CARS question pack to use for this purpose.

2. *Time*: Limit yourself to 90 minutes to complete all nine passages. If you find yourself unable to finish in that timeframe, also note down how long it takes for you to complete each passage. You may find that you are taking more than 10 minutes on average for each passage. You may also find that you are able to complete passages faster at the beginning, but slow down as you go due to fatigue. In both cases, what you need is more practice to i) increase your speed, and ii) build test-taking stamina.

3. *Other sections:* Of course, for your actual MCAT, you will be doing this section in conjunction with the other three sections, so you'll also want to do some full practice tests. Since CARS requires you to use a different set of skills, be sure you are able to quickly switch gears as you start this section. This will also put additional pressure on you to keep up your stamina, since you will be physically and mentally worn down by the previous section.

4. *Setting:* One thing often neglected by students when they prepare for the test is the setting in which they conduct their practice. When you begin to do full CARS sections and full practice tests with all four sections, make sure that you are doing so in a setting that mimics what you will experience at your actual test. This includes choosing a space where you will not be disturbed by others for the entire duration of the practice. Also ensure that it's relatively quiet, but not completely silent because you will likely hear some ambient noise in the testing facility. Do your practice at the same time of day as your actual MCAT. This will ensure that you are

habituated to that level of brain activity and mental engagement during that exact time. If you do all your practice in the morning but your actual test is in the afternoon, you may find yourself getting drowsy or struggling to focus during your test, which will undoubtably have a negative impact on your performance.

5. *Frequency:* This last point is not exactly about the practice environment, but it is still relevant to your practice routine. As much as possible, space out your full-length realistic practice so that you are only doing it once or at most twice a week. In between, you can still do your 30 minutes a day of reading. Spacing out the intensive practice tests will allow you time to integrate what you've learned. It will also prevent burnout right before your actual MCAT.

Controlling for all of these factors to mimic the conditions of your MCAT will enable you to prepare most accurately for the experience. It will help you to understand how you respond to test anxiety, noise, time constraints, and so forth, and give you the chance to get accustomed to these factors so they don't become distractions on your test day.

Once you've completed a whole CARS section for practice and counted up the number of correct answers, you can move on, right? Whether you are happy about your performance or discouraged, you will likely be mentally fatigued by the exercise. However, the immediate thing to do is not to walk away, but to review your answers.

First, flag the questions you got wrong or found difficult and determine if there is a pattern. Are you struggling primarily with Foundations of Comprehension questions, Reasoning Within the Text questions, Reasoning Beyond the Text questions, or is it a mixed bag? Then, think about *why* you got them wrong. Is it because you have a tendency to misconstrue the author's intentions? Is it because you have trouble seeing the relationship between different points presented within the passage? Or, do you have trouble applying and integrating new information?

Sometimes, you may have mastered the strategy for each question type but just be thrown off by the way the questions are posed. Other times, even when you have a good idea of what the answer would be, the options you are given may confuse you, making the task of choosing the right answer quite difficult. If you are someone who is easily distracted by the wording of a question, this is yet another area to work on.

The point is, until you sit down and analyze your answers, you will not know where your weaknesses are. Without knowing this, it would be impossible for you to work on them in a targeted way and improve your performance on CARS. So, to truly understand your performance potential on the CARS section, you must submit yourself to practicing in a realistic setting and analyze your results immediately.

5. Get Expert Feedback

Of course, it can sometimes be very difficult to identify your own weaknesses. When you're consistently getting a certain number of questions wrong, you may not be able to figure out what is holding you back. Even when you do know where you need to improve, you may not know how.

This is where an expert can step in and give you a competitive edge. An expert is someone who has a deep understanding of CARS, how the passages are modified, and how the test questions are constructed. Ideally, they would also have experience creating test questions themselves, so they understand the thought process from the test writer's perspective and give you insight about how to navigate tricky questions. Such an individual will be able to help you pinpoint your exact weaknesses when it comes to reading and reasoning about CARS passages. They will also be able to teach you tailored strategies on how to overcome your weaknesses. If you're able to work with an expert over a longer period of time, they will also keep you accountable to your study plan and make sure you remain consistent and improve steadily.

If you realize that this is what you need, BeMo is here to help! Our CARS experts will happily accompany you on your journey to ensure that you succeed on what is probably the most important and difficult test you are planning to take to date.

We hope that our discussion of these five important preparation strategies has encouraged you to get an early start on your CARS prep. Now that you have a good understanding of how to prepare and improve your reading skills, it's time to give you the final puzzle piece: how to approach each CARS passage! If you've been taking notes already, which we hope you were, let's be sure to carefully jot down our simple 7-step process, it will come in handy.

BeMo's 7 Steps to Ace Any CARS Passage

1. Understand the Author's Point of View

CARS is all about how well you understand the author's perspective on the subject they wrote about in the passage. Therefore, your first job when approaching a CARS passage is to get a solid grasp of their point of view and how they arrived at that conclusion.

To do this, you must first engage in *active reading*, which requires you to read with the intent of understanding not only the meaning but also its relevance. When you read a text actively, you are critically evaluating each phrase, sentence, paragraph, and section and asking yourself "What does the author mean here?" and "How does this contribute to the overall message of the piece?". You should always be thinking about whether the section you read was introducing a new idea or expanding on an old one, whether the author agrees or disagrees with it, whether the examples support or oppose the idea, and so forth. Active reading ultimately allows you to engage with the material more deeply and gain a richer understanding of its contents and the author's intent.

Once you have actively read the passage, you should be able to synthesize the ideas presented in each paragraph or section into a one-sentence statement that describes the ideas presented. By the end of the piece, you should be able to provide a compelling one- or two-sentence thesis of the work that accurately captures its message and significance. Think of it like a litmus test for yourself. If you are truly engaged in the text, comprehending it, and analyzing it as you should, then you should be able to generate summaries of what you are reading in your own words.

Summarizing what we're reading may sound fairly straightforward, but this is actually a very difficult task. Inexperienced readers will find themselves simply repeating everything that was said in a not-so-concise way without truly extracting the essence of the work from among the many details. Some will struggle to find their own words to express the thesis and end up borrowing words, phrases, and sentences directly from the text. Of course, this is not an effective way to summarize what you just read and is a sign of weak critical analysis and reasoning skills.

If this is an exercise you struggle with, we suggest you start with smaller chunks of text. Actively read a paragraph, put it away for a few minutes, then summarize it in a single sentence without looking at the original text. Giving yourself a time buffer allows you to truly process what you just read. Summarizing it without the paragraph in front of you removes the temptation of borrowing the original terminology and phrasing. Once you're more comfortable and proficient at summarizing short passages concisely and in your own words, you can begin to piece these together to come up with the central thesis of bigger passages you have read.. Recall, the approximate length of the passages you will encounter in the CARS section is between 500-600 words. Once you get to a point where you provide both summaries to individual paragraphs and synthesize them into a central thesis, you will be able to effectively answer all three CARS question types.

2. Identify the Question Type

As we discussed in *Chapter I: What is CARS?* I, there are three different question types and you need to learn to identify them. They are repeated below:

1. *Foundations of Comprehension:* Questions that ask you about the meaning of the passage or its subparts, the author's ideas, and the overall thesis.

2. *Reasoning Within the Text:* Questions that ask you to integrate more distant components of the text to generate a higher-level interpretation of the passage.

3. *Reasoning Beyond the Text:* Questions that ask you to apply ideas from the passage to a novel situation or to new information presented in the question.

"Why is identifying the question type important?" you might ask. Indeed, why not just answer the question? Well, different question types require you to use a different mode of thinking and employ different strategic approaches. To use the right approach, you absolutely must identify the question type correctly. Additionally, different people may struggle with different question types. Thus, being able to identify them allows you to engage in more targeted practice.

3. Apply the Right Strategy for Each Question Type

So, what is the right strategy for answering each of the three question types? Let's look at them in turn.

Foundations of Comprehension:

Comprehension questions are conceptually straightforward, but they can still trip you up if you're not careful. If you have been actively reading challenging material on a regular basis, you have already been preparing for questions that ask about the meaning of words, sentences, paragraphs, and the passage as a whole. The following are strategies to help you navigate these questions:

Understanding Basic Text Components:

- Know the central thesis before you read the question so you have a point of reference and are less likely to be swayed by the answer options.

- Be able to summarize the contents of each paragraph.

- Understand the purpose of each paragraph or sentence (e.g., providing an example, explaining a concept, countering an earlier idea)

- Look for transitions that indicate the logical relation between sections (e.g., "for example", "conversely", "as a result")

- If you are asked about a section or word that you do not know, use the immediate context to help you. At the very least, you should have a sense of the author's attitude, positive or negative, towards the idea they are conveying.

- Evaluate the options presented to you against the passage or paragraph summaries you came up with as you were reading the passage to determine whether they are consistent with each other.

Interfering Meaning from Context:

- Understand the structure of the passage (e.g., thesis + antithesis + synthesis, point and counterpoint, chronology). Knowing this structure and what paragraphs or points fall under each section will help you to understand the author's use of information.

- Use the immediate context to uncover the author's unstated intent or purpose.

- Be sensitive to the tone used by the author (e.g., humorous, rhetorical) as it can make the meaning of the text less transparent.

- Be able to identify connotations of words, rather than just know their denotations, to understand the author's attitude towards the ideas presented in the passage. While the denotation is the literal meaning of the word, the connotation is the implicit meaning associated with the word. For example, while "feedback" and "criticism" both denote forms of commentary on performance, the former has a neutral connotation while the latter has a negative connotation.

- Look for clues about the author's central thesis in the first and last paragraphs of the passage. These paragraphs form the bookends to the passage and will often contain crucial information for you to be able to infer the overall purpose of the passage, even if it's not stated explicitly.

If you find yourself struggling with this question type, it is likely because you have not established a solid understanding of the basic message of the passage and the meaning of its subcomponents. Once you can confidently give your own paragraph summaries and you know how each sentence contributes to the overall message, then you can attempt this question type again.

Reasoning Within the Text:

Reasoning Within the Text questions are the logical extension of Foundations of Comprehension questions. Rather than asking you about the surface meaning of the passage or parts of the passage, these questions ask you to draw meaning from the passage by combining, comparing, contrasting and evaluating different ideas presented within it.

Integrating distant components of the text:

- Make sure you have a good understanding of the author's overarching message and the overall purpose of the passage.

- Break down how each section of the passage contributes to that purpose and how they relate to each other. Some paragraphs may be presenting ideas or existing theories. These might be followed by an exposition of the author's own thoughts on those ideas. Other paragraphs may be providing examples as supporting evidence.

- Be sensitive to ideas that digress from or don't contribute to the author's main point.

- Know when the author is presenting their own perspective vs. the perspective of another person they are citing.

Recognizing and Evaluating arguments:

- Be sensitive to the credibility of the evidence presented by the author and the validity of their assumptions. Is the evidence factual or anecdotal? Does the author assume a causal relationship between two events when in fact there could be no relation at all?

- Become attuned to inconsistencies within the passage. Does the author present paradoxical or contradictory information?

- Know when the author's arguments are one-sided or biased. Does the author omit relevant information? Does the author present information with stereotypical labels?

If you struggle with Reasoning Within the Text questions, ask yourself these questions: How does the author feel about the topic of this essay? What evidence does the author use to support or oppose their main argument? How does each piece of information within the text help or hurt the author's main point?

Reasoning Beyond the Text:

This last question type can only be tackled successfully when you have fully understood the information presented within the text, since it asks you to take that information and apply it to new contexts.

Extrapolating Passage Ideas to New Contexts:

- Consider the bigger aspects of the text such as the framework or perspective the author uses. This will help you gauge how the new material fits in.

- Put yourself in the author's shoes. Ask yourself, "If I were the author, and held all the beliefs the author presents and implies in this passage, what would I most likely do or agree with, given this new information?"

- Know how the different options relate to the ideas in the passage by identifying their underlying common features. Carefully eliminate options that are similar on the surface but fundamentally different so that you can find the answer that is fundamentally analogous, even though it appears to be different.

Assessing the Impact of New Information on Passage Ideas:

- Have a solid grasp of what the author is saying so that you can determine whether the new idea supports or refutes, strengthens or weakens the author's argument.

- Consider the conclusions drawn in the passage to be changeable. This will give you the flexibility to consider the impact of the new ideas in presented in the question.

- Come up with a new central thesis given the new information. Does it stay the same or does it change?

If you are struggling with Reasoning Beyond the Text questions, ask yourself these questions about any text you read: If the author supports this point, what other points would the author support? What types of hypothetical evidence would the author use or not use?

You'll notice that the common thread behind all of these strategies is that you must absolutely have a good grasp of what the passage is saying in the first place. You cannot connect ideas within the text or generalize them to concepts outside the text if you don't understand the ideas themselves. This is why, even though comprehension questions make up the smallest proportion of questions in the CARS section, the skill you use to answer these questions are *foundational* to all questions you encounter in this section of the MCAT. So, the most important strategy to doing well on CARS is to simply to *understand the passage*, which is a skill you will hopefully be developing through actively reading challenging texts consistently and over a long period of time.

4. Only Use the Information Given

Regardless of which question type you are answering, the one thing you should *never* do is import outside information such as your own knowledge or opinions about the topic. This is especially dangerous if you do not agree with the author on some or all of the points. Since the questions are always centered on the author's opinions and stance, bringing in your own ideas can muddle your thought process. If one of the options you're given in a multiple-choice question presents an idea that is closer to your opinion but doesn't exactly fit with the author's opinion, you may unintentionally gravitate towards that answer, and as a result get the question wrong. Therefore, keep the author's ideas and your own ideas compartmentalized and draw only from what the author is saying.

This is true even for Reasoning Beyond the Text questions. Even though you may be presented additional information that was not part of the passage you read, you are still expected to use only the ideas given to you in the question.

5. Formulate Your Own Answer

After you read a question to a CARS passage, your first instinct will be to look at all of the answer choices. This will be especially true towards the beginning of your practice when you may feel less certain about your understanding of the passage or even the question you just read. Knowing the choices might make you feel safer momentarily, because at least you will have a finite set of options to choose from. However, if you don't have a solid grasp of the information from the passage and a good understanding of what the question is asking, reading the answers is more likely to *confuse* you than help you. Why might this be? Well, the answers to a CARS question are designed precisely for that purpose – to confuse you! Additionally, some of the options may be formulated to sound like the "common sense" answer, inviting you to pull in your own knowledge and experiences. As you already know, you must avoid doing this at all costs.

Since it's so easy to be swayed or confused by the answer choices provided to you, one of the best strategies to practice when answer CARS questions is to refrain from reading the answers right away and come up with your *own* answer to the question first. To do this, you must rely on the paragraph summaries and central thesis you came up with while activiely reading the passage. You must also have a clear understanding of the question. If you feel shaky on either of these, go back and review the passage and/or the question until you feel confident about them, then do your best to write down an answer that makes sense based on what the author said in the passage. Once you have formulated your own answer, read through the answer options and select the one that best approximates your response. Of course, also check to make sure that the other responses are definitely incorrect.

While you may struggle with this at first, using this approach to questions will increase your accuracy over time and ultimately make you a more confident test-taker!

6. Eliminate Obviously Wrong Answers

Of course, even when you are 100% certain of your understanding of both the passage and the question, you could still be faced with answer options that challenge your ability to make the right choice right off the bat. In such cases, you may need to rely on an old trick – the process of elimination. This can be done in several steps:

1. Eliminate the answers that do not align with the passage. If you have an accurate understanding of the passage, you should be able to spot these answers easily.

2. Eliminate the answers that are only partially correct. Sometimes, there will be answer options that begin with the correct idea, but end on an incorrect idea. Be sure to read the full answer and evaluate all components so you can eliminate these.

3. Eliminate the answers that are illogical. These are very similar to the partially correct options in that they may seem viable at first glance, but upon closer examination, you realize that the pieces don't fit together logically. For example, they might try to establish a causal relationship between two events with a transitional word like "because", even though the author did not imply it in the passage.

4. Eliminate the answers that are irrelevant. These are the trickiest to identify because they are often in line with information presented in the passage. The only reason they are incorrect is because they don't address the question at hand. If you are left with two options that both sound right based on the passage you read, one of them may fall into this category. In such cases, the immediate thing to do is to re-read the question. This will enable you to determine which answer is relevant and which one is not.

One additional tip when you are reading the questions and answers is to beware of negations, which can come in many forms. For example, a question may ask you to choose the answer that is *inconsistent* with the author's argument or *refutes* the main claim. In such cases, the negation is simply embedded in the word choice. There may also questions that are grammatically negated, such as a question asking you to identify the statement that does *not* constitute evidence supporting a claim. This second type can be easily missed if you're not paying attention to the small, yet significant functional word, "not". Any kind of negation in a question can add a layer of complexity to the exercise because you are now being asked to flip your thought process and do the opposite. Although this type of question may seem tricky at first glance, you will answer it as you do others; begin by coming up with your own answer, then ruling out all the incorrect answers. In examples above, you want choose the answer that is inconsistent with the passage and rule out answers that are consistent with it.

Knowing the common traps in the questions and answers and what to look for when eliminating the wrong answers will help you to avoid many unnecessary mistakes as you're practicing for CARS.

7. Don't Spend Too Much Time on Each Question

If you are working through a really tough CARS question while you are doing a timed practice test or during the real MCAT, remember not to spend too much of your time on that question. Simply pick the best answer, flag the question, and move on. You can always return to this question once you've completed all of the other questions for that same passage.

The obvious reason behind this strategy is that you have a time limit. Recall that you have 90 minutes for nine passage, so you should not be spending any more than 10 minutes on each passage and its questions. If you devote more time to a question you're unsure about, you could be taking time away from other more straightforward questions that you can almost certainly get right. This trade is obviously not worth it! Another reason for using this strategy is that sometimes, though not always, completing other questions for the same passage may actually clarify and enhance your understanding of the text or previous questions. If this happens, you can then easily go back and confirm the answer for that earlier question you struggled with.

When is a good time to take the test?

So, you've started preparing early and you've taken all the right steps, which means there is just one final question that needs to be addressed: When should you take the test? Of course, the answer to this question will depend in part on your preparedness for the other three sections of the MCAT, but beyond the bottom line that you should complete it before the deadline set by the schools you are applying for, you should take the test *when you're ready*. Sitting the MCAT is such a huge investment of time and money that ideally, you only want to do it once.

So, what counts as "ready"? Each person is different, as is their concept of a "good" CARS score. However, as a rule of thumb, if you're aiming for a score of about 128, then you'll need to get about 90% of the questions correct in each of your practice tests leading up to your MCAT. (Note that this is just approximate, as each MCAT section is scored on a curve, and your final score will depend on a host of factors.) Once you're able to achieve this score consistently across several practice tests, you should take the test. Another way to think about this is that you should take the test when you are consistently getting a few more correct answers than your target. That way, you will be able to get a satisfactory score even if the actual test is a little harder or your performance is affected by additional stress. The idea in both cases is to take the test at the peak of your performance, before your scores start to drop due to test prep fatigue or overpreparation. Take the test when you feel most confident about your ability to accurately represent your skill level.

We hope that the discussion of preparation strategies and steps to approach each CARS passage has been enlightening and that you now understand how implementing each of them will contribute to your success. If you will be taking the MCAT in the future and have not yet begun to prepare, let this be your inspiration to get started. If you have been preparing already but realize you have not been doing enough or you have been practicing incorrectly, let this be your motivation to correct your path. If you have done everything right and still feel that you can do better with a little guidance, let this be an invitation for you to reach out to us and get the help you need!

Let's not stop there! To help you get a better grasp of what you should be expecting on your CARS test, we will walk you through 10 sample passages and questions so that you can see exactly how each passage can be broken down and analyzed before choosing the correct answer. Also be sure to check out *Chapter VII: Long-term and Short-term Stress Management Strategies* for proven methods to help you overcome test and preparation anxiety.

Free Goodwill

A message from our CEO, Behrouz Moemeni

My mentor always used to say, "Behrouz, you should give until it hurts." What he meant by this is giving your time and resources to those who are less fortunate or experienced than you to empower them to get to the next level on their journey, whatever that may be. People who lend a hand to others with zero expectations for return experience higher life satisfaction and self-fulfillment and are generally more successful in their careers. However, I have learned that supporting others can be a lot simpler than what you may think. You don't have to spend a lot of time or money, and it doesn't actually have to "hurt" to help. It starts with the simple things and grows as you gain the resources to do more.

As you probably know, I created BeMo to provide as much information as possible to everyone. I think information should be available to all for little to no cost. That's why, at BeMo, we create books, videos, extensive blogs, and other resources at little to no cost to students, even though they cost us a lot to create. We only charge for our private consulting and preparation programs, and even then, the value we create for our students is infinitely more than the cost of our services. For example, think of the lifetime value of becoming a medical doctor, dentist, and so forth (e.g., by doing some quick math and multiplying only 20 years of work at an average of $250,000/year salary). Though the return on investment is crystal clear, we want students to start with a low-cost commitment to see the benefit first; we want students to choose us to be their private mentors only if they find value in our work and commit only when they are ready to invest in themselves, which we facilitate with interest-free installment plans. This is why we provide all the information necessary for anyone to do this on their own, if they choose to do so. However, the only way for us, at BeMo, to accomplish our audacious mission of helping one billion students is by reaching as many people as possible.

So, I'd like to create an opportunity for you to help others you don't know with a few minutes of your time. Think of those who will go through the same journey as you in the future. They are less experienced, have less resources, and maybe have no idea where to start. If you have found the information in this book valuable so far, would you please write us a quick review on Amazon?

Most people judge a book like this by its cover and its reviews. Your review will help someone...

get to the next level...

advance in their career...

achieve life fulfillment...

and...*help others*.

It will take you less than 60 seconds to make all of this happen...please leave a review on Amazon.

Thank you very much from the bottom of my heart for helping us with our mission.

To your success,

Behrouz Moemeni, Ph.D.
CEO @ BeMo

CHAPTER VI

10 Sample CARS Passages with Expert Responses and Analyses

I n this chapter, you will find 10 sample CARS passages, each with corresponding paragraph summaries and a central thesis. We also include three questions as well as the correct answers, explanations, and an expert analysis for each of the questions.

To get the most of these sample passages, we recommend that you pause after the passage and come up with your own paragraph summaries and central thesis before moving on to read the expert summaries and thesis on the next page. When you move on to read the questions, first identify the question types and answer them yourself. Only go on to read the answers, explanations, and discussions once you've given each question an honest attempt. If you get a question wrong, we encourage you to really study the explanations and make sure you can give them in your own words. Make sure you understand not only why the correct answer is right, but also why the incorrect answers are wrong.

As you go through the passages and questions, see if you can also identify any patterns in your performance. Note down what kind of question you are good at and which ones you tend to struggle with. Are you fairly consistent with Foundations of Comprehension questions, but tend to second-guess yourself on Reasoning Within the Text questions? Or, are you someone who finds the Reasoning Beyond the Text questions most challenging? Also, note down what aspects of the question or answer structure made the question challenging. Did the negation in the question slow you down, or were you confused by the fact that all the answers are mentioned in the passage? Once you begin identifying patterns in your performance, you can then engage in more targeted practice. If you need to, go back to *Chapter V: BeMo's Top Strategies & 7 Steps to ACE Any CARS Passage* to review the question types and how you can better navigate them.

Before we go on to the passages, here's a breakdown of what you can expect to see for each passage:

1. The passage. We recommend that you pause after this page to write down paragraph summaries and the central thesis.

2. The expert passage summaries and central thesis.

3. Three passage questions. We recommend that you pause after this page to identify the question types and answer the questions.

4. Question 1 answer, explanations and expert discussion

5. Question 2 answer, explanations and expert discussion

6. Question 3 answer, explanations and expert discussion

Are you ready? Let's begin!

SAMPLE PASSAGE 1

The Vietnamese epic poem Truyện Kiều (or Kiều) is written in the lục bát (six-eight) verse form, a famous meter popular for its regularity in rhythm, tone pattern, and rhyme. It is traditionally described as being composed of couplets containing a 6-syllable line followed by an 8-syllable line. Within each couplet, syllables are specified for one of two tone categories: flat tones (ngang or huyền), or sharp tones (sắc, nặng, hỏi, or ngã). The poet also employs a popular rhyming scheme of the lục bát verse form in which the sixth syllable of the 6-syllable line rhymes with the sixth syllable of the 8-syllable line, and the eighth syllable of the 8-syllable line rhymes with the sixth syllable of the following 6-syllable line.

The traditional description is fairly detailed in terms of tones and rhyme, but offers little in terms of rhythmic specifications. Apart from the macro-level rules on the number of rhythmic units in each line of the couplet, there are no further specifications on line-internal structure in the lục bát meter. However, as the theory of phrasing asserts, linguistic material is organized into a hierarchy in which rhythmic units of various sizes are nested under larger rhythmic units. Utterances are composed of one or more intonational phrases, intonational phrases are composed of one or more intermediate phrases, intermediate phrases are composed of one or more feet, and so forth. This is paralleled by the classical layering theory of structure in meter in which metrical units (i.e., syllable, foot, hemistich, line, couplet) are also hierarchically organized.

A closer analysis of the inter-syllabic syntactic breaks in the 3254 lines of Kiều reveals that it is no exception. In the 8-syllable line, larger breaks can be found after every other syllable, and an even larger break can be expected after the fourth syllable, indicating that this line can be subdivided into two hemistichs, which can be further divided into disyllabic feet. In the 6-syllable line, two patterns can be observed: larger breaks occur either after every other syllable, dividing this line into three disyllabic feet, or after every third syllable, dividing this line into two hemistichs. Thus, despite the lack of specificity in traditional descriptions of this meter, it is clear that it is not void of line-internal structure.

Paragraph Summaries and Central Thesis

Paragraph 1:
The epic poem Truyện Kiều is written in the lục bát meter, which has a regular rhythmic, tonal, and rhyme pattern. This paragraph introduces the traditional description of the lục bát meter to be contested by the author in subsequent paragraphs.

Paragraph 2:
The lack of rhythmic specificity in the traditional description of lục bát is inconsistent with theories of phrasing. In this paragraph, the author identifies a problem with the traditional description of the lục bát form.

Paragraph 3:
The lines of Kiều are revealed to contain internal rhythmic structure that are missed in the traditional description of the verse form. This paragraph provides evidence that the epic poem Kiều actually does adhere to linguistic theories of phrasing.

Central Thesis:
Though traditional descriptions of the lục bát meter portray line-internal structure as flat, there is evidence from an analysis of the syntactic breaks that there is line-internal hierarchical structure, which is more consistent with theories of linguistic phrasing.

Passage 1 Questions

Question 1: What is the author referring to by the phrase "macro-level rules" in the second paragraph?

    A. The rule that each syllable of the poem must have either a flat tone or a sharp tone.

    B. The rule that the 6th syllable in each line of a couplet must rhyme, and the 8th syllable in the second line of the couplet must rhyme with the 6th syllable of the first line in the next couplet.

    C. The first line in a couplet must have 6 syllables and the second line in a couplet must have 8 syllables.

    D. In order for a poem to be considered to have the lục bát verse form, it must adhere to each of the rules about rhyme, rhythm, and tone.

Question 2: Which of the following conclusions, drawn from the passage, is logically problematic?

    A. Traditional descriptions of the lục bát verse form are incorrect because they are missing crucial details about line-internal structure.

    B. Traditional descriptions of the lục bát verse form are inaccurate because couplets in Kiều do break from the 6-syllable-8-syllable model.

    C. The traditional description of the lục bát verse form should be updated given the newfound evidence for line-internal structure.

    D. The existence of line-internal structure, demonstrating the inadequacies of the traditional description of lục bát, calls for a reexamination of other specifications such as those about tone and rhyme.

Question 3: Which of the following findings would not weaken the author's conclusion?

    A. There is no evidence from poems other than Kiều that there is hierarchical rhythmic structure within each line.

    B. There is only one possible pattern in the 6-syllable line; it must be divided into two 3-syllable hemistichs.

    C. The patterns found in the lục bát meter are merely natural patterns of Vietnamese speech found in both written and spoken prose, and thus do not need to be specified as rules of poetry.

    D. The line-internal syntactic breaks described by the author are only found in some lines of Kiều and therefore not statistically representative of the broader patterns in the epic poem.

Passage 1 – Question 1 Answer & Discussion

Note: The explanation under each answer explains why it is correct or incorrect, and the correct answer is bolded.

Question 1: What is the author referring to by the phrase "macro-level rules" in the second paragraph?

Type: Foundations of Comprehension

A. The rule that each syllable of the poem must have either a flat tone or a sharp tone.

   Explanation: This is a rule about the tonal specification on each syllable, whereas the "macro-level" rules refer to the number of syllables in each line (see Answer C).

B. The rule that the 6th syllable in each line of a couplet must rhyme, and the 8th syllable in the second line of the couplet must rhyme with the 6th syllable of the first line in the next couplet.

   Explanation: This is a rule about the rhyme specification on specific syllables in each line, whereas the "macro-level" rules refer to the *number* of syllables in each line (see Answer C).

C. The first line in a couplet must have 6 syllables and the second line in a couplet must have 8 syllables.

   Explanation: The "macro-level rules" mentioned in the second paragraph refer to "the number of rhythmic units in each line of the couplet." In the previous paragraph, the author states that the lục bát is "composed of couplets containing a 6-syllable line followed by an 8-syllable line". Thus, the "rhythmic units" of the poem are the syllables, and the rule is that there are 6 of them in the first line of the couplet and 8 in the next line.

D. In order for a poem to be considered to have the lục bát verse form, it must adhere to each of the rules about rhyme, rhythm, and tone.

   Explanation: The "macro-level rules" refer specifically to rules about rhythm and does not include rules about rhyme or tone (see Answer C). Additionally, this statement is problematic because the author merely states that the lục bát is traditionally described as having a regular rhythm, tone pattern, and rhyme. She does not, however, assert that poems that deviate from the specifications indicated for this particular epic, Kiều, cannot be classified as having the lục bát verse form. In fact, she states that the poet of Kiều "...employs a popular rhyming scheme of the lục bát verse form...", suggesting that there are possible variations.

Discussion:

This is a Foundations of Comprehension question that tests your understanding of a basic component of the text by asking what a specific phrase is referring to. Though this may seem fairly straightforward, the answer options are either from the passage or could have plausibly originated from the passage. Therefore, it is not possible to simply eliminate options based on their absence from the passage.

To answer this question correctly, you must be able to link the phrase "macro-level rules" in the second paragraph to one of the specific rules detailed in the previous paragraph based on i) the previous sentence, and ii) the description of the term that follows in the same sentence. In the previous sentence, which says, "The traditional description is fairly detailed in terms of tones and rhyme, but offers little in terms of rhythmic specifications," is your first clue that the macro-level rules the author discusses refers to rhythm and not tones and rhyme. The information following the term in the second half of the sentence further indicates that it's about a numeric count in each line of the couplet. The only rule that fits this description from the previous paragraph is thus the one that states the number of syllables in each line of the couplet.

Passage 1 – Question 2 Answer & Discussion

Note: The explanation under each answer explains why it is correct or incorrect, and the correct answer is bolded.

Question 2: Which of the following conclusions, drawn from the passage, is logically problematic?

Type: Reasoning Within the Text

A. **Traditional descriptions of the lục bát verse form are incorrect because they are missing crucial details about line-internal structure.**

Explanation: We cannot logically draw this conclusion because the lack of additional specification does not invalidate the broader assertion that the lục bát meter is made up of couplets containing a 6-syllable and 8-syllable lines.

B. Traditional descriptions of the lục bát verse form are inaccurate because couplets in Kiều do break from the 6-syllable-8-syllable model.

Explanation: The author never states that couplets within the epic can deviate from the traditional rhythmic description. The conclusion is thus based on a faulty assumption, though it would be logically sound if the assumption were true.

C. The traditional description of the lục bát verse form should be updated given the newfound evidence for line-internal structure.

Explanation: This is conclusion is based on the information given in the passage, and it is logically sound.

D. The existence of line-internal structure, demonstrating the inadequacies of the traditional description of lục bát, calls for a reexamination of other specifications such as those about tone and rhyme.

Explanation: This is simply not a conclusion that can be drawn from the passage. The author does not find other parts of the traditional description problematic, as can be seen in the sentence, "The traditional description is fairly detailed in terms of tones and rhyme, but offers little in terms of rhythmic specifications." Thus, this is not a conclusion we can draw from the passage.

Discussion:

This Reasoning Within the Text question asks you to evaluate the logical soundness of conclusions drawn from the text. The correct answer must fulfill two criteria: It must be a conclusion that one can draw from the passage, and it must be logically flawed. Answers B and D are incorrect because either the whole conclusion or the assumptions within the conclusion are not consistent with the passage. Answer C is wrong because even though it is a conclusion we can reasonably draw from the passage, it does not have any logical inconsistencies. Answer A is correct because it is the only option that fulfills both of the criteria listed above.

This question is difficult because at first glance, the correct answer seems to be a conclusion that the author would draw, so you may be inclined to rule it out quickly. However, if you analyze the internal logic of this conclusion, you will discover that the traditional description of lục bát is not *incorrect*; at best we can say it is *incomplete*. Keep in mind that Reasoning Within the Text questions ask you to think about the passage beyond the ideas that are presented literally. This particular question requires you to think about the soundness of the arguments and the reasonableness of the conclusion.

Passage 1 – Question 3 Answer & Discussion

Note: The explanation under each answer explains why it is correct or incorrect, and the correct answer is bolded.

Question 3: Which of the following findings would not weaken the author's conclusion?

Type: Reasoning Beyond the Text

A. There is no evidence from poems other than Kiều that there is hierarchical rhythmic structure within each line.

   Explanation: If Kiều was the only example of poetry with line-internal structure, this would weaken the author's claim that all poetry written in the lục bát verse form should have line-internal structure.

B. There is only one possible pattern in the 6-syllable line; it must be divided into two 3-syllable hemistichs.

   Explanation: This finding would only invalidate the author's claim that there are two possible rhythmic patterns in the 6-syllable line. However, such a finding would still be consistent with the author's conclusion that there is line-internal rhythmic structure in the lục bát meter.

C. The patterns found in the lục bát meter are merely natural patterns of Vietnamese speech found in both written and spoken prose, and thus do not need to be specified in the rules of poetry.

   Explanation: This finding would also weaken the author's claim as it would mean that the patterns the author describes are not unique to the lục bát meter, but are present in all instances of Vietnamese text, spoken and written.

D. The line-internal syntactic breaks described by the author are only found in some lines of Kiều and therefore not statistically representative of the broader patterns in the epic poem.

   Explanation: Discovering that there is little supporting evidence for the claim within the example text used to validate it would certainly weaken the author's conclusion about line-internal structure in the lục bát meter.

Discussion:

This question is difficult for two reasons. First, as a Reasoning Beyond the Text question, it asks you to use new information to re-evaluate the author's claim made in the passage. Second, the question is negated, adding another logical layer to undo and thus increasinges your cognitive load. Rather than looking for one finding that weakens the author's conclusion, you are required to rule out all the findings that weaken the author's conclusion to find the one that does not. To make this more difficult, the correct answer is actually inconsistent with one of the author's findings, but ultimately it does not invalidate the author's overall claim.

In order to answer this question correctly, you must first have a clear idea of what the author's conclusion is – that the traditional description of the lục bát meter lacks line-internal specification. Once you have established this, and you have undone the logical knots in the question, you can begin to go through the answers one by one and ask yourself whether the new information would weaken this claim.

SAMPLE PASSAGE 2

Martin Luther's doctrine of justification purports that human salvation is possible only through Christ's righteousness, which has been bestowed upon the human race through his sacrifice. Thus, human souls are saved without merit, through faith in Christ. In his view, humanity does not possess any remnants of the image of the divine and the initial creation of humankind in God's likeness has been completely destroyed by continued sinfulness.

The depravity of humankind is highlighted in Luther's comparison of human law and God-given law. The former requires the mere works of the body. It is not essential for the human heart to participate in obedience to the laws that are constructed socially or politically. The only motivations for obedience to human law are fear of punishment or personal gain. Such obedience increases sin, since it is done out of viciousness and does nothing to improve the state of the human soul. God-given law is foreign to humanity: the law is pure goodness and to fulfill the law is to accomplish works with love for the law; this is incompatible with human sin.

The righteousness of human hearts, according to Luther, has been imputed to humankind, but humankind is not righteous on its own. It is impossible for humankind to possess or grow in righteousness, since only God has righteousness that he has mercifully ascribed to humanity. Only faith can transform a person and faith in Christ necessarily makes one a participant in God's righteousness.

If humankind is enveloped in sin and cannot possibly overcome this sinfulness on its own, if we are so removed from the divine that everything God-given is foreign and painful for us, in what possible way can one have faith in such a state? How can one receive grace and be receptive to it? How does it find "space" to work in the muddled, corrupted human soul? The answer, for Luther, lies in agency. He speaks about two environments of self-experience in *Preface to Galatians*. In active righteousness, the external circumstances of the law have developed the ego in human consciousness. The law has led humanity to take an active role to become participants in acquiring righteousness before God. Passive righteousness requires even the well-intended ego to be relinquished, the falsely constructed consciousness to be discarded, so that the transformation of the human soul can take place by the work of the Holy Spirit.

What, then, causes the corrupt being to loosen his grip on his ego in the first place? Whom should we accredit for this very foundational decision? If indeed God's Spirit only begins his work after the ego has been relinquished by man, perhaps man is not so meritless after all.

Paragraph Summaries and Central Thesis

Paragraph 1: Luther's doctrine of justification states that humans are sinful and can only be saved through faith in Christ, who is righteous. This paragraph introduces the contrast of human sinfulness and God's righteousness, which will be explored further in subsequent paragraphs.

Paragraph 2: Luther states that the motivations for obeying human law can only be wicked while the motivations for obeying God's laws can only be good, so humans are incapable of obeying God's law. This paragraph gives an example from Luther to support the second half of the first paragraph.

Paragraph 3: According to Luther, righteousness does not originate from humans but is imputed on humankind by God when we have faith in Christ. This paragraph makes a connection between two seemingly incompatible entities, humankind and God, and returns to the idea explored in the first half of the first paragraph.

Paragraph 4: Luther claims that righteousness must be obtained passively, by letting go of the self and allowing the Holy Spirit to do its work. Here, the author points out a gap in the theology and draws on more of Luther's interpretations of Biblical text to answer his own questions.

Paragraph 5: If man has to make the decision to relinquish his ego, then he has some merit in becoming righteous. The final paragraph reveals the author's own attitudes towards the claim that man has no merit in being righteous.

Central Thesis: For Luther, being righteous in the eyes of God is not the result of our own works but the result of the Holy Spirit working in us. However, the author does not agree that man has no merit in achieving righteousness.

Passage 2 Questions

Question 1: For which of the following reasons does the author disagree with Luther about man's involvement in his own salvation?

    A. Man has no role in saving his own soul because he participates in passive righteousness.

    B. Man must allow the Holy Spirit to work in him.

    C. Even though man is not able to fulfill God-given law, he is still able to obey human law.

    D. It is impossible for man to overcome his own sinfulness.

Question 2: Which of the following is inconsistent with Martin Luther's idea of the nature of humankind?

    A. The Holy Spirit helps humankind attain righteousness by removing human consciousness.

    B. Even human motivations to obey the law are corrupted by sin.

    C. Humankind is incapable of good due to our sinful nature.

    D. Humankind bears only mild likeness to God, our Creator, because of our continued sinfulness.

Question 3: The idea of predetermination – i.e., God determines who believes in Jesus and goes to heaven – would do what to the author's argument?

    A. It would strengthen the author's argument because this is in direct opposition to the doctrine of free will.

    B. It would strengthen the author's argument because God would give man the ability to take his salvation into his own hands.

    C. It would weaken the author's argument because the decision for an individual to relinquish his own ego would be made by God.

    D. It would weaken the author's argument because salvation cannot be obtained without the work of God.

Passage 2 – Question 1 Answer & Discussion

Note: The explanation under each answer explains why it is correct or incorrect, and the correct answer is bolded.

Question 1: For which of the following reasons does the author disagree with Luther about man's involvement in his own salvation?

Type: Reasoning Within the Text

A. Man has no role in saving his own soul because he participates in passive righteousness.

Explanation: The author's argument is that IF man participates in passive righteousness, then he does have a role in saving his own soul. See the explanation for Answer B.

B. Man must allow the Holy Spirit to work in him.

Explanation: This is consistent with the author's rebuttal, which is most clearly laid out in the very last sentence of the passage, "If indeed God's Spirit only begins his work after the ego has been relinquished by man, perhaps man is not so meritless after all." For the author, relinquishing the ego is an autonomous act, for which the merit belongs to man himself. This goes against Luther's idea that God is solely responsible for man's salvation.

C. Even though man is not able to fulfill God-given law, he is still able to obey human law.

Explanation: The author does not make any statement about whether obedience to human law counts towards one's salvation.

D. It is impossible for man to overcome his own sinfulness.

Explanation: This point does not directly address the question of whether man could be (partly) responsible for his own salvation.

Discussion:

This Reasoning Within the Text question requires you to understand the author's central thesis, which is presented in the final paragraph of the passage, and the reasoning behind his conclusion. The options you are given may confuse you because upon a first read, you might notice that three of them (Answers B-D) are actually points that Luther might agree with. You might then be inclined to choose the only point that is not made by Luther, that is, Answer A. However, this is incorrect because the author would also disagree with this idea.

To arrive at the correct answer, you must then reassess Answers B-D to identify the one the author uses as his argument against Luther. Answer D is not relevant to the question at hand, and the author does not comment on the relationship between Answer C and the idea of merit for salvation. Answer B is correct because it is most consistent with the author's reasoning for his position presented in the final paragraph.

Passage 2 – Question 2 Answer & Discussion

Note: The explanation under each answer explains why it is correct or incorrect, and the correct answer is bolded.

Question 2: Which of the following is inconsistent with Martin Luther's idea of the nature of humankind?

Type: Foundations of Comprehension

A. The Holy Spirit helps humankind attain righteousness by removing human consciousness.

Explanation: This statement is indeed inconsistent with the information presented in the final sentence of this passage, which asserts that humans need to get rid of their own falsely constructed consciousness so that the Holy Spirit can do its work. However, it does not actually comment on human nature.

B. Even human motivations to obey the law are corrupted by sin.

Explanation: This statement is consistent with Luther's idea of human nature. It is stated in the second paragraph that "The only motivations for obedience to human law are fear of punishment or personal gain."

C. Humankind is incapable of good due to our sinful nature.

Explanation: This is statement is also consistent with Luther's idea of human nature. Throughout the passage, the idea that sin has deprived humanity of self-attained righteousness is continuously reinforced.

D. Humankind bears only mild likeness to God, our Creator, because of our continued sinfulness.

Explanation: Though Luther would agree that humankind is plagued by continued sin, he would disagree with the idea that humankind bears a mild likeness to God, as can be seen in the sentence where he states, "...humanity does not possess any remnants of the image of the divine..."

Discussion:

This question simply tests your understanding of a basic component of the text; however, the way it is set up could make it tricky for some. First, note that there is in fact a negation in the question. Rather than asking you to look for a statement that is *consistent* with Luther's beliefs about human nature, it asks you to look for a statement that is *inconsistent* with Luther's beliefs. Therefore, you need to first rule out any answers that are in line with Luther's ideas about humanity.

By doing this, you should be able to easily eliminate Answers B and C. This leaves you with Answers A and D, both of which seem to contradict information in the passage. Oftentimes, when this happens, you can rule out one of the options by its relevance to the question. At this point, it is always a good idea to go back and reread the question to make sure you have a solid understanding of what it's asking for. This question specifically asks you to identify a statement that is inconsistent with Martin Luther's beliefs about *human nature*. We already know both are inconsistent with Martin's beliefs, so you need only to choose the answer that specifically addresses *human nature*. In doing so, you can rule out Answer A and select Answer D.

Passage 2 – Question 3 Answer & Discussion

Note: The explanation under each answer explains why it is correct or incorrect, and the correct answer is bolded.

Question 3: The idea of predetermination – i.e., God determines who believes in Jesus and goes to heaven – would do what to the author's argument?

Type: Reasoning Beyond the Text

A. It would strengthen the author's argument because this is in direct opposition to the doctrine of free will.

Explanation: While this statement captures an agreeable relationship between redetermination and free will, it would not strengthen the author's argument. An element in the author's conclusion is that man has the free will to make the initial decision to relinquish his ego. Thus, predetermination opposes that and would weaken the author's argument.

B. It would strengthen the author's argument because God would give man the ability to take his salvation into his own hands.

Explanation: The idea of predetermination, as defined above, does not suggest that God gives man ability to do anything. It simply states that God determines what man believes in and his ultimate fate.

C. It would weaken the author's argument because the decision for an individual to relinquish his own ego would be made by God.

Explanation: The author argues that man partakes in achieving his own salvation because he makes the decision to relinquish his own ego. The idea of predetermination removes that agency from man and gives it to God, thus weakening the author's argument.

D. It would weaken the author's argument because salvation cannot be obtained without the work of God.

Explanation: The reason cited is incorrect. It assumes that God is necessarily involved in man's salvation, but not that

He is necessarily the sole orchestrator of it. Simply making the first assumption does not weaken the author's argument that man is partly responsible for his own salvation because it does not exclude man in the justification process.

Discussion:

This Reasoning Beyond the Text question asks you to consider a new piece of information and how it alters the author's conclusion. Two of the answers say that it would strengthen the author's conclusion, while the other two say that it would weaken it. If you have a clear idea of whether the author's argument is strengthened or weakened, you can easily eliminate two of the options. However, if you are unsure at the outset, you can still arrive at the right answer by simply considering the reason provided in each answer.

Answer A can be eliminated because the reason cited is logically flawed. Answer B can be eliminated because it presents an inaccurate interpretation of predetermination. That leaves Answers C and D. Though they both seem plausible, we must again, consider the logic behind the assumptions of the reasons cited. The author's argument is that man is not excluded from the work of his salvation. Thus, the correct answer is one in which man has no part in this enterprise. As explained above, the assumption made by the statement in Answer D does not exclude man from the process. We can therefore rule this answer out and select Answer C as the correct option.

SAMPLE PASSAGE 3

Project Based Learning (PBL) is gaining major headway in the realm of teaching as a primary learning tool. While there are many advantages to such an approach, many do not view PBL as teaching. When utilized incorrectly or in an inauthentic way, students are left with scant teacher guidance and minimal content covered; however, gold standard PBL, a comprehensive research-based model, addresses these concerns and makes a case for the use of PBL in education.

With traditional teaching methods, students are driven mainly by external factors, such as pleasing their parents and achieving high marks. Most find traditional teaching methods monotonous and prefer to interact with educators and peers. Projects are often introduced into traditional teaching as a reward or a hands-on extension of the material taught, but lack the rigor needed to qualify as PBL. They merely serve as a secondary instructional method; a lack of authenticity causes students to be disengaged and unable to view the project as meaningful.

Gold standard PBL strives to increase student knowledge and understanding by establishing a highly authentic learning process. When learning is connected to real-world experiences – such as solving a problem or meeting a design challenge – student engagement is increased. Studies show that students who participate in PBL learn more information and retain that information longer. Students display a 60% higher long-term retention rate and perform better on assessments because they are able to apply in-depth knowledge, demonstrating true understanding and learning of content rather than rote memorization.

Beyond teaching content, gold standard PBL aims to teach students life skills, such as problem-solving and successful collaboration. By allowing students to refine these skills in the classroom, they can utilize them more successfully in their future endeavors. PBL is designed to develop independent learners that are prepared to self-advocate and take the initiative necessary to succeed. For teachers that aspire to prepare students for life-long learning, and to instill in them a passion for learning, PBL is an ideal approach and a win-win for everyone.

Paragraph Summaries and Central Thesis

Paragraph 1: Project Based Learning (PBL) has been criticized for its lack of teacher guidance and content covered, but gold standard PBL addresses the issues. The author's first paragraph sets the stage for these major arguments in favor of using PBL as a learning tool.

Paragraph 2: Introducing projects to break up traditional teaching methods does not qualify as PBL and creates problems for the student. The author outlines an approach that is often considered PBL but is not true PBL, and she argues against this approach.

Paragraph 3: Gold standard PBL is an effective teaching strategy that leads to a more authentic learning process, and thus greater student engagement and academic success. The author provides statistics to make a case for the effectiveness of PBL-style teaching.

Paragraph 4: PBL develops independent learners and teaches life skills applicable to students' future endeavors. Here, the author provides additional arguments for the use of PBL in education.

Central Thesis: Gold standard PBL should be utilized to increase student engagement and learning, as well as to help students refine skills for future success. PBL must be implemented in the correct way to be an effective teaching method.

Passage 3 Questions

Question 1: Which of the following new pieces of evidence would discredit the author's main thesis?

    A. A new study revealed that students who participated in PBL were more adept at problem-solving in the first year of their careers.

    B. Additional statistics are published that quantify a decrease in rote memorization despite student success on examinations after PBL.

    C. After five years of consistent implementation, PBL is shown to increase the number of parents that engage with teachers throughout the school year.

    D. It is found that teachers utilizing PBL incorporate less learning targets into their curriculum.

Question 2: Which of the following claims is best supported by the passage?

    A. PBL can easily be implemented correctly.

    B. PBL involves the use of projects to incentivize students and increase their involvement.

    C. PBL is a tool for increasing student participation and fostering self-sufficiency.

    D. PBL draws upon students' external motivations to boost content retention.

Question 3: Which of the following is not merely an assumption made by the author when comparing traditional teaching methods with PBL?

    A. PBL relates to students' intrinsic motivations while more traditional methods greatly rely on external factors.

    B. Students can achieve higher content retention with PBL compared to traditional teaching methods.

    C. Students who participate in PBL do not resort to rote memorization in preparation for assessments.

D. Students who refine skills in the classroom will be successful in applying these skills in their future.

Passage 3 – Question 1 Answer & Discussion

Note: The explanation under each answer explains why it is correct or incorrect, and the correct answer is bolded.

Question 1: Which of the following new pieces of evidence would discredit the author's main thesis?

Type: Reasoning Beyond the Text

A. A new study revealed that students who participated in PBL were more adept at problem-solving in the first year of their careers.

    Explanation: Rather than discredit the author's thesis, this new study would support the author's thesis that PBL should be utilized to help students refine skills for future success in addition to increasing student engagement and learning.

B. Additional statistics are published that quantify a decrease in rote memorization despite student success on examinations after PBL.

    Explanation: As it is currently written, the passage assumes that students who participate in PBL are not utilizing rote memorization in preparation for assessments and that it is the change in teaching style that results in greater success on exams. These statistics would support the author's thesis by providing additional evidence that PBL creates a more authentic and meaningful learning process in which students do not resort to memorization.

C. After five years of consistent implementation, PBL is shown to increase the number of parents that engage with teachers throughout the school year.

    Explanation: This statement would neither discredit nor support the author's thesis as the author does not comment on the involvement of parents in the education process.

D. It is found that teachers utilizing PBL incorporate less learning targets into their curriculum.

    Explanation: In the first paragraph, one of the main arguments against PBL is that this teaching method can lead to "minimal content covered." The author refutes this with statements such as "...students who participate in gold standard PBL learn more information and retain that information longer." If evidence found that that teachers utilizing PBL incorporate less learning targets into their curriculum, this would weaken the author's thesis that PBL increases student learning as it would show that less content is covered in the curriculum.

Discussion:

This is a Reasoning Beyond the Text question which asks you to evaluate new information and how it relates to the author's main thesis. You are looking for one finding that would weaken the author's claims to the point of discrediting it. Firstly, before answering a question about the thesis of a passage, be sure to take a moment to write out your own one sentence summary of the author's main idea. It is important to collect your thoughts about the author's thesis before reading the answer choices presented in the question.

In order to answer this question correctly, first think about the possible answer choices that you may come across. You may find answer choices that are unrelated to the author's thesis and would therefore neither support nor discredit it, you may find answer choices that support the author's thesis, and, lastly, there should be one answer choice that would discredit the author's thesis. Start by determining if any of the answer choices can be easily ruled out because they are unrelated to the thesis of the passages. For example, the author never discusses the role of parents in education, so the Answer C can be eliminated. Next, work through the remaining answer choices one at a time, each time refer back to the thesis you have written down and evaluate whether this new piece of evidence would support it. This would help you to rule out Answers A and B, leaving you with Answer D, which is the only one that weakens the author's claim.

Passage 3 – Question 2 Answer & Discussion

Note: The explanation under each answer explains why it is correct or incorrect, and the correct answer is bolded.

Question 2: Which of the following claims is best supported by the passage?

Type: Foundations of Comprehension

A. PBL can easily be implemented correctly.

Explanation: This answer is incorrect because the author does not comment on how easily PBL can be implemented. The author indicates in the first two paragraphs that PBL is often "utilized incorrectly," as inauthentic projects that "...lack the rigor needed to qualify as PBL," which implies that PBL may be harder to implement correctly than many teachers realize.

B. PBL involves the use of projects to incentivize students and increase their involvement.

Explanation: The author does state that "student engagement is increased" with PBL, but argues against the use of projects "as a reward" to incentivize students.

C. PBL is a tool for increasing student participation and fostering self-sufficiency.

Explanation: This is the correct answer choice as both points can be found within the passage. In paragraph three, the author states that "student engagement is increased" when PBL is done in an authentic way. In the conclusion paragraph, the author explains that PBL is designed "...to develop independent learners that are prepared to self-advocate and take the initiative necessary to succeed," skills that indicate PBL fosters self-sufficiency in students.

D. PBL draws upon students' external motivations to boost content retention.

Explanation: While PBL has been shown to result in "...a 60% higher long-term retention rate," it does not do so through external motivations. In paragraph two, the author argues that it is "...with traditional teaching methods [that] students are driven mainly by external factors." In paragraph three, the author contrasts this with PBL, saying that students are engaged in "...a highly authentic learning process...connected to real-world experiences." When students see the meaning and value in what they are learning through PBL, they no longer need external motivations.

Discussion:

This is a Foundations of Comprehension question that tests your understanding of the author's claims presented in the text. At first glance, each of the answer choices seems reasonable as each incorporates phrases that will sound familiar after reading through the passage. Therefore, it will require close reading and in-depth analysis of the choices to determine the correct answer.

In order to answer this question correctly, you must dissect each option. This is a question about basic components of the passage, not one that asks you to extrapolate what you have read. First you can eliminate any answer choices that could be true, but are not actually substantiated by the passage, such as Answer A. Then, look at each of the remaining answer choices and rule out those that have pieces that are supported by the passage as well as pieces that are not supported, such as Answers B and D. What you are left with is the only answer that has a claim that would be fully supported by the passage – Answer C.

Passage 3 – Question 3 Answer & Discussion

Note: The explanation under each answer explains why it is correct or incorrect, and the correct answer is bolded.

Question 3: Which of the following is not merely an assumption made by the author when comparing traditional teaching methods with PBL?

Type: Reasoning Within the Text

A. PBL relates to students' intrinsic motivations while more traditional methods greatly rely on external factors.

   Explanation: This assumption is made in paragraph two when the author states that "...with traditional teaching methods, students are driven mainly by external factors, such as pleasing their parents and achieving high marks." The author assumes that with PBL students are no longer driven by external factors like high marks.

B. Students can achieve higher content retention with PBL compared to traditional teaching methods.

   Explanation: In paragraph three, the author includes statistics from studies that show "...students who participate in PBL learn more information and retain that information longer" with a "...60% higher long-term retention rate." Therefore, this is not an assumption made by the author, but rather an explicit argument made by the author using the data presented.

C. Students who participate in PBL do not resort to rote memorization in preparation for assessments.

   Explanation: In paragraph three, the author states that students "...perform better on assessments because they are able to apply in-depth knowledge...rather than rote memorization." This statement assumes that students who participate in PBL are not utilizing rote memorization in preparation for assessments although this is not directly examined by the study presented.

D. Students who refine skills in the classroom will be successful in applying these skills in their future.

Explanation: In the conclusion paragraph, the author makes the assumption that students who "...refine skills in the classroom," such as problem solving and collaboration, will be "...successful in their future endeavours." However, there is no evidence or data to back up this statement, so the author is assuming that classroom skills are translatable to the real world, but does not provide evidence that this is the case.

Discussion:

This Reasoning Within the Text question asks you to evaluate the author's writing for evidence-based assumptions. The key word in the question is "merely," which tells us that the correct answer must not only be a claim the author supports, but also a claim explicitly presented in the passage and backed up with evidence or statistics. Claims that can be found in the passage that are not validated are assumptions or inferences made by the author. Missing this crucial word may cause you to read the answers with the mindset that you are looking for the one option that is not supported by the passage. We hope you were not led down this path!

In order to answer this question correctly, you must evaluate the author's writing to determine if each claim is backed up with evidence or statistics. All of the answers will sound familiar or even correct, because they are claims that are supported by the passage. In this case, there are no answer choices that can be immediately eliminated as a statement that is not found within the text. To tackle this question, work through it one answer at a time: find each claim in the passage and determine if there is a statistic or cited evidence that the author uses to validate the claim. You may have to return to the passage to see what was said for each statement in the answers, and in doing so, you would discover that only Answer B was stated explicitly and supported by quantitative evidence.

SAMPLE PASSAGE 4

Searle developed an experiment designed to refute the mechanization of computer functionalism based on a hypothetical simulation called the Chinese Room thought-experiment. According to Searle, the theory of computer functionalism is flawed because the human mind cannot be replicated through the functions and mechanics of a programmed system. Computational inputs and outputs are not equivalent to the mental states of the human mind; thus, Searle largely refutes the idea of strong artificial intelligence (AI).

Within the thought-experiment, a human stands in for the devised mechanisms of a computer. Isolated from all external relations, their only interactions with the exterior environment are through an input and output slot. Through the input slot, the human receives a string of words written in Chinese symbols from a Native Chinese speaker. This human is given a ruling guidebook that allows them to construct a response using Chinese symbols. The ability to read these symbols and devise a response using the guide is mechanic in nature; the human is simply wired to follow a rote circuit. The human within the thought-experiment follows and processes the patterns of symbols with no understanding of what these symbols convey. This forms the basis of Searle's reasoning that strong AI does not have the means to understand information therefore it cannot replicate the human mind.

However, the human within Searle's thought-experiment does not fully represent the complex mechanics of strong AI. Assuming that strong AI is possible, it would be more fitting to see how the understanding of the experiment's subject would perform in an open environment, considering that strong AI not only generates information from a controlled linear assembly line of processed information, but from all external relations.

Searle deduces that the human within his thought-experiment does not understand Chinese; however, he fails to address the possibility that they could come to understand the language in time. Language is a human construct; humans assign and designate meaning to words and use symbol manipulation. Language and communication precede understanding. In relation to computer functionalism, language operates through codes; just as we implement language and communication into our lives, computers function through coded language. If humans are able to learn language, perhaps strong AI could learn to adopt these conventions as well.

Paragraph Summaries and Central Thesis

Paragraph 1: Searle designed the Chinese Room thought-experiment to demonstrate that the idea of strong AI is flawed. In this paragraph, the author introduces the thought-experiment and why it was conceived.

Paragraph 2: In the thought-experiment, a human acts as a stand in for the mechanisms of a computer and must respond to text written in Chinese symbols. The author uses this paragraph to explain how the thought-experiment works.

Paragraph 3: Searle's thought-experiment is flawed as it does not accurately replicate strong AI's complex mechanics. This paragraph reveals the author's stance on Searle's argument and his favorable attitudes towards AI.

Paragraph 4: Just as humans can learn coded language, AI too may learn these patterns over time. The author uses this paragraph to point out another hole in Searle's argument against strong AI.

Central Thesis: Searle's thought-experiment does not accurately replicate the complex mechanics of strong AI, thus his experiment cannot refute the future possibility of strong AI that can learn complex human functions such as language.

Passage 4 Questions

Question 1: Which of the following is the only assertion from the passage that does not conflict with the author's point?

A. The intricacies of human psychology cannot be captured by AI systems.

B. Strong AI processes non-linear information to generate outputs.

C. AI can learn complex systems except conventions with manipulated symbols that are associated to meanings in the real world.

D. Strong AI does not have the means to understand information in different languages.

Question 2: If Searle had two versions of the thought-experiment, one version as described in the passage and a second version in an environment with external relations, and he demonstrated that the human stand-in would not have a better understanding of the language it was processing in the second version, how would this affect the author's argument?

A. This would weaken the author's argument.

B. This would strengthen the author's argument.

C. This would neither weaken nor strengthen the author's argument.

D. This would remove the possibility that strong AI could come to understand language.

Question 3: Someone who agreed with the author's main point would likely also agree with which of the following?

A. In the future, strong AI has the potential to replicate all aspects of the human mind.

B. No type of AI, even strong AI, can replicate the intricacies of the human mind.

C. AI has the capacity to build upon its programming, essentially learning new skills such as language.

D. A human given limited inputs within a closed system accurately represents the linear mechanics of a computer.

Passage 4 – Question 1 Answer & Discussion

Note: The explanation under each answer explains why it is correct or incorrect, and the correct answer is bolded.

Question 1: Which of the following is the only assertion from the passage that does not conflict with the author's point?

Type: Reasoning Within the Text

A. The intricacies of human psychology cannot be captured by AI systems.

    Explanation: This answer is based on an assertion made in the first paragraph, where it states that "The theory of computer functionalism is flawed because the human mind cannot be replicated through the functions and mechanics of a programmed system." However, this assertion is in conflict with the author's argument in the final paragraph of the passage that the human in the experiment "...could come to understand the language in time" and thus AI too "...could learn to adapt these conventions." For these reasons, this is not the correct answer.

B. **Strong AI processes non-linear information to generate outputs.**

    Explanation: This is the only answer choice that includes an assertion from the passage that is not in conflict with the author's central thesis. As the author states in the third paragraph, "...strong AI not only generates information from a controlled linear assembly line of processed information, but from all external relations." This is the basis for the author's argument that Searle's thought-experiment cannot refute the future possibility of strong AI.

C. AI can learn complex systems except conventions with manipulated symbols that are associated to meanings in the real world.

    Explanation: "...conventions with manipulated symbols" refers to human language, which the author states is "...a human construct; humans assign and designate meaning to words and use symbol manipulation." In the same paragraph, he suggests that human language should be learnable by AI, thus this statement conflicts directly with the author's point.

D. Strong AI does not have the means to understand information in different languages.

Explanation: This assertion is not made by Searle or the author in the passage. Though the thought-experiment involved Chinese symbols, the author does not suggest that this should be treated differently from any other language. More importantly, an assertion like this would go against the author's point that strong AI has the power to learn language in general.

Discussion:

This is a Reasoning Within the Text question that asks you to integrate distant components of the text. You must have a firm grasp on the central thesis of the passage, which the question refers to as "the author's point." To answer this doubly negated question correctly, you must select the answer that does *not* conflict with the author's point, i.e., the answer that *is* in line with the author's point.

Be sure to determine the author's thesis before proceeding to read through the choices. Crucially, you must not confuse the author's stance with that of Searle. Each of the answer choices will sound familiar as they all draw on information from the passage. You can first rule out answer choices that are not made at all by either the author or Searle, such as Answers C and D. Then, you will need to identify the options that represent Searle's ideas but not the author's, like Answer A. You are then left with Answer B, which is narrow in scope, but is the only choice that does not conflict with the author's point.

Passage 4 – Question 2 Answer & Discussion

Note: The explanation under each answer explains why it is correct or incorrect, and the correct answer is bolded.

Question 2: If Searle had two versions of the thought-experiment, one version as described in the passage and a second version in an environment with external relations, and he demonstrated that the human stand-in would not have a better understanding of the language it was processing in the second version, how would this affect the author's argument?

Type: Reasoning Beyond the Text

A. This would weaken the author's argument.

> *Explanation:* This answer choice is correct because one of the flaws the author cites in regard to Searle's thought-experiment is that it is performed in an environment "...isolated from external relations" which "...does not fully represent the complex mechanics of strong AI." The existence of a different version with better representation of strong AI and the same lack of true understanding weakens the author's argument that Searle cannot refute the possibility of strong AI based on his thought-experiments because they are inaccurate representations of AI's complexities.

B. This would strengthen the author's argument.

> *Explanation:* The existence of a thought-experiment that better represents the complexities of AI does not strengthen the author's argument. [See Answer A]

C. This would neither weaken nor strengthen the author's argument.

> *Explanation:* [See Answers A and B]

D. This would remove the possibility that strong AI could come to understand language.

> *Explanation:* This answer is very similar to Answer A because it is saying that one of the author's points – that AI could come to adopt the convention of language – is being

weakened. However, the possibility that strong AI could come to understand language is not affected by the existence of a second version of Searle's thought-experiment; what is affected is only the author's claim that Searle's thought-experiment is a poor representation is affected.

Discussion:

This Reasoning Beyond the Text question asks you to evaluate new information and how it affects the author's argument. Your first step should always be to determine the author's argument before reading the answer choices. In this case, the author argues that Searle's thought-experiment does not accurately replicate human intricacy nor the complex mechanics of strong AI, thus his experiment cannot refute the future possibility of strong AI.

In order to answer this question correctly, first think about what types of new evidence might discredit or weaken the author's argument. For example, if it was found that Searle's thought-experiment was well designed and did accurately represent the complexity of AI, the author's position would be weakened. This is precisely what is described in the question. You can thus quickly eliminate both Answers B and C, leaving you with Answers A and D. To eliminate D, you must recognize that this answer is targeting a fact that is beyond the author's argument against Searle specifically; it is a comment on the strength of AI itself, which we cannot assess based on the information provided here.

Passage 4 – Question 3 Answer & Discussion

Note: The explanation under each answer explains why it is correct or incorrect, and the correct answer is bolded.

Question 3: Someone who agreed with the author's main point would likely also agree with which of the following?

Type: Foundations of Comprehension

A. In the future, strong AI has the potential to replicate all aspects of the human mind.

   Explanation: While the author does propose that "...if humans are able to learn language, perhaps strong AI could learn...as well," the author never states that it could replicate all aspects of the human mind. Based on the information presented within passage, we cannot make an inference about the author's ideas beyond language.

B. No type of AI, even strong AI, can replicate the intricacies of the human mind.

   Explanation: Again, the author ends the passage with the idea that "...if humans are able to learn language, perhaps strong AI could learn...as well," so someone who agreed with the author's main point would not likely agree with the idea that strong AI cannot replicate intricacies of the human mind, as language is quite intricate.

C. **AI has the capacity to build upon its programming, essentially learning new skills such as language.**

   Explanation: This answer choice expresses the main points of the author's thesis, which is that Searle's flawed experiment cannot refute the possibility of strong AI that can learn complex human functions such as language. The author ends the passage stating "...if humans are able to learn language, perhaps strong AI could learn to adapt these conventions as well;" thus, someone with similar views to the author would agree with this statement.

D. A human given limited inputs within a closed system accurately represents the linear mechanics of a computer.

Explanation: In paragraph three, the author argues that Searle's experiment "...does not fully represent the complex mechanics of strong AI" and that it would be more fitting to perform the experiment in an "...open environment, considering that strong AI not only generates information from a controlled linear assembly line of processed information, but from all external relations." Therefore, someone with similar views to the author would not agree with this statement because the author does not claim that AI is simply linear mechanics in a closed system, but rather the opposite.

Discussion:

This is a Foundations of Comprehension question that tests your understanding of the author's main point as it is presented in the text. Here you are presented with several statements that each use similar terminology to the passage. Therefore, you cannot simply eliminate answer choices based on their absence from the passage. Rather you must rely on your understanding of the author's position.

In order to answer this question correctly, you will need to analyze each option. First, you can eliminate Answer B, which most clearly opposes the position taken by the author. Then, you can eliminate any answers that seam feasible, but are not actually corroborated by the passage, such as Answers A and D. You would then be left with Answer C, which is the only choice that would be fully supported by someone who agrees with the author's main point.

SAMPLE PASSAGE 5

The vulnerability of refugees, asylum seekers, and undocumented migrants living in Morocco to violence and the political, economic, and social structures of both Moroccan and international societies have placed them into liminal states where they have few options but to remain in Morocco. What structures create this instability and what are the consequences? Structural violence and liminality must be examined first.

Arnold Van Gennep first coined the term *liminality* in reference to a three-staged rite of passage, which he documented in tribal societies. The first stage is a separation from one's society while the final stage is that person's reintroduction into society. The middle stage is that of the limen, where the person is neither attached to his or her kin or former self, nor is she yet transformed and accepted into her new role. She inhabits, instead, a world in limbo, where her only social connections are with those undergoing the same ritual. This results in othering and segregation, often creating loneliness among those in the midst of this liminal state.

Refugees, asylum seekers and undocumented migrants flee their home countries for varying reasons, usually a mixture of structural and physical violence. Structural violence results from the structures in place (be they economic, social, institutional, etc.), that disadvantage certain groups of people. The migrant's political, social and/or economic systems no longer support them, and they are on a bridge to an ambiguous future which may never arrive. Unable or unwilling to return to their former life, and equally unable to legally migrate to Europe, they find themselves stuck in Morocco. These migrants now face an unexpected reality in their new home. The reality is that Morocco is not equipped to handle them, but does so anyway. This is due to a plethora of factors mainly stemming from the European Union's externalized border controls. This includes incentives for the Moroccan government to keep the migrants on African soil, such as giving billions of euros to Morocco to deal with the migrant "problem". The EU has turned a blind eye to the way Morocco manages this difficult task. The result for migrants in Morocco is a precarious situation in which they are vulnerable to violence, harassment, poverty, and discrimination from a variety of perpetrators.

In this space of the limen migrants find themselves essentially ungoverned, their social position not yet affirmed by state or international law. With no legal status such as citizenship, and therefore no actionable rights, they have little avenues forwards or backwards, and they inhabit what Giorgio Agamben calls "bare life." It is the ultimate exclusion from the social and political, and thus creates a vulnerability to violations and violence. Structural violence is the architect of this liminal state and "bare life," and leads to various other forms of violence. Violence acts in every step of the journey from the home country of migrants, up-to and including their stay in Morocco, and acts to constrain mobility and oppress life-worlds.

Paragraph Summaries and Central Thesis

Paragraph 1: Refugees, asylum seekers and undocumented migrants are in precarious situations in Morocco. In this paragraph, the author introduces a problem and sets the scene of the later paragraphs, which will explore the cause.

Paragraph 2: Liminality is the middle state of a journey of transformation in which the person is only attached to those undergoing it with them. The author defines the first important concept for understanding vulnerability of the migrants.

Paragraph 3: Migrants become stuck in Morocco where they experience precarity due to the structural violence in their home countries and from the EU and Morocco. The author defines the second important concept for understanding vulnerability of the migrants.

Paragraph 4: Structural violence places migrants into a liminal state where they experience "bare life", which makes them vulnerable to other forms of violence. In this final paragraph, the author explores the relationship between structural violence and the liminal state.

Central Thesis: Structural violence in migrants' home countries forces them into liminality in Morocco, where they experience "bare life" and become vulnerable to discrimination, poverty and physical violence.

Passage 5 Questions

Question 1: Which of the following best captures the author's main argument?

    A. The European Union causes "bare life" by externalizing its border controls to Morocco and turning a blind eye to the way the Moroccan government deals with migrants.

    B. Migrants in Morocco lack rights and are vulnerable to various forms of violence due to the structural violence they experience at home and abroad.

    C. Migrants in Morocco experience "bare life," in which they are reintroduced to society and therefore face discrimination.

    D. Morocco receives billions of euros from the EU, but is unable to provide migrants safety from violence or discrimination.

Question 2: Aristotle makes the distinction between *zoe* (from zoologos), which is the body in nature without rights, and *bios*, "the good life" which is attached to political life. Which of the statements from the passage is evidence of *zoe*?

    A. She inhabits, instead, a world in limbo, where her only social connections are with those undergoing the same ritual.

    B. With no legal status such as citizenship, and therefore no actionable rights, they have little avenues forwards or backwards...

    C. Unable or unwilling to return to their former life, and equally unable to legally migrate to Europe, they find themselves stuck in Morocco.

    D. Migrants face "...a precarious situation in which they are vulnerable to violence, harassment, poverty, and discrimination from a variety of perpetrators."

Question 3: If it were now known that some of the migrants were economic migrants and were leaving their home countries to find employment, how would this affect the conclusions reached by the author?

A. This would change the author's conclusion because the author assumes that the migrants are unable to return to their home countries out of fear of violence, not economic issues.

B. This would not change the author's conclusion because the passage states that the EU gave billions of euros to Morocco to deal with the migrants.

C. This would not change the author's conclusion because the author states that migrants flee their home countries for a number of reasons, including structural violence.

D. This would change the author's conclusion because the author implies that only real refugees should be considered deserving of European and Moroccan aid.

Passage 5– Question 1 Answer & Discussion

Note: The explanation under each answer explains why it is correct or incorrect, and the correct answer is bolded.

Question 1: Which of the following best captures the author's main argument?

Type: Foundations of Comprehension

A. The European Union causes "bare life" by externalizing its border controls to Morocco and turning a blind eye to the way the Moroccan government deals with migrants.

Explanation: This is incorrect because the European Union is not the sole cause of "bare life." As mentioned in paragraph four, "bare life" is caused by general exclusion from the social and political world.

B. **Migrants in Morocco lack rights and are vulnerable to various forms of violence due to the structural violence they experience at home and abroad.**

Explanation: This answer is correct. We know that the author wants to answer the question posed in paragraph 1, "What structures create this instability and what are the consequences?" This answer accounts for the cause of migration (structural violence), and the consequences (discrimination, etc.).

C. Migrants in Morocco experience "bare life" in which they are reintroduced to society and therefore face discrimination.

Explanation: This sentence is incorrect because "bare life" represents the liminal phase rather than the reintroduction phase, as evidenced by the phrase, "...migrants find themselves essentially ungoverned, their social position not yet affirmed by state or international law."

D. Morocco receives billions of euros from the EU, but is unable to provide migrants safety from violence or discrimination.

Explanation: While the author would agree with this statement, it is evidence used to support the argument, rather than the argument itself.

Discussion:

This is a Foundations of Comprehension question that tests your understanding of the author's central thesis. The options you are given may confuse you because they all sound like passages from the text.

To answer this question correctly, you can begin by eliminating any statements that are clearly incorrect, like Answer C, and those that are only partially correct, like Answer A. You are then left with Answers B and D, both of which are true based on the passage. To select the right answer, you much recognize that these statements have different functions in the passage. Answer D serves as a supporting point to the thesis; thus Answer B is correct.

Passage 5 – Question 2 Answer & Discussion

Note: The explanation under each answer explains why it is correct or incorrect and the correct answer is bolded.

Question 2: Aristotle makes the distinction between *zoe* (from zoologos), which is the body in nature without rights, and *bios*, "the good life" which is attached to political life. Which of the statements from the passage is evidence of *zoe*?

Type: Foundations of Comprehension

A. She inhabits, instead, a world in limbo, where her only social connections are with those undergoing the same ritual.

   Explanation: This statement discusses a lack of social connections, rather than a lack of rights.

B. With no legal status such as citizenship, and therefore no actionable rights, they have little avenues forwards or backwards...

   Explanation: This excerpt outlines the lack of one kind of legal status, leading to a lack of rights.

C. Unable or unwilling to return to their former life, and equally unable to legally migrate to Europe, they find themselves stuck in Morocco.

   Explanation: Though this excerpt mentions the migrants' inability to "...legally migrate to Europe," we cannot assume from this statement that they lack the rights to migrate elsewhere or even return to their home countries.

D. Migrants face "...a precarious situation in which they are vulnerable to violence, harassment, poverty, and discrimination from a variety of perpetrators."

   Explanation: Though vulnerability to violence and poverty can be caused by a lack of rights, the latter is not directly addressed in this statement.

Discussion:

As soon as you saw that a new idea was introduced in the question, you may have assumed that this is a Reasoning Beyond the Text question. However, the question is simply asking you to identify the idea from the passage that best represents *zoe*, the state of lacking rights, making it a Foundations of Comprehension question. The task of identifying the correct response is made difficult by the fact that many of the factors described in the passage are related to or may even cause migrants to be without rights, but they may not inherently describe that condition.

Answer A can be eliminated fairly easily as it focuses on social connections rather than rights. Answer D can also be eliminated because it does not address the question of rights directly. This would leave you with Answers B and C, both of which include ideas pertaining to rights or legality. However, Answer C narrowly describes migrant's lack of legal rights to go to Europe, thus Answer B most closely describes the general state of *zoe*.

Passage 5 – Question 3 Answer & Discussion

Note: The explanation under each answer explains why it is correct or incorrect, and the correct answer is bolded.

Question 3: If it were now known that some of the migrants were economic migrants and were leaving their home countries to find employment, how would this affect the conclusions reached by the author?

Type: Reasoning Beyond the Text

A. This would change the author's conclusion because the author assumes that the migrants are unable to return to their home countries out of fear of violence, not economic issues.

   Explanation: This answer fails to take into account the author's view that structural violence (which includes economic violence), is the main reason that migrants are unable to go home.

B. This would not change the author's conclusion because the passage states that the EU gave billions of euros to Morocco to deal with the migrants.

   Explanation: The author did not make any connection between the funding provided by the EU and the kind of migrants trying to leave Morocco.

C. **This would not change the author's conclusion because the author states that migrants flee their home countries for a number of reasons, including structural violence.**

   Explanation: As stated in the second paragraph, economic violence is a sub-type of structural violence. Therefore, the author's argument that structural violence leads to the "bare life" of these migrants is still valid.

D. This would change the author's conclusion because the author implies that only real refugees should be considered deserving of European and Moroccan aid.

   Explanation: This statement is false as the author made no such claims.

Discussion:

This Reasoning Beyond the Text question asks you to re-evaluate the author's claim given new information. To answer this question correctly, you must understand that migrants fleeing economic insecurity are part of the group that the author discusses.

With this understanding, we can begin to look at the answer choices. Since the author already includes this group of migrants in her discussion, knowing that some of them are economic migrants would not change her conclusion. We can thus eliminate Answers A and D. Answer B is partially correct in that it would not change the author's conclusion, but the reasoning behind the answer is problematic; thus we are left with Answer C.

SAMPLE PASSAGE 6

Few would contest that medical education alters a person's knowledge and understanding of the human body. Medical schools around the country create an environment to learn the academic essentials of medicine through basic sciences and clinical rotations. Courses on biochemistry, human anatomy, and physiology are nearly universal across contemporary medical school curricula. The sheer number and frequency of exams is designed to ensure knowledge retention, but the moral reasoning or formation of medical students cannot be overlooked.

Over the course of their training, medical students learn more than just the basic medical and clinical sciences. They also learn the cultural norms, important principles, professional commitments, and ethical dimensions of medicine, all of which have a significant impact on the moral formation of medical practitioners. In effect, medical students undergo a re-formation of their attentive faculty, learning to disregard features of patients' stories that might once have commanded their attention and learning to attend carefully to other aspects that they would not have noticed before. Medical education, in other words, is a powerfully formative experience.

Formation is the act of doing. Through hard study and iterative practice under the guidance of competent teachers, students become clinicians capable of consistently knowing and doing good. The methods of medical student formation and means of transformation are often debated in medical literature. Surveyors of medical education have frequently noted the many unacknowledged or "hidden" lessons embedded within medical training that influence the formation of physicians. Recognition of the hidden curriculum does not imply a normative judgment of its value. Rather, depending on the content of its "lessons," the curriculum can lead to positive and constructive, or negative and destructive effects. The hidden curriculum, if misaligned and unchallenged can lead to the progressive decline of moral reasoning during medical training.

Paragraph Summaries and Central Thesis

Paragraph 1: There is more to the formation of medical doctors than the courses they take in medical school. Here, the author introduces the "hidden curriculum" to be expanded on in subsequent paragraphs.

Paragraph 2: Medical students transform through medical school, learning cultural, ethical, and professional aspects of medicine. In the second paragraph, the author expands on the additional elements acquired through medical school that impact the moral formation of practitioners.

Paragraph 3: Hidden lessons within medical training can be beneficial or detrimental to medical students' formation as moral and reasonable practitioners. The author introduces the idea that hidden lessons are not unequivocally beneficial.

Central Thesis: Hidden lessons in training play a large role in the formation of medical practitioners and, depending on the context, can have positive or negative effects.

Passage 6 Questions

Question 1: Someone who agrees with the author's assertion that "Through hard study and iterative practice under the guidance of competent teachers, students become clinicians capable of consistently knowing and doing good" would not agree with which of the following:

   A. Repeating clinical actions takes time away from learning important new lessons from competent teachers.

   B. Teachers need to be competent, but it is through practice and study that clinicians become experts.

   C. Doing and knowing good stem from both coursework and clinical rotations.

   D. Once a student becomes a competent and knowledgeable physician, they too could teach.

Question 2: According to the author, medical students can become good and capable clinicians though which of the following?

   A. Understanding the "hidden lessons" taught to them.

   B. Learning how to be moral, which comes through extensive course study.

   C. Listening attentively to all their teachers.

   D. Engaging in repeated hands-on clinical work and diligent study.

Question 3: When the author stated, "Recognition of the hidden curriculum does not imply a normative judgment of its value," he meant that:

   A. The norms of the lesson are dependent upon the person teaching it, and probably relate to that person's own mores and experiences.

   B. A hidden lesson is not inherently good or bad.

   C. Only a medical student who has gotten the lesson can decide if it was helpful to them or not.

   D. Hidden lessons within curriculums should never be judged.

Passage 6 – Question 1 Answer & Discussion

Note: The explanation under each answer explains why it is correct or incorrect, and the correct answer is bolded.

Question 1: Someone who agrees with the author's assertion that "Through hard study and iterative practice under the guidance of competent teachers, students become clinicians capable of consistently knowing and doing good" would not agree with which of the following:

Type: Foundations of Comprehension

A. **Repeating clinical actions takes time away from learning important new lessons from competent teachers.**

   Explanation: The author asserts that "iterative practice," i.e., repetition, is important. The statement therefore contradicts the assertion.

B. Teachers need to be competent, but it is through practice and study that clinicians become experts.

   Explanation: Although the quoted text does not explicitly state that a clinician becomes an expert due to their study and practice more than based on the competence of their teachers, this statement does not directly contradict the text in the question.

C. Doing and knowing good stem from both coursework and clinical rotations.

   Explanation: This answer is clearly expressed in the text when the author states, "...hard study and iterative practice."

D. Once a student becomes a competent and knowledgeable physician, they too could teach.

   Explanation: Though this is not expressed in the quote, it also does not contradict it directly.

Discussion:

This Foundations of Comprehension question tests your understanding of the word "iterative" from the passage. This word means "to do repeatedly" and it refers to a cyclical process through which learning is achieved over time. The question is made more difficult by the negation, forcing you to looking for the answer that goes against this notion, rather than answers that are in line with the notion.

To answer this question correctly, you can begin by ruling out the answers that definitely do not contradict the author's statement. Answer D can be eliminated quickly because the excerpt does not address the student's ability to teach at all. Answers B and C can be ruled out next because they are both in line with the statement in the question. That leaves us with Answer A, which states that iterative practice does not aid learning, a clear contradiction to the author's statement.

Passage 6 – Question 2 Answer & Discussion

Note: The explanation under each answer explains why it is correct or incorrect, and the correct answer is bolded.

Question 2: According to the author, medical students can become good and capable clinicians though which of the following?

Type: Foundations of Comprehension

A. Understanding the "hidden lessons" taught to them.

 Explanation: We cannot conclude this because the author states that these hidden messages can be either "...positive and constructive, or negative and destructive." Therefore, if a student understood a hidden message but it was destructive, they may not become a good and capable clinician.

B. Learning how to be moral, which comes through extensive course study.

 Explanation: This is incorrect because the notion that becoming moral is gained through extensive study contradicts the author's point that formation comes, in part, through practice.

C. Listening attentively to all their teachers.

 Explanation: While the author would agree that listening to *competent* teachers contributes to the success of a medical student, this answer states *all* teachers. It furthermore overlooks the main assertations in paragraph three of study and practice.

D. **Engaging in repeated hands-on clinical work and diligent study.**

 Explanation: The answer can be found in paragraph three when the author states, "Through hard study and iterative practice under the guidance of competent teachers, students become clinicians capable of consistently knowing and doing good." Here iterative means repeated practice.

Discussion:

This is a Foundations of Comprehension question that tests your understanding of an idea from the passage. To answer this question correctly, you need to find the section that the author is referring to, then see if each of the answer choices adequately addresses the question.

All of the answers may seem plausible at first because they all come from the passage. However, upon closer inspection, you will realize that some of them do not answer the question at hand. Answer A can be eliminated because the author makes it abundantly clear that hidden lessons are not always beneficial to medical students. We can also rule out Answers B and C on the account of incompleteness. We are therefore left with Answer D.

Passage 6 – Question 3 Answer & Discussion

Note: The explanation under each answer explains why it is correct or incorrect, and the correct answer is bolded.

Question 3: When the author stated, "Recognition of the hidden curriculum does not imply a normative judgment of its value," he meant that:

Type: Reasoning Within the Text

A. The norms of the lesson are dependent upon the person teaching it, and probably relate to that person's own mores and experiences.

   Explanation: While the author alludes to the fact that some teachers are more competent than others, the point of this sentence must be understood through reading the next sentence, which states, "...depending on the content of its "lessons," the curriculum can lead to positive and constructive, or negative and destructive effects". Therefore, we can assume that the author was not referring to the mores of the teacher.

B.   A hidden lesson is not inherently good or bad.

   Explanation: The author goes on to mention in the next sentence, "...depending on the content of its "lessons," the curriculum can lead to positive and constructive, or negative and destructive effects". Therefore, we can conclude that by not implicating normative judgements, the lessons are valued as neither good nor bad.

C. Only a medical student who has gotten the lesson can decide if it was helpful to them or not.

   Explanation: This answer is a logical conclusion to the question of normative judgement, but it fails to account for the content of the lessons, which cannot necessarily be judged by the student as positive or negative, but rather by the outcome. This is further elaborated in the next two sentences: "Rather, depending on the content of its "lessons," the curriculum can lead to positive and constructive, or negative and destructive effects. The hidden curriculum, if misaligned and unchallenged can lead to the progressive decline of moral reasoning during medical training."

D.   Hidden lessons within curriculums should never be judged.

Explanation: The author is not saying this. In fact, if we look at the final sentence of the passage, we can see that only through judging and challenging bad hidden curricula can we fight against moral decline: "The hidden curriculum, if misaligned and unchallenged can lead to the progressive decline of moral reasoning during medical training."

Discussion:

This Reasoning Within the Text question asks you to determine the meaning of a quote by integrating ideas presented in other parts of the passage, crucially, the following sentence.

Answer A can be discounted because upon reading the sentence that follows, we can conclude that it does not refer to teachers. You may also quickly rule out Answer D, which contradicts a point the author makes later on in that paragraph. We are thus left with Answers B and C, both of which express the idea that hidden lessons could be good or bad depending on X. However, Answer C makes a false assumption by adding more than is mentioned or implied in the text. Therefore, this answer can also be eliminated, leaving us with Answer B.

SAMPLE PASSAGE 7

Everything in this world exists as a dichotomy: good and evil, right and wrong, men and women, even love and hate. Instead of addressing the standard duality of love and hate, Shakespeare emphasizes the interesting correlation between love and reason. You would think that love and reason complement one another, yet the two become conflicting issues which initially seem to inhibit one another, but ultimately play important roles in controlling the other. Shakespeare uses this seemingly controversial idea as a basis for his comedy, showing just how reasonless pure love can be, and how loveless honest reason can be. Of all the relationships in his plays, none can be explained by reason or logic; likewise, none of the reason and law seems to have any components of compassion or understanding.

Shakespeare's plays are riddled with passionate lovers, all of whom commit unreasonable and reckless acts in the name of love. Shakespeare's continued motif of reasonless love further demonstrates its destructiveness. The characters affected fall into deep and passionate yet inexplicable and irrational love. These unfounded relationships ultimately result in chaos, thereby illustrating the damaging effects of such love. By incorporating motifs and the effects of love on characters, Shakespeare effectively presents a dramatic counterexample for what a balanced relationship might be. The love that blooms between them reveals the necessity for reason to temper passionate love.

Just as extreme love calls for a certain degree of reason in order to avoid disarray, reason also needs components of compassion and understanding. Shakespeare presents us with counterexamples of this crucial balance to demonstrate the need for love and reason to coexist. He demonstrates how one force, when presented too strongly, seemingly drives the other to factor to the other extreme. Shakespeare indicates that reason and love simply cannot and do not exist on the same level; rulings which are based on reason should incorporate more aspects of love and understanding. By using examples of reason that go unchecked by love, one realizes that excessive reason would be ameliorated once issued in the light of compassion, understanding, and love.

Each dichotomy needs the other in order to exist. Although the duality of each relationship in Shakespeare's plays presents two polar extremes, each aspect balances the other and thus allows for both features to exist in tempered yet optimal conditions. Similarly, love and reason also share such a relationship; love that contains no reason and reason that contains no love result in chaotic and unbalanced situations. Although Shakespeare fails to present a balanced relationship as proof of its success and importance, the gravity of his counterexamples implies the necessity of such a balance between love and reason. Coexistence might seem improbable to some and elusive to others, but success for one implies the participation of the other.

Paragraph Summaries and Central Thesis

Paragraph 1: Shakespeare examines the duality of love and reason through his plays. In this paragraph, the author introduces the topic of the essay and sets it apart from other more conventional dualities.

Paragraph 2: Shakespeare's characters who are in love commit irrational acts that result in chaos, demonstrating that love needs to be tempered by reason. This paragraph expands on the idea of irrational love, which calls for reason.

Paragraph 3: Shakespeare shows how rulings guided by reason alone can be improved when guided by love and compassion. This paragraph expands on the idea that reason also cannot be without love.

Paragraph 4: Although Shakespeare does not present a relationship balanced in love and reason, his extreme counterexamples demonstrate the need for this balance. In this paragraph, the author presents his interpretation of what the duality in Shakespeare's plays is telling us.

Central Thesis: Shakespeare uses the duality between love and reason to show that each without the other results in chaotic imbalances.

Passage 7 Questions

Question 1: What do Shakespeare's extreme characters who embody either only love or only reason allow us to understand?

   A. Irrational love eventually ends in an irrational way.

   B. In order for the two factors to exist, they actually need the other as a regulating force.

   C. Reason that includes love is chaotic, so the two should not mix.

   D. In order for love to truly exist, it requires some measure of hate.

Question 2: Based on the information presented in this passage, it is reasonable to conclude:

   A. A crime of passion is the result of love left unchecked by its counterbalance: hate.

   B. A crime of passion is the result of love not tempered by reason.

   C. A crime of passion is the result of reason not tempered by love.

   D. A crime of passion is the result of the intimate relationship between love and hate.

Question 3: Which of the following assertions is not presented as support for the author's point?

   A. Shakespeare uses this seemingly controversial idea as a basis for his comedy, showing just how reasonless pure love can be, and how loveless honest reason can be.

   B. Shakespeare's continued motif of reasonless love further demonstrates its destructiveness.

   C. Everything in this world exists as a dichotomy: good and evil, right and wrong, men and women, even love and hate.

   D. Shakespeare presents us with counterexamples of this crucial balance to demonstrate the need for love and reason to coexist.

Passage 7 – Question 1 Answer & Discussion

Note: The explanation under each answer explains why it is correct or incorrect, and the correct answer is bolded.

Question 1: What do Shakespeare's extreme characters who embody either only love or only reason allow us to understand?

Type: Foundations of Comprehension

A. Irrational love eventually ends in an irrational way.

Explanation: This can be drawn from paragraph two in which author states, "The characters affected fall into deep and passionate yet inexplicable and irrational love. These unfounded relationships ultimately result in chaos..." However, it does not address the other side of the duality – extreme reason.

B. In order for the two factors to exist, they actually need the other as a regulating force.

Explanation: The author explores this idea throughout the whole passage. In paragraph four, he writes, "Each dichotomy needs the other in order to exist...Similarly, love and reason also share such a relationship; love that contains no reason and reason that contains no love result in chaotic and unbalanced situations." In other words, love and reason need the other as a regulating force, so B is the correct answer.

C. Reason that includes love is chaotic, so the two should not mix.

Explanation: In paragraph three, the author argues that reason needs love: "Just as extreme love calls for a certain degree of reason in order to avoid disarray, reason also needs components of compassion and understanding."

D. In order for love to truly exist, it requires some measure of hate.

Explanation: In the first paragraph of the passage, the author introduces different dualities such as good and evil and love and hate, but then goes on to say, "Instead of addressing the standard duality of love and hate, Shakespeare emphasizes the interesting correlation between love and reason." The rest of the passage goes on to discuss the correlation between love and reason, so D is incorrect.

Discussion:

This is a Foundations of Comprehension question that asks you to understand the basic components of the text. It is challenging because it requires you to have a firm grasp on the central thesis of the passage, which isn't explicitly stated. Furthermore, there is more than one answer that the author would agree with, but only one of them captures the full understanding we are supposed to have after reading the passage.

Working through the answers, you can quickly eliminate Answer D because it talks about a duality that is not the focus of this passage. You can also easily rule out Answer C if you recognize that it goes against the author's central thesis. At this point, we are left with Answers A and B, both of which would accurately reflect ideas presented in the passage. However, only Answer B fully addresses both sides of the duality.

Passage 7 – Question 2 Answer & Discussion

Note: The explanation under each answer explains why it is correct or incorrect, and the correct answer is bolded.

Question 2: Based on the information presented in this passage, it is reasonable to conclude:

Type: Reasoning Beyond the Text

A. A crime of passion is the result of love left unchecked by its counterbalance: hate.

   Explanation: In the first paragraph of the passage, the author introduces different dualities such as good and evil and love and hate, but then goes on to say, "Instead of addressing the standard duality of love and hate, Shakespeare emphasizes the interesting correlation between love and reason." The rest of the passage goes on to discuss the correlation between love and reason, so A can't be the correct answer.

B. A crime of passion is the result of love not tempered by reason.

   Explanation: In paragraph 2, the author writes, "Shakespeare's plays are riddled with passionate lovers, all of whom commit unreasonable and reckless acts in the name of love." If we equate "unreasonable and reckless acts" to "crimes of passion," then the passage suggests that such acts are guided by love without reason, so B is the correct answer.

C. A crime of passion is the result of reason not tempered by love.

   Explanation: See the explanation for B. Since a crime of passion is the result of love not tempered by reason, C can't be the correct answer because it is the reverse.

D. A crime of passion is the result of the intimate relationship between love and hate.

   Explanation: In the first paragraph of the passage, the author introduces different dualities such as good and evil and love and hate, but then goes on to say, "Instead of addressing the standard duality of love and hate, Shakespeare emphasizes the interesting correlation between love and reason." The rest of the passage goes on to discuss the correlation between love and reason, so D can't be the correct answer.

Discussion:

This is a Reasoning Beyond the Text question that asks you to evaluate statements that are not directly presented in the passage against the passage information. It is challenging because of the high degree of similarity between the answer options, thus requiring you to be acutely aware of what distinguishes them in order to determine the correct response.

The introductory paragraph of the passage helps you to eliminate Answers A and D immediately because both draw on the duality of love and hate, rather than love and reason. To choose between Answers B and C, you would need to first understand what "a crime of passion" refers to – acts driven by love and lacking in reason. Once that is clear you can easily rule out C in favor of B

Passage 7 – Question 3 Answer & Discussion

Note: The explanation under each answer explains why it is correct or incorrect, and the correct answer is bolded.

Question 3: Which of the following assertions is not presented as support for the author's point?

Type: Reasoning Within the Text

A. Shakespeare uses this seemingly controversial idea as a basis for his comedy, showing just how reasonless pure love can be, and how loveless honest reason can be.

Explanation: The author's whole argument involves the interaction between love and reason, namely how pure or overly passionate love, devoid of reason, can result in chaos and destruction and how reason, when untampered by love or compassion is unbalanced. Therefore, this quote is used to support the author's point.

B. Shakespeare's continued motif of reasonless love further demonstrates its destructiveness.

Explanation: The author's whole argument involves the interaction between love and reason, and how pure or overly passionate love, devoid of reason, can result in chaos and destruction. Therefore, this quote is used to support the author's point.

C. Everything in this world exists as a dichotomy: good and evil, right and wrong, men and women, even love and hate.

Explanation: This statement is about the interaction and balance of love and reason's coexistence, but love and reason are not a classic dichotomy like love and hate, so this quote is not used to support the author's main point.

D. Shakespeare presents us with counterexamples of this crucial balance to demonstrate the need for love and reason to coexist.

Explanation: In paragraph three, the author writes, "Just as extreme love calls for a certain degree of reason in order to avoid disarray, reason also needs components of compassion and understanding." Throughout the passage, the author discusses the interaction and balance of reason and love's coexistence, so this is also used to support the author's main point.

Discussion:

This is a Reasoning Within the Text question that asks you to integrate distant components of the text. It requires you to have a firm grasp on the central thesis of the passage (the author's point), which isn't explicitly stated. Further, this question is complicated by the negation; you have to find the answer that is *not* presented as support for the author's point. Finally, all the answer choices are taken from the text, so simply relying on your memory of what was in the passage vs. what was not in the passage will not help you.

The author's central argument here is that just like he does with dualities such as love and hate or good and evil, Shakespeare uses love and reason throughout his plays to show how each aspect balances the other. Understanding this, you can begin to eliminate the answers that support this thesis – Answers A, B, and D – so that you are left with the correct answer: C.

SAMPLE PASSAGE 8

The population of industrialized countries is aging rapidly, leading to increased pressure on both health and social systems to provide care for these citizens. Estimates indicate that by the year 2036, 24% of the Canadian population will be over the age of 65 years. Similar statistics in the United States predict that by 2030, approximately 20% of residents will be aged 65 years and older. Increased life expectancy has led to an increase in interdisciplinary approaches to care in the community for older adults living with chronic conditions or requiring palliative care. Advances in medicine, palliative care practices, and homecare supports allow people who are dying the option of staying at home longer than in the past.

In 2005, it was estimated that only 5% of Canadians receive integrated palliative services, and for rural residents, this number is estimated to be even lower. Integrated palliative care is person-driven holistic care provided in a setting of their choice and addresses family needs. The small percentage of individuals receiving integrated palliative care is worrying because bucolic areas tend to have a higher proportion of elderly individuals than urban areas, indicating a greater need for services. In North America, the largest palliative care programs are often in cities and they are often very expensive to operate.

Canada and the United States are faced with weaker prospects for economic growth, which combined with fiscal deficits could have grave implications for the opportunity to grow health spending. Price inflation for core health-related costs and services has been and will continue to drive costs higher, possibly limiting access and availability of health-care services. As populations age, decision-makers will be confronted with the responsibility of how to best care for older adults, such as palliative care, especially in rural places.

Palliative care volunteers (PCV) have an essential role in the palliative care team, where programs rely heavily on volunteers and few programs could afford to provide quality end-of-life care without their services. There is a developing appreciation for the vital role volunteers can occupy in palliative care, especially regarding personal, respite, and emotional support to older adults and their families.

There is considerable variability in the use of PCV across developed countries and restrictions in their role. In many settings, including patient's homes, volunteers are restricted in the direct care they can provide. This variability leads to ambiguity regarding volunteer boundaries and the training required to provide consistent care. There is a definite need for palliative care services in provincial areas; however, resources are limited. Volunteers may be a feasible option to fill the growing resource gap in rural community palliative care.

Paragraph Summaries and Central Thesis

Paragraph 1: Increased life expectancies in industrialized countries like Canada and the U.S. will lead to larger elderly populations in the decades to come, which leads to an increased need for palliative care. In this introductory paragraph, the author introduces the statistics that necessitate the discussion of the topic of this passage.

Paragraph 2: In North America, integrated palliative care is most available in urban areas, but the elderly patients in need tend to live in rural areas. This paragraph presents one challenge of accessing integrative palliative care.

Paragraph 3: Weak economic prospects and increasing health costs may further limit the access to health services such as palliative care. This paragraph presents a second challenge of accessing integrative palliative care.

Paragraph 4: Palliative care volunteers (PCV) play a vital role in palliative care programs. This paragraph introduces a potential solution to the access issues discussed in previous paragraphs.

Paragraph 5: There is ambiguity surrounding qualification process and scope of PCVs, but these volunteers are needed to fill in the resource gap. In the final paragraph, the author discusses a barrier faced by PCVs, underscored by the need for their services.

Central Thesis: Palliative care volunteers (PCV) face constraining regulations, yet they are needed to fill the healthcare gap for providing rural palliative care to the growing elderly population in Canada and the U.S.

Passage 8 Questions

Question 1: Which of the following assumptions did the author have to make in order to come to his conclusion that PCVs would fill in the healthcare gap in Canada and the U.S.?

    A. PCVs tend to serve in rural areas.

    B. PVCs face fewer restrictions in less developed countries.

    C. PCVs do not need extensive training to provide consistent care.

    D. PVCs are drawn to urban areas where more residents receive integrated palliative services.

Question 2: The author uses the word "bucolic" in paragraph two to mean:

    A. Impoverished

    B. Privileged

    C. Rural

    D. Urban

Question 3: Someone who agreed with the author's main point would also be likely to agree with which of the following?

    A. Combatting litter pollution in local streams will be best achieved through political advocacy efforts to elect officials who can make change.

    B. Combatting litter pollution in local streams will be best achieved by employing private sector waste removal companies.

    C. Combatting litter pollution in local streams is only going to get more difficult as populations grow.

    D. Combatting litter pollution in local streams can be tackled by organizing weekly neighborhood stream clean ups.

Passage 8 – Question 1 Answer & Discussion

Note: The explanation under each answer explains why it is correct or incorrect, and the correct answer is bolded.

Question 1: Which of the following assumptions did the author have to make in order to come to his conclusion that PCVs would fill in the healthcare gap in Canada and the U.S.?

Type: Reasoning Within the Text

A. PCVs tend to serve in rural areas.

> *Explanation:* In the final paragraph, the author states, "Volunteers may be a feasible option to fill the growing resource gap in rural community palliative care," but he does not explicitly provide evidence that PCVs serve in rural areas. Therefore, he had to make this assumption to arrive at this conclusion.

B. PVCs face fewer restrictions in less developed countries.

> *Explanation:* Though the sentence "There is considerable variability in the use of PCV across developed countries and restrictions in their role," might suggest that there is less variability and restrictions elsewhere, the nature of the system in place for PCVs outside of North America is irrelevant to the conclusion that PCVs would fill a gap within North America.

C. PCVs do not need extensive training to provide consistent care.

> *Explanation:* Though the author says there is variability in the training required to provide consistent care, he never assumes how much training is necessary. The amount of training needed also does not factor into the fact that PCVs can fill a gap in the Canadian and U.S. healthcare system.

D. PVCs are drawn to urban areas where more residents receive integrated palliative services.

> *Explanation:* The author does not make this assumption. If he did, he would not be able to conclude that PCVs would fill in a gap in rural areas of North America.

Discussion:

This is a Reasoning Within the Text question that asks you to identify a piece of information that is missing from the passage but crucial for making an argument. You must begin with a full understanding of that argument, which is only partially included in the question.

After you have recognized that the healthcare gap mentioned is specifically in rural areas, you may be able to easily zero in on A as the correct answer. If you missed this little detail, you can still arrive at the correct answer by a process of elimination. Answers B and C can both be ruled out on the account of being irrelevant to the argument. You are then left with Answers A and D, which seem to be opposites. To figure out which is the correct answer, you need simply to go back to the passage and find the relevant statement in the final paragraph where the author specifies that the resource gap is in "...rural community palliative care." You would then be able to eliminate Answer D, which would hurt rather than support the author's argument, leaving you with Answer A.

Passage 8 – Question 2 Answer & Discussion

Note: The explanation under each answer explains why it is correct or incorrect, and the correct answer is bolded.

Question 2: The author uses the word "bucolic" in paragraph two to mean:

Type: Foundations of Comprehension

A. Lacking in financial resources.

Explanation: Although the author indicates that large palliative care programs are expensive to operate, this paragraph focuses on elderly populations in rural vs. urban settings.

B. Having additional rights and advantages.

Explanation: The author states that there are more elderly people living in bucolic areas and more of a need for palliative care there. If bucolic means privileged, then there would be more resources to provide palliative care in that area, so this definition doesn't make sense.

C. Being distant from city centers.

Explanation: This paragraph states that there is a higher need for services in bucolic areas than urban areas and that the largest palliative care programs are in cities, so you can deduce that if there are services available in urban areas while on the other hand services are in need in "bucolic" areas, bucolic must mean rural or farther away from those services in city centers.

D. Being proximal to city centers.

Explanation: The author contrasts "bucolic" areas with the urban areas where there are fewer elderly people. Since the author establishes a contrasting relationship between bucolic and urban areas, bucolic cannot mean proximal (close) to city centers.

Discussion:

This is a Foundations of Comprehension question that asks you to infer meaning from rhetorical devices, word choice, and text structure. In this case, the question asks you what the word "bucolic" means based on the immediate context in which you find the word. Here, it is helpful to have a summary of the relevant paragraph in mind to guide you. The main idea of paragraph two is: In North America, integrated palliative care is expensive and most available in urban areas, but the elderly patients in need tend to live in rural areas, which indicates a large need for expanded integrated palliative care. The word "bucolic" is used in opposition to the word "urban," which should give you a big clue to its meaning. If you are not sure about the main idea of the second paragraph due to the use of the word "bucolic," you can still refer to the central thesis of the passage, which is that PCVs can fill in a healthcare gap and provide rural palliative care. In both paragraph two and the overall thesis of the passage, palliative care is referenced as being a large issue in rural areas, or in the very least, is compared to palliative care in urban areas, so the most likely meaning of "bucolic" must be C – being distant from city centers!

Passage 8 – Question 3 Answer & Discussion

Note: The explanation under each answer explains why it is correct or incorrect, and the correct answer is bolded.

Question 3: Someone who agreed with the author's main point would also be likely to agree with which of the following?

Type: Reasoning Beyond the Text

A. Combatting litter pollution in local streams will be best achieved through political advocacy efforts to elect officials who can make change.

   Explanation: Although the author does mention, "As populations age, decision-makers will be confronted with the responsibility of how to best care for older adults…" there is no significant discussion of political advocacy or officials being the ones who can best address the issue of inadequate palliative care for growing elderly populations.

B. Combatting litter pollution in local streams will be best achieved by employing private sector waste removal companies.

   Explanation: There is no mention of private sector involvement in the passage at all, so there is no evidence that this could be the correct answer.

C. Combatting litter pollution in local streams is only going to get more difficult as populations grow.

   Explanation: This passage does discuss the growth of elderly populations as a cause for the growing gap in care, but this was a point to support the need of more PCVs, not the main thesis itself.

D. Combatting litter pollution in local streams can be tackled by organizing neighborhood volunteer stream clean ups.

   Explanation: This answer makes the most sense because the author views PCVs as a viable solution to inadequate palliative care. The wording in the answer does not say that neighborhood volunteer stream cleanups is the best solution or the most effective, but that litter pollution "can be tackled" by such clean ups, so this makes the most sense in relation to the author's main point.

Discussion:

This is a Reasoning Beyond the Text question that asks you to apply ideas from the passage to a new context, which is challenging because you not only need to have a firm grasp of the central thesis, but you also need to be able to identify the commonalities between the passage and the new situation presented. You must be careful not to draw in your own knowledge or biases, even if you have your own ideas about how to resolve the litter pollution issue.

As you read through each answer choice, look for elements that it shares with the central thesis. All answer choices contain "combatting litter pollution in local streams," but each choice provides a different solution to litter pollution in local streams. So, the solution to litter pollution in local streams will contain a similarity to the proposed solution to palliative care in rural areas. Recall that the solution proposed by the author is to increase the number of volunteers in this sector. We can thus rule out Answer B because the solution outlined involves the private sector. We can also rule out Answer A because the author does not discuss systemic change involving the government in the passage. You are then left with Answers C and D, both of which the author may agree with. However, you must remember that you are looking for an answer that provides a solution to the problem, rather than discuss the cause. You can therefore rule out Answer C and be confident that Answer D is correct. Weekly neighborhood stream clean ups do not imply any sort of monetary transaction, so the effort must be completed by volunteers, just like the PCV who help provide care to the elderly in rural areas!

SAMPLE PASSAGE 9

The production *I Call Myself Princess* showcases a compelling theatrical narrative about Indigenous performers. In presenting tales, a discussion is opened about the importance of Native stories and storytelling. While the play navigates through different worlds, the intercultural politics of Indigenous work also operates within the seen and unseen; visibility and representation has become a contentious subject for Indigenous work, especially within Canada. The city of Toronto has been posited as a "contested space." The Native Earth Performing Arts (NEPA) Theatre provides an exemplary physical space that integrates and works against many different modes of "space" – political space, economic space, social space, and ultimately artistic space. But how do these different spaces manifest and even work against one another?

Creating spaces for the visibility and recognition of Indigenous people and Indigenous work has been a slow process of reclamation and redress. Aboriginal people across Canada pushed back against forces that had silenced them and began to seize platforms from which to speak. A vast history of Canadian neglect has translated into the many stories of Canada's Indigenous population, which express how the Eurocentric model of history works against the Native story. Performatively, theatre presents an outlet for the telling and re-telling of Native stories. It presents a stage and a platform for the Native voice.

History is embedded within culture and institutionalized spaces, thus in establishing spaces that performatively present distinct perspectives of Native stories, one can argue that there is inherent politicization that occurs within theatre. *I Call Myself Princess* asks the ultimate question: now that Aboriginal people are speaking, is anybody listening? This story is being told at NEPA; more than just a building, the space is "open to the world" and welcomes anyone and everyone as a community cultural hub. More than anything, it embodies an intercultural space for integration and revitalization. It is the many stories that welcomingly come and go within this space that transcends the confinements of the physical space. It can be argued that it is necessary to outline the many groups within

Toronto in order to recognize the intercultural politics of space at play within theatre and our city.

Paragraph Summaries and Central Thesis

Paragraph 1: The play *I Call Myself Princess* occupies various, sometimes conflicting theoretical spaces simultaneously through its presentation of native storytelling in Canada's NEPA Theatre. This paragraph introduces a new idea through a specific example.

Paragraph 2: Utilizing the theatrical stage as a vehicle for reclamation, indigenous peoples in Canada tell their stories through performance in an environment that used to silence their voices. This paragraph broadens the focus of the new idea introduced in the first paragraph.

Paragraph 3: The NEPA theater is characterized as a physical space in which the intercultural politics of space transcend the theater's boundaries, presenting the opportunity for native stories like *I Call Myself Princess* to be told, seen, and heard. This paragraph narrows the focus of the broader idea discussed in paragraph two back to the example introduced in the first paragraph.

Central Thesis: The play *I Call Myself Princess* exemplifies the use of theatrical productions by Canadian Indigenous peoples to reclaim their voices through the occupation of intercultural political spaces like the NEPA Theatre.

Passage 9 Questions

Question 1: The author would be most likely to agree with which of the following statements:

A. Ballet challenges long-held gender norms by having both male and female dancers exhibit grace and other traits associated with femininity.

B. The modern art form of the Instagram "selfie" challenges the role of the photographer, making them both the artist and the art form at the same time.

C. Spoken word poetry dismantles the Eurocentric idea of the literary canon through its performative nature, incorporating rhythmic jazz elements that developed in communities of color.

D. All of the above.

Question 2: The author uses the word "intercultural" in paragraph three to mean:

A. Within a culture.

B. Native to a particular area.

C. Relating to two or more cultures.

D. Of traditional culture.

Question 3: Which conclusion does the author use the example of *I Call Myself Princess* to support?

A. The suppression of Indigenous theatrical productions demonstrates the silencing of Canada's Native peoples.

B. Indigenous theatrical productions are efforts to reclaim previously silenced Native voices and spaces.

C. Indigenous theatrical productions are about the struggle for Native peoples' autonomy in Canada.

D. None of the above.

Passage 9 – Question 1 Answer & Discussion

Note: The explanation under each answer explains why it is correct or incorrect, and the correct answer is bolded.

Question 1: The author would be most likely to agree with which of the following statements:

Type: Reasoning Beyond the Text

A. Ballet challenges long-held gender norms by having both male and female dancers exhibit grace and other feminine traits.

Explanation: The central thesis of the passage involves an art form that challenges or disrupts a norm in some way. When you examine this answer choice in detail, it becomes clear that the statement itself supports gender norms. Stating that the trait of grace is feminine upholds structures that dictate how each gender should act.

B. The modern art form of the Instagram "selfie" challenges the role of the photographer, making them both the artist and the art form at the same time.

Explanation: This answer choice focuses on blurring the lines between the artist and the art being created, which is not the main point of Indigenous theatre as described by the author.

C. Spoken word poetry dismantles the Eurocentric idea of the literary canon through its performative nature, incorporating rhythmic jazz elements that developed in communities of color.

Explanation: The passage focuses on the art form shaped by the cultural norms of Canada's indigenous peoples, while this answer choice focuses on the art form shaped by the cultural norms of communities of color – both marginalized social groups. Additionally, both the passage and this answer choice mention a rejection of dominant Eurocentric ideas by a marginalized group through the art form.

D. All of the above.

Explanation: See Answers A and B.

Discussion:

This is a Reasoning Beyond the Text question that asks you to apply ideas from the passage to a new context. It is challenging because it requires you to have a firm understanding of the central thesis of the passage in order to apply it to an unfamiliar context.

As you read through each answer choice, look for elements that it shares with the central thesis. Broadly, Answers A, B, and C all include an element of crossing existing boundaries (i.e., between male and female, art and artist, and Eurocentric and non-Eurocentric musical traditions). However, upon closer examination, you would be able to see that one of these is more representative of the issues the author writes about in this passage, so Answer D can be eliminated. If you noticed the theme of a historic power imbalance in the passage, you may be able to rule out Answer B, which highlights two roles that are not plagued with this imbalance. This would leave you with Answers A and C. You can then rule out Answer A as it reinforces the norms of femininity rather than breaking them down. You would then be left with Answer C, which mirrors the author's advocacy for creating intercultural spaces.

Passage 9 – Question 2 Answer & Discussion

Note: The explanation under each answer explains why it is correct or incorrect, and the correct answer is bolded.

Question 2: The author uses the word "intercultural" in paragraph three to mean:

Type: Foundations of Comprehension

A. Within a culture

Explanation: The author states that, "More than anything, [the NEPA theatre] embodies an intercultural space for integration and revitalization." Since integration implies the combination of different parts, or in this case, cultures, it would not make sense for the "intercultural space" to be constrained to a single culture.

B. Native to a particular area

Explanation: In the sentence before the one in which the word "intercultural" appears, the author states that the NEPA is "open to the world." It would go against this notion for the NEPA to be a space native to a particular area.

C. Relating two or more cultures

Explanation: In the previous sentence, NEPA theatre is presented as a "...community cultural hub". Based on context, we understand that the NEPA theatre embodies a space in which two or more cultures can be integrated and revitalized.

D. Of traditional culture

Explanation: Though the passage focuses on lending a voice to traditional Indigenous art and culture, this definition would not fit with the immediate context of the sentence for reasons similar to Answer A since it implies only one culture is being integrated.

Discussion:

This is a Foundations of Comprehension question that asks you to infer meaning from rhetorical devices, word choice, and text structure. In this case, the question asks you what the word "intercultural" means based on the context.

Though it is used in two sentences in paragraph three, one of them is more informative of its meaning. In addition to the immediate context, you may also use the information in the sentence before or after to aid you. From the context, we know that the NEPA is a "cultural hub" that is "open to the world" that is used for cultural "integration." Thus, we can rule out Answers A, B, and D, which restrict the scope of the space to just one (type) of culture.

Passage 9 – Question 3 Answer & Discussion

Note: The explanation under each answer explains why it is correct or incorrect, and the correct answer is bolded.

Question 3: Which conclusion does the author use the example of *I Call Myself Princess* to support?

Type: Reasoning Within the Text

A. The suppression of Indigenous theatrical productions demonstrates the silencing of Canada's Native peoples.

Explanation: In paragraph two, the author writes, "Performatively, theatre presents an outlet for the telling and re-telling of Native stories. It presents a stage and a platform for the Native voice." Nowhere in the passage does the author claim that this production is suppressed, even though it may highlight the historic silencing of Native voices.

B. Indigenous theatrical productions are efforts to reclaim previously silenced Native voices and spaces.

Explanation: In paragraph one, the author tells you that *I Call Myself Princess* "...showcases a compelling theatrical narrative about Indigenous performers. In presenting tales, a discussion is opened about the importance of Native stories and storytelling." You also know that the play *I Call Myself Princess* is staged at the NEPA Theatre where "...creating spaces for the visibility and recognition of Indigenous people and Indigenous work has been a slow process of reclamation and redress." This conclusion is therefore well-supported by this example.

C. Indigenous theatrical productions are about the struggle for Native peoples' autonomy in Canada.

Explanation: Though the author states that "...a vast history of Canadian neglect has translated into the many stories of Canada's Indigenous population, which express how the Eurocentric model of history works against the Native story," he never implies that Native people seek autonomy.

D.   None of the above.

Explanation: See Answer B.

Discussion:

This is a Reasoning Within the Text question that asks you to integrate distant components of the text to evaluate the example discussed in two paragraphs against the conclusions presented in the answer choices. You must identify the author's central thesis even though that thesis is not explicitly stated, and verify that the example *I Call Myself Princess* supports that conclusion.

Scanning through the answers, you can rule out Answer C immediately, since the author does not address issues of autonomy in this passage. You can also rule out Answer A because the author does not say that the production *I Call Myself Princess* is in anyway being suppressed. You must then decide whether Answer B is supported by the example or not in order to choose between B and D. Recognizing that *I Call Myself Princess* is used by the author as an example of a theatrical production that strives to project previously suppressed Native voices, you can confidently choose Answer B as the correct response.

SAMPLE PASSAGE 10

Prose fiction was one of the best-selling literary genres of the Elizabethan age, despite (or perhaps because of) its uncertain status as a literary genre. Almost all of the prose fictional narratives of the time included dedicatory material by the author that negotiated both the status of their work and the readers' response to it. Robert Greene prescribes his 1588 work *Pandosto. The Triumph of Time* as "pleasant for age to avoid drowsy thoughts, profitable for youth to eschew other wanton pastimes, and bringing to both a desired content." According to Farmer and Lesser, prose fiction, including romance, had a larger share of the London book trade than drama in the years between 1592 and 1612, at 6.7%, clearly indicating that the genre had the attention of early modern readers in London. It is impossible to trace a history of the genre in England without taking into account the massive readership that placed it, problematically, at the heart of early modern culture.

Some scholars have investigated the readership of late sixteenth- and early seventeenth- century prose fiction. To date there has been no study focused specifically on the ways in which early modern readers extracted passages of prose fiction in their commonplace books, even though such books provide a vital form of evidence about the readership and cultural function of these texts. We can extend our understanding of the readership of Elizabethan prose fiction by tracing the nature and placement of extracts from some of the most popular and controversial narratives in both manuscript commonplace books and printed anthologies of miscellanies. Studying the ways in which readers commonplaced passages from prose fiction narratives will be especially important in understanding the ways in which readers interpreted the genre, particularly keeping in mind the hermeneutic challenges that many of these texts contained. These narratives required an intense intellectual engagement from its readers, as texts such as Thomas More's *Utopia* entirely depend upon the reader's hermeneutic intervention to understand the text's careful metafiction.

By analyzing the contexts in which extracts from authors such as Gascoigne, Lyly, and Greene appeared in commonplace books we can see that, despite the controversial nature of these texts, they were also part of a movement to create a literary role for a genre that has now become synonymous with literature. According to Moss, commonplace books were compilations of extracts from various literary sources, used as pedagogical tools in a humanist training, as they provided the compiler ready access to the stores of knowledge and expertise.

Paragraph Summaries and Central Thesis

Paragraph 1: The authors of prose fiction were attuned to the readers that made prose fiction a commercially successful genre in Elizabethan England. This paragraph introduces information about the commercial status of prose fiction in the period.

Paragraph 2: We need to study how prose fiction excerpts were placed in manuscripts and printed in commonplace books in order to understand how Elizabethan readers approached and interpreted these texts. In this paragraph, the author suggests a method for studying early modern readerships of prose fiction.

Paragraph 3: Commonplace books are collections of extracts from various sources that gave purpose to prose fiction. In this paragraph, the author provides a definition of commonplace books and how they can shed light on readers' approaches to prose fiction.

Central Thesis: We should study commonplace books to gain insight into how readers interpreted prose fiction texts because the readership of the genre was such an important aspect of the genre, making it a commercial success.

Passage 10 Questions

Question 1: According to the author, how can researchers use commonplace books today?

 A. Researchers can understand the differences between readers' approaches to manuscript and print culture and how they appreciated each medium differently.

 B. Researchers can use them to trace the responses that the various readers had to texts, and the ways in which readers situated these interpretation-demanding narratives within a larger literary culture.

 C. They can give researchers insight into the personal lives of readers and their ability to interpret texts.

 D. They are important indicators of the educational system of the period and pedagogical approaches to reading.

Question 2: According to the author, why do we need to keep readers in mind when studying Elizabethan fiction?

 A. Analysis of the early modern London book market demonstrates that readers significantly invested in the genre, as sales of prose fiction constituted at least a third of all book sales.

 B. Prose fiction readers were more committed to the genre than audiences of drama.

 C. Prose fiction authors often addressed their readers in the prefatory matter, mentioning how the works could be of use to them.

 D. Thomas More's *Utopia* tells us about the importance of readers.

Question 3: Based on this passage, which of the following would reflect the author's views on literature and literary genres?

 A. Literature is a form of art that is independent from the contexts surrounding it.

 B. We must study literary works through the lens of authors' lives to understand how to interpret them.

C. The author's intention is the only important aspect of a literary piece of writing.

D. Literature is a commercial enterprise.

Passage 10 – Question 1 Answer & Discussion

Note: The explanation under each answer explains why it is correct or incorrect and the correct answer is bolded.

Question 1: According to the author, how can researchers use commonplace books today?

Type: Foundations of Comprehension

A. Researchers can understand the differences between readers' approaches to manuscript and print culture and how they appreciated each medium.

Explanation: The author mentions manuscript commonplace books and printed miscellanies as equal forms of evidence, writing: "We can extend our understanding of the readership of Elizabethan prose fiction by tracing the nature and placement of extracts from some of the most popular and controversial narratives in both manuscript commonplace books and printed anthologies of miscellanies." As such, differences in media are not important considerations for the author in this case.

B. Researchers can use them to trace the responses that the various readers had to texts, and the ways in which readers situated these interpretation-demanding narratives within a larger literary culture.

Explanation: Because the central thesis of the passage is that commonplace books offer valuable insight into how readers viewed the prose fiction genre, researchers can use commonplace books to situate the genre into the larger literary culture of the period and understand readers' approaches to these texts.

C. They can give researchers insight into the personal lives of readers and their ability to interpret texts.

Explanation: Though the author argues that commonplace books can shed light on how readers interpreted texts, there is no demonstrated interest in the readers' personal lives nor their interpretive abilities.

D. They are important indicators of the educational system of the period and pedagogical approaches to reading.

Explanation: The passage states that "...commonplace books were compilations of extracts from various literary sources, used as pedagogical tools in a humanist training, as they provided the compiler ready access to the stores of knowledge and expertise." Here, the author explains that commonplace books were important pedagogical tools, but does not elaborate on how researchers could understand how reading was taught in that period.

Discussion:

This is a Foundations of Comprehension question that tests your understanding of the central argument of the passage. As such, it is designed to test your comprehension of the various claims made by the author, as well as your ability to decipher what the author is *not* claiming.

The key to the question is to carefully compare the language of each answer option to the portions of the passage to see whether the underlying meaning matches what the author has claimed. Though the answer options may not be necessarily incorrect outside the context of this passage, we must ensure that the claim of answer option is articulated by the author for it to be correct. As such, we can proceed through a process of elimination. We can see that the author makes no claims about media, eliminating Answer A, does not delve into readers' abilities to interpret text, eliminating Answer C, and makes no claims about the pedagogical system of the era, eliminating Answer D. We are then left with Answer B, and must compare the claim of the answer option against the arguments of the passage, finding that the two do align.

Passage 10 – Question 2 Answer & Discussion

Note: The explanation under each answer explains why it is correct or incorrect, and the correct answer is bolded.

Question 2: According to the author, why do we need to keep readers in mind when studying Elizabethan fiction?

Type: Reasoning Within the Text

A. Analysis of the early modern London book market demonstrates that readers significantly invested in the genre, as sales of prose fiction constituted at least a third of all book sales.

Explanation: Studies of early modern London's book trade demonstrate that prose fiction "had a larger share of the London book trade than drama in the years between 1592 and 1612, at 6.7%," not a third of all sales.

B. Prose fiction readers were more committed to the genre than audiences of drama.

Explanation: Though the author does cite a study that found that prose fiction outsold publications of drama, there is no mention of the audiences of dramatic works (see quoted passage above).

C. Prose fiction authors often addressed their readers in the prefatory matter, mentioning how the works could be of use to them.

Explanation: The author cites a passage from the dedicatory material of Robert Greene's *Pandosto*, in which Greene mentions that the book could be "...pleasant for age to avoid drowsy thoughts, profitable for youth to eschew other wanton pastimes, and bringing to both a desired content." This is used as evidence that prose fiction authors were very aware of their readers, supporting the idea that those studying the genre should also be aware of its readers in that era.

D. Thomas More's *Utopia* tells us about the importance of readers.

Explanation: The author references the hermeneutic challenges that make up the metafiction of More's *Utopia*. However, *Utopia* does not explicitly discuss readers, nor does the author state so.

Discussion:

This is a Reasoning Within the Text question that assesses your ability to understand the evidence provided within the passage. The question tests your critical analysis of the information and rhetorical formulations used by the author to draw the conclusions that are presented by the passage. The key to answering this question correctly lies in your ability to differentiate the various claims used by the author to determine what is actually used as evidence for the claim in question.

As a first step, it is integral to consider the claims of each answer option against the passage to verify whether they accurately reflect the information from the text. This would enable you to eliminate Answer A. The subsequent answer options are less straightforward to tease apart because they are all taken from the passage. Thus, you must assess them carefully to see how fully they articulate the reason we must study readers of prose fiction. Though the author mentions More's *Utopia*, the passage does not make the study of prose fiction readers dependent on that text. Similarly, the author does not make audiences of drama an important reason for why we must study prose fiction readers. However, the author does quote a passage from an author of a prose fiction text and discusses how these authors were concerned with the readership of their material, which closely aligns with Answer C.

Passage 10 – Question 3 Answer & Discussion

Note: The explanation under each answer explains why it is correct or incorrect, and the correct answer is bolded.

Question 3: Based on this passage, which of the following would reflect the author's views on literature and literary genres?

Type: Reasoning Within the Text

A. Literature is a form of art that is independent from the contexts surrounding it.

Explanation: Since the passage is focused on the ways in which literature is consumed, and the context in which it is created, the approach that literature is independent of these forces does not coincide with the author's perspective on literature.

B. We must study literary works through the lens of authors' lives to understand how to interpret them.

Explanation: Though the author of the passage is interested in the historical contexts surrounding texts' production and consumption, there is no mention of the importance of biographical information about the texts' authors.

C. The author's intention is the only important aspect of a literary piece of writing.

Explanation: The author of the passage values readers' approaches and interpretations, thereby demonstrating that the author's intention is not the only important aspect of a literary piece of writing.

D. Literature is a commercial enterprise.

Explanation: The author is mindful of the market in which literary works are created and disseminated, citing book trade statistics.

Discussion:

This is a Reasoning Within the Text question that asks you to demonstrate your understanding of the author's views on a topic based on the passage. In this case, you are asked to infer the author's overall stance on literary genres. This is a difficult question that tempts you to bring in your own views about the topic at hand. You may find yourself agreeing with one or more of the answers, even though it might not reflect what the author would think or say.

To successfully navigate this question, you must stay guarded against your own knowledge and views and not allow them to cloud your judgment. In doing so, you can systematically eliminate Answers A, B, and C, which are all views that could be plausibly held by another author or literary critic, but ultimately do not reflect the views of the author of this passage. We are thus left with Answer D, which may at first seem too limiting in scope for a discussion about literature, but actually captures the author's views on the matter.

Now that you have gone through 10 sample CARS passages with expert guidance, we hope you have a better understanding of the types of questions you will encounter, a grasp of the level of difficulty of the passages and questions, and also a clearer idea of your own strengths and weaknesses. If these 10 passages took you a long time to go through, not to worry, this is all part of the learning process. In *Chapter VIII: 40 Practice CARS Passages with Questions and Answers*, you will have another 40 practice passages, giving you many more opportunities to not only refine your strategies, but also to increase your speed!

However, before we get there, we would like for you to take a well-deserved break from practicing so we can teach you about something just as important for acing your MCAT: stress management.

CHAPTER VII

Long-Term and Short-Term Stress Management Strategies

One of the most common reasons good students perform poorly on CARS is because they let their nerves get the best of them. When they encounter a difficult passage on the MCAT they start to panic, lose confidence, and can no longer apply the practice they did leading up to the exam. If you let stress get the best of you on test day, this can translate into a low CARS score that does not reflect your true critical thinking and reasoning skills.

Therefore, it is absolutely critical for you to develop strategies to cope with stress. These strategies will help you with CARS and also throughout the rest of your professional and personal life. In this chapter, we are going to teach you both long-term and short-term strategies to manage your stress as you prepare to ace CARS. We encourage you to experiment with each strategy and choose the ones that work best for you.

Long-term Strategies

Let's begin by discussing some long-term solutions. These are strategies that you can begin to implement in the weeks and months leading up to your MCAT.

First, it goes without saying that going through the preparation process we suggest in this book, including reading challenging texts, understanding CARS question types, completing practice passages, and getting expert feedback, will make you feel more at ease during your actual MCAT. The more realistic your practice is, the more comfortable you will be.

We also recommend that you visit the testing site prior to your MCAT. This is extremely helpful for a few reasons. First, you can familiarize yourself with the testing site and surrounding area. That way, you will know exactly where you need to be and how to get there. We even recommend that you take multiple trips to and from the testing site and your home so you can figure out traffic patterns and any shortcuts. Immersing yourself in the actual environment and atmosphere will also put you at great ease on your MCAT day because being it will no longer be a novel experience. If you have time, engage in an enjoyable activity close to the testing site, such as having a nice meal, listening to your favorite music, reading a book, or socializing with a friend. This helps to encourage a positive mindset when you return to this location for your test.

In the time leading up to your MCAT, be sure to research and understand how each school you are applying to evaluates CARS. An important step in managing your stress is setting realistic goals for your score. What is a good CARS score? Well, it depends on the schools you are applying to. A CARS score that is competitive at one school may not be competitive at another. Some schools weigh your MCAT score heavily when determining whether or not to invite you for an interview or offer you a spot in their program, while other schools take a more holistic approach in reviewing your application. While most medical schools like to see strong scores across the board in each MCAT section, some schools place higher importance on CARS and certain medical schools will *only* look at CARS. Understanding how the schools you are applying view CARS is crucial knowledge to have as you design your study plans for the MCAT. This information can give you piece of mind and will help you to remain confident that you are tackling your preparation in the way that makes sense for your applications.

Keep yourself healthy with proper nutrition, regular exercise, and adequate rest. In the months leading up to this exam, you may find yourself neglecting your physical wellbeing to put in extra hours in an attempt to boost your score just a couple of points. Know that this may actually have the opposite effect! If you allow your physical state to deteriorate while you are preparing for your test, you are putting yourself at risk of falling ill, or at the very least of not achieving your peak performance on the test. If you are not well-rested, you may not be able to effectively retrieve the knowledge you have so painstakingly memorized and you may not be able to engage in the level of critical thinking necessary to ace the test. Keeping yourself in good physical condition is therefore just as important as ensuring that you are mentally prepared for the test. Make sure you are eating small, well-balanced meals every few hours during your waking hours. Make sure you take short breaks to stand up, walk around, and let your eyes rest. Work in longer breaks during your day to do some light exercise. Similar to working out our muscles, we need to create a routine whereby we exercise at least a few times a week in order to see lasting effects. Last but not least, ensure that you are getting at least eight hours of sleep each night, and keep your sleeping schedule consistent.

Short-term Strategies

Having done everything you can to manage your stress in the long-term, you may still find that your stress levels rise shortly before your MCAT. This is normal, so here are some stress management strategies that you can draw upon in the days or hours leading up to your test. Since different individuals conceptualize stress differently, each person will also find some coping mechanisms more effective than others.

Before we discuss healthy stress management strategies, we want to draw your attention to some unhealthy habits that will harm you in the long run. These include:

- Smoking

- Alcohol consumption

- Unhealthy eating (e.g., bingeing, not eating enough, overconsumption of caffeine or sugar)

- Self-isolation (i.e., withdrawing from or taking your stress out on friends and family, discontinuing hobbies, and so forth). Of course, if someone is the source of your stress, limiting the time you spend around that person will help.

- Sleeping too much or too little.

- Lack of exercise or excessive exercise. A moderate amount of physical activity, such as weight training, running, swimming, and so forth, has proven psychological benefits like relieving stress. However, exercising to avoid other responsibilities, or over-exercising such that it results in drastic weight loss is not healthy.

Naturally, our recommendation is for you to avoid resorting to the above for stress relief. These habits are both ineffective and detrimental to your overall health.

Let's now discuss some healthy short-term stress management strategies that you can draw on, starting with what you can do to reduce anxiety and stress the night before your MCAT.

The night before your MCAT should *not* be spent reviewing or preparing for the test. Cramming the night before or on the day of your MCAT can have detrimental effects on your performance. By then, you should be well-prepared, so relax, enjoy your day, and complete the following to ensure test day runs as smoothly as possible: lay out some comfortable clothes to wear, pack nutritious snacks that will sustain your energy throughout the test, and get a water bottle ready to go. Throughout the day visualize your success on CARS and the MCAT as a whole. This may sound cheesy, but this is a proven way to build your confidence and is a wonderful final thought to focus on as you fall asleep the night before your test. Visualizing success helps your mind to practice success and can actually help you perform better.

Aim to go to bed early, get a good night's sleep, and wake up early. The minute you wake up on the day of your MCAT, fill your mind with a positive thought, remind yourself of all the right things you have done in preparation for CARS and the entire test, and think of the great opportunity that is ahead of you. Again, visualize your success! If it helps, write yourself a motivational note the night before and read it in the morning. One positive thought in the morning can transform your whole day. Of course, take time to have a good breakfast, get ready, and give yourself ample time to travel to your destination. This is not the time to start something new, so if you do not normally drink coffee now is not the time to start. We recommend that you plan to arrive at least 30 minutes before your MCAT is scheduled to begin. You should have mapped out several routes in advance so you know how long the commute will take and what other options you have if the primary route is unavailable due to traffic.

If you feel nervous before your MCAT, place a clean pen or pencil into your mouth horizontally and gently bite down on it with your back molars. This will force your facial muscles into a smile. Leave the pen or pencil in your mouth for about two minutes, take it out for a few minutes, and then repeat for another two minutes. Doing this will trick your brain into thinking that you are smiling, and the neurotransmitters that are released in this process will actually put you in a better mood and will help you maintain a positive state of mind. The results are even stronger if you do it in front of a mirror. Alternatively, stand in front of the mirror and watch yourself smile. Your brain physiology will change, and you will begin to feel more positive. You can also try leaning back in a chair with your hands behind your head and your feet up, or standing with your arms outstretched, chest out, and head raised. As with the smiling exercise, you can trick your brain into thinking you are relaxed and confident by holding these positions for 30 seconds or more.

Box breathing is a simple, yet powerful exercise that helps to reduce stress and return your breathing to its normal rhythm if you start to experience nerves. To do it effectively, take a deep breath in through your nose for 5 to 6 seconds, ensuring that you are using your diaphragm so that your belly puffs out, hold that breath for 4 seconds, and then exhale through your mouth for a prolonged 7 to 10 seconds, again using your diaphragm to push the air out. It should sound like an audible sigh as you breathe out. Repeat this a few times. As you may know, the prolonged exhalation causes your parasympathetic nervous system to activate and simultaneously tones down your sympathetic nervous system. If you have access to a stethoscope, test this out by monitoring your heart rate as you perform this breathing exercise. As you take a deep breath in through your nose, notice your heart rate increasing. Then, exhale very slowly and notice your heart rate slowing down. Prolonged diaphragmatic exhalation also occurs after a good laugh, yawn, or sigh of relief, which is why you feel more relaxed after engaging in one of these gestures. This evolutionary tool has been harnessed by professionals such as basketball players who take a few deep breaths before shooting a free throw, or soccer players who do breathing exercises before taking a penalty kick. Military snipers are also trained to do breathing exercises before taking a shot because it reduces their heart rate and breathing rate to give them a more accurate shot. You also can take advantage of this evolutionary tool to aid your performance on CARS and during your MCAT!

On test day, you will have breaks where you are able to eat snacks and drink water to replenish your energy and focus throughout this lengthy test. Staying hydrated is critical to your brain functioning at full capacity and becoming dehydrated means that your body cannot function as well and test day nerves are more likely to take hold. If you are prone to panic attacks or anxiety, it is important to know that these can be triggered by dehydration. How you drink water on test day actually matters! Take small sips of water rather than chugging a lot of water at once. Water has been shown to have natural calming properties, can promote feelings of relaxation, and is an important step in managing your stress – so avoid rushing your hydration on test day!

We hope that some, if not all, of these long- and short-term stress management strategies will become useful for you as you gear up for your big day. Thus far, we have focused on need-to-know facts about CARS, our top strategies for acing CARS, and what you should be doing before and during your MCAT to perform your best. In the next chapters, you will find 40 practice CARS passages to use in your preparation as well as some bonus resources to ensure you have all of the information you need for success!

CHAPTER VIII

40 CARS Practice Passages

Now that you have familiarized yourself with the do's and don'ts of CARS prep, read through expert analyses of CARS questions and answers, and reviewed stress management strategies, you are ready to tackle more CARS passages! This is a great opportunity for you to take the strategies you've been learning throughout the book and implement them while reading and analyzing new texts and questions. If you need to, refer to the strategies outlined in *Chapter V: BeMo's Top Strategies & 7 Steps to ACE Any CARS Passage* intermittently so that you are putting them into practice consistently as you work through this chapter.

In this chapter, you will find 40 additional practice passages on a variety of different topics, including the humanities and social sciences, but also some science-related topics. The science passages are there to help you see that the same critical thinking skills you are honing for CARS are useful for interpreting texts in every domain. If you come from a science background, these passages will additionally challenge you to leave all of your prior knowledge behind and focus solely on the information and perspectives contained within the passage and accompanying questions.

For each passage, we have left space for you to note down paragraph summaries and the central thesis. Continuing this exercise will help you to feel confident in your basic understanding of the passages you read so that you can more comfortably tackle the questions that come with each passage. We recommend that you split these passages up and complete them in batches. After each batch, check the answers using the Answer Key at the end of the chapter. Though there are no explanations for why each answer is correct or incorrect, we encourage you to revisit each passage for which you answered one or more questions wrong and come up with your own explanation for why each answer is correct or incorrect. Doing this will help you to further exercise those critical analysis and reasoning skills that you will need to succeed on this section of the MCAT.

As you go through these practice passages, we also recommend you work on reducing the amount of time you need to complete each passage. Since you will have slightly longer passages in the official CARS section and 5-7 questions instead of 3, you'll want to work towards completing these passages within 5-6 minutes. To track your progress, time yourself for each passage, and ensure that over the course of your preparation, your times are decreasing. Remember, if your time is decreasing at the expense of accuracy, slow yourself back down again. Only work on reducing your time if you are getting all or at least a majority of the questions correct.

Take a deep breath. Ready, set, go!

PRACTICE PASSAGE 1

The Malay language is known for having two interacting sound change processes: full reduplication (e.g., buŋa 'flower, singular' → buŋa-buŋa 'flowers, plural') and nasal substitution (e.g., məŋ+tari → mənari 'dance'). This latter process occurs when a nasal sound immediately precedes a voiceless consonant that is produced in a different location in the mouth. When this happens, that nasal sound and the following consonant are replaced by a single sound that is both nasal and produced in the same location as the consonant.

These two processes interact when the məŋ- prefix attaches either to the first component of the reduplicated verb, giving the verb a continuous meaning, or to the second component of the reduplicated verb, giving the verb a reciprocal meaning. When məŋ- attaches to the first component, the copy that doesn't bear the prefix surfaces with a nasal produced in the same location as the consonant (e.g., mənari+nari 'dance continuously'). However, when məŋ- attaches to the second component, the copy that doesn't bear the prefix surfaces with consonant instead of the nasal sound (e.g., tari+mənari 'dance with each other').

This pattern is difficult to account for under any derivational account that must consider the order of reduplication and məŋ- prefixation, and therefore the order of reduplication and nasal substitution. If reduplication happens first, then the non-prefixed component should always surface with the consonant, regardless of whether it occurs first or second. If məŋ- prefixation happens first, then the non-prefixed component should always surface with the nasal, regardless of whether it occurs first or second. Resolving this ordering paradox thus seems to require an arbitrary separation of the two prefixations into different operations with different orderings.

The interaction between verbal reduplication and məŋ- prefixation is better accounted for in a parallel system, which takes a verb, complete with the prefix and both reduplicants, and evaluates the overall well-formedness of the string of sounds. Under this approach, we pursue a simpler analysis. To ensure that the correct form of the verb is produced, regardless of where the prefix attaches, we introduce two independently motivated rules. The first of these

175

ensures that the two copies of the reduplicated verb begin with the same sound and is based on the general intuition that speakers across different languages prefer the two reduplicants to be identical. The second of these prohibits words in Malay from beginning with a nasal sound, and is based on widespread restrictions against word-initial nasals in Austronesian languages of Southeast Asia. When in conflict with each other, the second rule supersedes the first such that when the məŋ- prefix attaches to the second copy, the first copy surfaces not with the nasal, but with the consonant.

Paragraph Summaries and Central Thesis

Instructions: For each paragraph, write a one-sentence summary of its contents and also note down what its function is in the passage (e.g., example, counterargument, alternative point of view). At the bottom, write in one or two sentences what the central thesis of the passage is.

Paragraph 1:

_____

_____

_____

Paragraph 2:

_____

_____

_____

Paragraph 3:

_____

_____

_____

Paragraph 4:

_____

_____

_____

Central Thesis:

_____

_____

_____

Passage 1 Questions

Instructions: For each question, identify the question type and circle the correct answer. The answer key can be found at the end of this chapter.

Question 1: Which of the following can be reasonably inferred from the passage?

Type: _____

    A. In certain languages, nasal sounds dictate the meaning of a word.

    B. Malay is a language within the Austronesian family.

    C. Verbal reduplication is more intuitive than word-initial nasal duplication.

    D. Prefixes do not change word meaning in Malay, just tone.

Question 2: Considering the passage's definition of the parallel system, what is the most likely definition of the serial system?

Type: _____

    A. A system that analyzes a verb in its form with the prefix and a verb with both reduplicants independently.

    B. A system that analyzes a verb in its form with the prefix and a verb with both reduplicants at the same time.

    C. A system that evaluates the overall well-formedness of the string of sounds.

    D. A system that primarily analyzes instances in which a nasal sound immediately precedes a voiceless consonant.

Question 3: What does the author mean by "independently motivated" in paragraph 4?

Type: _____

    A. The author is referring to the difference between full reduplication and nasal substitution.

B. The author is referring to the independence of the overall well-formedness of the string of sounds from the motivation of the speaker.

C. The author is referring to the arbitrary separation of the two prefixations into different operations with different orderings.

D. The author is referring to the fact that the rules have separate, unshared motivations behind each of their regulations.

PRACTICE PASSAGE 2

Letters play a big role in *Sense and Sensibility*, perhaps bigger than some of the other narratives by Austen. Indeed, the letters in this novel have often been read as part of the epistolary novel convention. For example, Ian Jack's chapter "The Epistolary Element in Jane Austen," argues that if "we are in doubt about how to interpret one of her characters, it is as well to look closely at any letter that we may be given."

The argument is certainly true, though we do not only need to look at the letters that we are given – simply paying attention to what kind of letters the characters send provides us with a treasure trove of information about the characters already. For instance, Marianne's character in *Sense and Sensibility* can be better understood when we pay attention to the letters she writes while in London. When the two sisters first arrive to London in Chapter 5 of the second volume, the narrative almost immediately turns to the writing of letters in which we see a number of letter-writing etiquettes: that the eldest of the sisters is expected to take on the responsibility of informing her mother of their trip; that the number of letters sent to their mother should be limited due to the expense incurred to the recipient; and, most importantly, that Marianne's decision to write a letter to Willoughby leads to the assumption that they must be engaged.

Elinor's confidence in the fact that Marianne must be following the strict guidelines of the male-female letter communication highlights not only the convention of the time, but also the breach of propriety that Marianne is willing to undergo to communicate with Willoughby. Unlike Jane Bennet from *Pride and Prejudice*, who does not permit herself to open a line of communication between herself and Mr. Bingley, and who is as a result left at the mercy of Miss Bingley, Marianne risks her reputation by starting the correspondence. Moreover, the transgressive actions are observed openly by the people around Marianne, as Mary A. Favret observes: "In all, Marianne's letters to Willoughby are reported as seen four times in the novel; her loss of privacy grows proportionally."

Once the inappropriateness of the letters is revealed, the "imprudent" letters serve as a metaphor for Marianne's loss of virtue overall. The letters provide Austen with a safer subject to discuss a more scandalous topic that she could not have otherwise breached openly in the novel. Moreover, the decisive moment of Marianne's loss of reputation is what seals her fate with regards to her matrimonial expectations.

Paragraph Summaries and Central Thesis

Instructions: For each paragraph, write a one-sentence summary of its contents and also note down what its function is in the passage (e.g., example, counterargument, alternative point of view). At the bottom, write in one or two sentences what the central thesis of the passage is.

Paragraph 1:

_____

_____

_____

Paragraph 2:

_____

_____

_____

Paragraph 3:

_____

_____

_____

Paragraph 4:

_____

_____

_____

Central Thesis:

_____

_____

_____

Passage 2 Questions

Instructions: For each question, identify the question type and circle the correct answer. The answer key can be found at the end of this chapter.

Question 1: The author uses the word "epistolary" in paragraph 1 to best mean:

Type: _____

    E. Related to letters or letter writing

    F. Related to history or past social developments

    G. Related to character development

    H. Related to literary interpretation in the academic sense

Question 2: According to the information in the passage, Austen would be most likely to agree with which of the following statements:

Type: _____

    A. Social norms create real behavioral restrictions that can only be confronted through covert means.

    B. Social norms are socially constructed and therefore must be addressed through examination of social relationships.

    C. Social norms are oppressive and must be questioned and ultimately abolished.

    D. All of the above

Question 3: Which of the following passage assertions is NOT presented as evidence of the author's point?

Type: _____

    A. Marianne's indiscreet letters represent her loss of virtue.

    B. When the narrative takes the two sisters to London, much of the action revolves around the letter-writing norms of the time.

    C. Elinor being convinced that Marianne is abiding by the gendered letter-writing norms of the time emphasizes the rigid rules of such communication as well as Marianne's courage to act outside social expectations of her role to speak with Willoughby.

D. None of the above.

PRACTICE PASSAGE 3

Molecular motors utilize the cytoskeleton, a protein network of tubules in the interior of cells, as tracks for the directed transport of cargos. These molecular motors, or motor proteins, are natural machines that use energy to move along the cytoskeleton. Microtubules are inherently polar structures, which allows directional movement of along these cellular tracks. Specialized motor proteins have been shown to localize to a subset of microtubules that target adhesion complexes and facilitate their turnover and formation. These motor proteins have been implicated in the regulation of macrophage adhesions and their ability to degrade extracellular matrix (ECM) for migration to locations of infection within the body.

Macrophages are a type of phagocytic cell, which function to engulf other cells or particles within the body. A typical function of macrophages is the engulfment of infectious agents as one of the immune system's major lines of defense against disease. While macrophages naturally degrade the scaffolding ECM beneath them for immune response, overactivity or mis-regulation of this type of migratory cell can lead to detrimental effects on the body.

In order for cells to migrate, adhesion complexes must be disassembled and reassembled at new locations within the cell. Movement of components of adhesion complexes within cells to accomplish this is dependent upon molecular motors. In overactive migratory cells, which can result in pathologic states, small molecule inhibitors designed to specifically target molecular motors may help to disable the migratory function of invasive cells.

Paragraph Summaries and Central Thesis

Instructions: For each paragraph, write a one-sentence summary of its contents and also note down what its function is in the passage (e.g., example, counterargument, alternative point of view). At the bottom, write in one or two sentences what the central thesis of the passage is.

Paragraph 1:

_____

_____

_____

Paragraph 2:

_____

_____

_____

Paragraph 3:

_____

_____

_____

Central Thesis:

_____

_____

_____

Passage 3 Questions

Instructions: For each question, identify the question type and circle the correct answer. The answer key can be found at the end of this chapter.

Question 1: If it were discovered that molecular motors are downregulated in migratory cells such that fewer motor proteins are present, how would this affect the conclusion made by the author?

Type: _____

    A. This discovery would weaken the rational for the author's conclusion.

    B. This discovery would completely discredit the author's conclusion.

    C. This discovery would support the author's conclusion.

    D. This discovery would have no impact on the author's conclusion.

Question 2: Which of the following passage assertions is used to support the author's main point?

Type: _____

    A. Macrophage mis-regulation leads to detrimental effects and pathologic states in the body.

    B. Microtubules are inherently polar structures.

    C. Macrophages characteristically engulf agents as a principal defense against disease.

    D. Motor proteins have been connected to the regulation of macrophage adhesions.

Question 3: Which of the following best captures the main goal of the passage?

Type: _____

    A. To educate the reader on the body's main immune defenses.

    B. To propose a novel approach to restricting disease-state macrophages.

C. To inform the reader on the role of small molecule inhibitors in regulation of overactive molecular motors.

D. To enumerate the many functions of motor proteins.

PRACTICE PASSAGE 4

Austen's letters have been instrumental in providing details about the life of the middle class, to which Austen belonged, Austen's own life experiences, and contextual analysis of her novels. And yet, critics' displeasure with the letters persists, partially due to the way they differ from other literary correspondences in print, such as the letters of William Wordsworth and John Keats, and remain focused on the minutiae of daily life instead of literary considerations.

What this bias against the letters fails to comprehend, however, is the difference between Austen and these other literary figures. Jane Austen was a professional writer, one who published anonymously, and who was very interested in the monetary result of her work. Her letters include many references to the amounts that Austen earned from the copyright and sale of her novels, and there is even a letter that humorously complains about people's tendency to borrow rather than purchase the books. Moreover, Austen stood out from most of the literary figures from and before her time due to the fact that she was not engaged in a literary social milieu, and was surrounded by the reading public instead. Unlike earlier authors such as Samuel Johnson, Lady Mary Wortley Montagu, Mrs. Hester Piozzi (all of whom had literary correspondences published during or after their lifetimes), Austen was not a part of the British literary elite, nor did she seek to join it.

In fact, we see her own awareness of this fact in one of her letters to Cassandra in which she refers to Hester Piozzi (a woman who was a part of the London literary milieu due to her association with Samuel Johnson, and whose primary contribution to literature was merely her correspondence and biography of Johnson) and demonstrates Austen's familiarity with her letters. Austen's decision to experiment with Piozzi's style points to a self-awareness on Austen's part regarding her own status as an author and a so-called "woman of letters." Her consideration of one female writer brings her to consider her own writing and position as an author (or at least, the ways in which her friend could, humorously, warp her authorship status). And yet, just as Austen decides that she "shall not" write her letters in Piozzi's style, she also decides to remain anonymous and excluded from the literary milieu of her time. In this way, we see Austen emerge as a new type of writer in English literature, one who shunned the all-encompassing identity of an author, and who instead maintained a personal life outside of the profession. Indeed, the non-literary quality of Austen's letters points to the very emergence of writing as a profession.

Paragraph Summaries and Central Thesis

Instructions: For each paragraph, write a one-sentence summary of its contents and also note down what its function is in the passage (e.g., example, counterargument, alternative point of view). At the bottom, write in one or two sentences what the central thesis of the passage is.

Paragraph 1:

_____

_____

_____

Paragraph 2:

_____

_____

_____

Paragraph 3:

_____

_____

_____

Central Thesis:

_____

_____

_____

Passage 4 Questions

Instructions: For each question, identify the question type and circle the correct answer. The answer key can be found at the end of this chapter.

Question 1: If it were known that Austen did not write her letters anonymously, how might the author's argument change?

Type: _____

    A. The author would not be able to explain Austen's inclusion of minute details of her daily life in her letters.

    B. The author would have to conclude that Austen did not write her letters anonymously in order to sell more of her books.

    C. The author would not be able to definitively conclude that Austen did not desire to be a member of the British literary elite.

    D. The author could assume that Austen was imitating the style of Hester Piozzi, who also did not write her letters anonymously.

Question 2: What is an assumption that the author makes in the passage?

Type: _____

    A. The author assumes that Austen shunned the all-encompassing identity of an author when in fact she was concerned with the monetary result of her work, so she her identity as an author was actually all-encompassing.

    B. The author assumes that Austen was familiar with Hester Piozzi's work simply because she referenced Piozzi in a letter.

    C. The author assumes that Austen was concerned with the monetary result of her work because she published anonymously so that readers would not be put off by the fact that she was a female author.

    D. The author assumes that Austen's anonymity reflects her lack of desire to be part of the British literary circles simply because women included at the time did not write anonymously.

Question 3: What does the inclusion of minute details in Austen's letters indicate?

Type: _____

A. Austen wanted to be considered a member of the literary elite, like other male authors of her time.

B. Austen's consideration of her writing as a profession.

C. Austen's fictional characters, who also write such letters, are a reflection of herself.

D. Austen was unconcerned with critics' perceptions of her writing.

PRACTICE PASSAGE 5

Williams-Beuren Syndrome (WBS), is a disorder caused by a hemizygous deletion of genes located on chromosome 7q11.23. Although the deletion ranges in size from 1.55Mb to 1.85Mb, the elastin gene, ELN, is lost in all affected individuals. A wide variety of clinical manifestations have been seen among WBS patients including cardiovascular defects, cognitive impairment, metabolic changes, and distinctive facial features. The condition is usually diagnosed clinically at birth then confirmed with genetic testing.

Being a chromosomal genetic disorder there is currently no cure for Williams-Beuren syndrome. Management is therefore aimed at improving the patient's quality of life and lessening their symptoms. Annual physical exams with blood pressure measurements, cognitive assessments, and visual and hearing testing is recommended. Many patients find both physical and speech therapy effective in improving their fine motor coordination and social interactions. Additionally, early screening for hypertension should be performed and treated with calcium channel blockers and/or beta-blockers. In cases of uncontrolled hypertension, arteriography is the gold standard to identify renovascular stenosis. Life expectancy is less for individuals with Williams syndrome than the general population, mainly due to the increased rates of cardiovascular disease.

In the case of a 22-year-old female with previously diagnosed WBS, both common and uncommon sequelae were noted. Her common manifestations included supravalvular aortic stenosis, renal artery stenosis hypertension, congenital hypothyroid, dental and eye abnormalities, impaired cognitive development, failure to thrive and overly friendly character. Around 30% of children with WBS have subclinical hypothyroidism. This patient also suffered from concomitant CVID, Mitochondrial Oxidative Phosphorylation Disorder, Demonier Syndrome, Asthma, Crohn's Disease, Seizure Disorder and Panhypopituitarism. The case of Panhypopituitarism in a patient with WBS is uncommon, with no current cases available in the literature.

Due to insurance complications and the extreme complexity of her case, access to subspecialist providers was very limited. Therefore, the majority of her care was managed by her primary care physician including continuing current treatment, follow up after multiple hospitalizations, medication management, and social work involvement when needed. As the only option for management involves lessening symptoms, we must ensure that insurance obstacles are not the reason patients cannot achieve a reasonable quality of life.

Paragraph Summaries and Central Thesis

Instructions: For each paragraph, write a one-sentence summary of its contents and also note down what its function is in the passage (e.g., example, counterargument, alternative point of view). At the bottom, write in one or two sentences what the central thesis of the passage is.

Paragraph 1:

_____

_____

_____

Paragraph 2:

_____

_____

_____

Paragraph 3:

_____

_____

_____

Paragraph 4:

_____

_____

_____

Central Thesis:

_____

_____

_____

Passage 5 Questions

Instructions: For each question, identify the question type and circle the correct answer. The answer key can be found at the end of this chapter.

Question 1: Which of the following is likely to be the author's view on common and uncommon sequelae?

Type: _____

A. The author views sequelae as complications from a genetic disorder that will likely never see a cure; thus, better treatment options must be secured.

B. The author views sequelae as a cause of suffering in WBS patients and therefore is an issue that must be addressed.

C. The author views sequelae as manifestations of an inadequate medical insurance system which cannot easily be addressed.

D. The author views sequelae as the root cause of uncommon Panhypopituitarism in severe cases of WBS which warrants further literature investigation.

Question 2: Which new example is most consistent with the author's definition of a chromosomal disorder?

Type: _____

A. An eighty-year-old man acquires a deletion of a large segment of genetic material that results in a health condition that is uncurable.

B. An individual has inherited a congenital, altered genetic code which manifests in symptoms that are difficult to treat.

C. A two-month-old infant is born with a transformed chromosome which genetic testing gradually restores over time to address the varied manifestations of the resulting condition.

D. A malformed chromosome at birth causes an individual to experience wide-ranging, complex symptoms once an adult.

197

Question 3: Why does the author introduce the seemingly disparate topic of insurance?

Type: _____

A. The author includes this topic to juxtapose social issues with medical issues faced by WBS patients.

B. The author includes this topic as another example of the vast diversity of clinical manifestations faced by WBS patients.

C. The author includes this topic to illustrate an extreme yet uncommon impediment for WBS patients.

D. The author includes this topic to highlight another varied factor that affects the quality of life for WBS patients.

PRACTICE PASSAGE 6

When Edward Norton's character in *Fight Club* creates Tyler Durden, he finds a way to do what every person wishes and dreams to do: say what he wants to say and be heard by those around him. By acting as such, Norton's character arguably follows an example set by Miguel de Cervantes centuries earlier.

Cervantes uses his ability to weave commentary and story together into incredible yet readable novellas; these novellas essentially provide a medium through which Cervantes expresses his critique on society. E. C. Riley claims that "Cervantes never wrote down his ideas in anything resembling a treatise, but directly and indirectly he made a great many critical and theoretical comments in the course of his writings" (v). Such a claim is easily demonstrated by the apparent influence of Cervantes and his experiences on the main character in his short story "The Glass Graduate." The novella's main character, Tomás, mirrors his creator in hardships and in lifestyle so much that one forms connections between the character's piercing criticisms and Cervantes' ideas regarding Spanish society. Although proper literary analysis generally warns against a direct association between any character in a piece and the author, in the case of "The Glass Graduate," Cervantes undoubtedly uses Tomás as his own Tyler Durden through whom he can freely criticize society.

Cervantes projects himself through Tomás by subjecting Tomás to the same adversity as himself. The author led an unpleasantly lonely life, an experience which caused him to put Tomás into an isolated situation that ultimately has detrimental effects on Tomás' life. Cervantes' disapproving, almost depressing, perspective on isolation comes from having been imprisoned multiple times and from having a lonesome profession as a tax collector. Furthermore, his life as a tax collector deprived Cervantes of close friends and a social lifestyle. These events, which left Cervantes bitter towards the limitations and loneliness of solitude, appear in "The Glass Graduate" with isolation being the root cause of Tomás' inability to become a scholar. In the short story, Tomás naively induces his own seclusion, hoping that such solitude will ultimately aid him in achieving excellence in academia. Although well intentioned, this state of isolation ruins

Tomás and his aspirations by estranging the very audience that Tomás needs in order to be a successful scholar. Throughout the entire story, Tomás distances himself from others by keeping his parentage secret and by preventing the formation of any bonds between him and those around him. Such extreme psychological isolation initially and physical detachment as the glass graduate demonstrate Tomás' perpetual efforts to remove the presuppositions that would be associated with his background.

Given the confines of Spanish society during the 16th and 17th centuries and its heavy emphasis on lineage and honor, one recognizes Tomás' actions as a defense mechanism against the limitations that society would assign to him due to his heritage and place of birth. Nevertheless, despite all his efforts, Tomás fails miserably. Cervantes ends the short story with Tomás "leaving behind him the reputation of having been a prudent and very valiant soldier" (130) rather than as a scholar. Tomás' failure, having resulted from a lifetime of isolation, therefore effectively casts a pall on the entire concept of reclusion. Cervantes' poor encounters with solitude cause him to make isolation the downfall of his main character who endures the negative effects of isolation.

Paragraph Summaries and Central Thesis

Instructions: For each paragraph, write a one-sentence summary of its contents and also note down what its function is in the passage (e.g., example, counterargument, alternative point of view). At the bottom, write in one or two sentences what the central thesis of the passage is.

Paragraph 1:

_____

_____

_____

Paragraph 2:

_____

_____

_____

Paragraph 3:

_____

_____

_____

Paragraph 4:

_____

_____

_____

Central Thesis:

_____

_____

_____

Passage 6 Questions

Instructions: For each question, identify the question type and circle the correct answer. The answer key can be found at the end of this chapter.

Question 1: Which of the following best represents a weak point in the author's argument?

Type: _____

- A. The author acknowledges the prudence of the advice to avoid direct association between any character in a piece and the author, only to engage in that practice directly after.

- B. The author bases their argument about a centuries-old piece of literature on the character in a contemporary, mainstream film.

- C. The author uses a quote from E. C. Riley without first establishing who Riley is, what their viewpoint is, and if they are a reliable source.

- D. The author chooses to analyze the lesser-known "The Glass Graduate" instead of Cervantes' masterpiece *Don Quixote*.

Question 2: If the passage did not include the example of *Fight Club*'s Tyler to compare with Cervantes' Tomás, how would the author's argument change?

Type: _____

- A. The author's argument would be more logically sound.

- B. The strength of the author's argument would stay the same.

- C. The author's argument would have less of a universal application.

- D. The author's argument would be less logically sound.

Question 3: Which of the following best describes the function of the author's mention of the movie *Fight Club*?

Type: _____

- A. The author introduces the passage with a reference to *Fight Club* to inform the reader that the movie is actually based on an obscure short story by Cervantes before describing the short story in question.

B. The author introduces the passage with a reference to *Fight Club* to generate interest in the drier literary critique that constitutes the rest of the passage.

C. The author introduces the passage with a reference to *Fight Club* to familiarize the reader with a way in which an individual can use a character to explore their true feelings without repercussion.

D. The author introduces the passage with a reference to *Fight Club* to reveal Cervantes' true desire to combat, or fight, the social structures that led to his isolation through clever word play.

PRACTICE PASSAGE 7

At the end of his Third Meditation, leading into the Fourth, Descartes is left with a seemingly insurmountable contradiction: if God is perfect, then why would that which comes from him (e.g., Descartes himself) not also be perfect?

Descartes begins his Fourth Meditation with just two certainties: he is a thinking thing which exists, and the cause for that is the existence of a more perfect being, God. These two certainties leave Descartes with the conundrum of how error and falsehood could arise if all that is derived from a perfect being. Using himself as an example, Descartes states at the beginning of his Fourth Meditation: "if everything that is in me comes from God, and he did not endow me with a faculty for making mistakes, it appears that I can never go wrong". This inconsistency threatens Descartes' original two certainties, therefore driving Descartes to contemplate the source of error itself before he can move on to other meditations.

He presents his first argument in the Fourth Meditation that error is the mark of non-being rather than actual imperfection. This he describes as "the negative idea of nothingness" which is supposedly the direct opposite of perfection. This train of thought ultimately culminates in Descartes stating that "God is immense, incomprehensible and infinite". Descartes asserts that from this, it follows that as a mere mortal, Descartes himself wouldn't be able to understand his own imperfections. His own lack of full "being" and perfection therefore inherently prevents him from understanding the contradictory error which he is trying so hard to explain.

The fundamentals of this line of reasoning draw from the classic ideology that there is a great chain of being – a hierarchy for the universe based on levels of perfection. Given Descartes' deference to this attitude about items in the world, it makes sense that he would claim humans, which are ranked lower in the great chain of being, to be incapable of comprehending that which comes from a higher level. By claiming that humans are simply lower in the great chain of being and therefore cannot comprehend all the workings of God, Descartes effectively avoids having to delve too deeply into the actual qualities of God's perfectness or man's imperfection.

Paragraph Summaries and Central Thesis

Instructions: For each paragraph, write a one-sentence summary of its contents and also note down what its function is in the passage (e.g., example, counterargument, alternative point of view). At the bottom, write in one or two sentences what the central thesis of the passage is.

Paragraph 1:

_____

_____

_____

Paragraph 2:

_____

_____

_____

Paragraph 3:

_____

_____

_____

Paragraph 4:

_____

_____

_____

Central Thesis:

_____

_____

_____

Passage 7 Questions

Instructions: For each question, identify the question type and circle the correct answer. The answer key can be found at the end of this chapter.

Question 1: If it were known that God was imperfect, how would this affect Descartes' argument (as the author presents it)?

Type: _____

- A. Descartes would have to explain why God was capable of errors.

- B. Descartes would then actually be equivalent to God, making him certain not only that he exists, but that there is no hierarchy among beings.

- C. Descartes would not need to explain why he himself is capable of error.

- D. Descartes would be unable to prove his own existence.

Question 2: According to the author's portrayal of his argument, why does Descartes employ the ideology of a universal hierarchy based on levels of perfection?

Type: _____

- A. This ideology allows Descartes to show that if God is incomprehensible, man is also just as incomprehensible.

- B. This ideology allows Descartes to establish that men, though flawed, are nearly perfect because they come from a perfect being: God.

- C. This ideology allows him to deduce that God is a perfect being by virtue of being superior to the imperfect man in this hierarchy.

- D. This ideology allows him to establish man as inferior to the omnipotent, omniscient God, and therefore incapable of identifying why he is imperfect yet comes from a perfect God.

Question 3: Based on the author's word choice in paragraph 3, what is most likely their attitude towards Descartes' reasoning?

Type: _____

A. Although the author follows the general logical progression of Descartes' argument, they might be slightly skeptical about error being the mark of non-being.

B. The author is indifferent about Descartes' reasoning and how it functions in the progression of Descartes' argument.

C. Although the author clearly identifies a lack of sound reasoning in the progression, they are inclined to believe it due to its intuitive nature.

D. The author admires the clever way with which Descartes uses logic to explain that his error is actually the result of non-being.

PRACTICE PASSAGE 8

Dyslexia is a language-based learning disability that typically manifests as a difficulty with reading, but can impact other skills as well such as spelling, writing, and speech. Dyslexia impacts people of all ages, but is referred to as a learning disability because it is often discovered as a child experiences difficulty in school. While dyslexia is not related to academic ability, traditional teaching methods are often unsuccessful. Referred to as a hidden learning disability, dyslexia cannot be seen and often goes undiagnosed despite one in five children being affected.

Described as a gap between a student's ability and achievement, modified teaching and remediation can allow dyslexic students to achieve the same academic achievement as their peers. While the exact cause has not yet been elucidated, this learning disability is attributed to a decoding issue in the brain that materializes in a cluster of symptoms. Those with dyslexia struggle with identifying speech sounds and learning how they relate to letters and words. Parents or teachers of children with dyslexia will notice reading below the expected level for a child's age and avoidance of activities that involve reading. Other common manifestations include difficulty finding the appropriate words and an inability to determine pronunciation of words. Training teachers to screen for such symptoms is essential to early intervention and to combating the social and emotional impacts of dyslexia.

As students struggle to read and keep up with their peers, they experience complex emotions associated with learning and school. Many students feel inferior and do not understand why they struggle academically. In particular, children with undiagnosed dyslexia have been shown to suffer from poor self-esteem. Much of the work that is done to get them back on the road to success centers around rediscovery of their academic potential and belief in themselves.

An additional struggle for dyslexic students arises when academics broach increasingly complex topics. To cope with unfamiliar vocabulary, many students with learning differences will memorize vocabulary and can perform well with certain tasks, but cannot apply vocabulary meanings within the context of assessments. As more studies are published, it has become increasingly evident that images connect to the language center of the brain. Students with reading disabilities often have weak concept imagery. Multisensory instruction, alongside emotional support, has proven to be a useful tool in building academic success for those with dyslexia.

Paragraph Summaries and Central Thesis

Instructions: For each paragraph, write a one-sentence summary of its contents and also note down what its function is in the passage (e.g., example, counterargument, alternative point of view). At the bottom, write in one or two sentences what the central thesis of the passage is.

Paragraph 1:

_____

_____

_____

Paragraph 2:

_____

_____

_____

Paragraph 3:

_____

_____

_____

Paragraph 4:

_____

_____

_____

Central Thesis:

_____

_____

_____

Passage 8 Questions

Instructions: For each question, identify the question type and circle the correct answer. The answer key can be found at the end of this chapter.

Question 1: The author states that dyslexia affects people of all ages, but the passage is focused on children. Why did the author make this decision?

Type: _____

    A. To make a case for the use of modified teaching methods to help dyslexic students find self-confidence and academic success.

    B. To convince the reader that Dyslexia is more prevalent in children than in adults.

    C. To argue for a shift towards academic support for children with dyslexia, rather than emotional support once they reach adulthood.

    D. To examine the efficacy of individualized instruction in bridging the gap between ability and achievement for children with dyslexia.

Question 2: If recent findings indicate that one in ten students suffer from Dyslexia, how would this affect the author's main argument?

Type: _____

    A. This would strengthen the author's main argument.

    B. This would discredit the author's main argument.

    C. This would neither strengthen nor discredit the author's main argument.

    D. This would weaken the author's main argument, but not discredit it entirely.

Question 3: Which of the following passage assertions is not evidence for the author's central thesis?

Type: _____

A. Modified teaching and remediation can allow dyslexic students to achieve the same academic achievement as their peers.

B. Training teachers to screen for dyslexia symptoms is essential to early intervention.

C. Those with dyslexia struggle with identifying speech sounds and learning how they relate to letters and words.

D. Multisensory instruction, alongside emotional support, has proven to be a useful tool in building academic success for those with dyslexia.

PRACTICE PASSAGE 9

Chinese languages have developed a variety of rich and complex tone systems, ranging from three-tone languages to nine-tone languages. Adding to the complexity of these systems is a widely attested process called tone sandhi, in which a tone can be altered, sometimes drastically, by adjacent tones in connected speech.

A classic example is Tone Three (T3) Sandhi in Standard Mandarin. Standard Mandarin has four citation tones: T1 high-level, T2 high-rising, T3 fall-rising, T4 falling. Given a context in which there are two consecutive T3 syllables with fall-rising tones, the first is realized with a high rising tone. In strings of three or more syllables, T3 Sandhi applies in the two closest syllables that form a meaningful unit and gradually expands its domain outward. In a phrase with the structure [[xx]x], where "x" represents a syllable and the brackets indicate the cohesiveness between the syllables, first two syllables undergo tone sandhi first, and the sandhi would appear to spread from left to right. In a phrase with the structure [x[xx]], the second and third syllables undergo tone sandhi first, so the sandhi would appear to spread from right to left. Thus, the direction of this sandhi process is determined by syntactic structure.

This is not the case in other types of sandhi processes. Directional tone sandhi, found in dialects like Tianjin, Boshan, and Hakka-Lai, are characterized by two traits: 1) The directionality of the sandhi remains consistent, regardless of any syntactic structure within the phrase, and 2) both left-to-right and right-to-left directions of application can be observed depending arbitrarily on the specific combination of underlying tones. Thus, for the same tone sequence with differing syntactic structures, [[xx]x] or [x[xx]], tone sandhi should apply in the same direction.

However, variability in the application of tone sandhi in the Chengdu dialect calls into question the syntactic insensitivity of 'directional' tone sandhi. Given trisyllabic sequences with the same tone, there are instances of underapplication and differences in directionality. Moreover, both underapplication and the direction of application in outlying tokens are conditioned by structure; it is more likely for sandhi to underapply when two syllables are separated by a syntactic break, and it is more likely for sandhi to apply in the opposite direction to avoid making a change that would cross a syntactic boundary. Thus, it would seem that even in sandhi processes that should be completely lexically determined, speakers are still attending to the syntactic cohesion between constituents.

Paragraph Summaries and Central Thesis

Instructions: For each paragraph, write a one-sentence summary of its contents and also note down what its function is in the passage (e.g., example, counterargument, alternative point of view). At the bottom, write in one or two sentences what the central thesis of the passage is.

Paragraph 1:

_____

_____

_____

Paragraph 2:

_____

_____

_____

Paragraph 3:

_____

_____

_____

Paragraph 4:

_____

_____

_____

Central Thesis:

_____

_____

_____

Passage 9 Questions

Instructions: For each question, identify the question type and circle the correct answer. The answer key can be found at the end of this chapter.

Question 1: Which of the following best describes the notion of "syntactic structure"?

Type: _____

    A. The underlying tones in a syllable string.

    B. The cohesion between syllables within a phrase.

    C. The directionality of tone sandhi application.

    D. The underapplication of tone sandhi across a syntactic break.

Question 2: Which of the following discoveries would weaken the author's conclusion?

Type: _____

    A. The finding that speakers Chengdu speakers are aware of the syntactic boundaries between syllables.

    B. The finding that directional sandhi is acquired faster by infants than non-directional sandhi.

    C. The finding that there are syntactically determined sandhi processes other than Mandarin T3 sandhi.

    D. The finding that the sandhi processes in Boshan and Tianjin are invariable.

Question 3: What assumption is the author making in her conclusion with regards to directional tone sandhi?

Type: _____

    A. What was discovered in the Chengdu dialect will also likely be found in other dialects with directional tone sandhi.

    B. Only one of the two traits is necessary for a language to classify as having directional tone sandhi.

C. The description of T3 sandhi in Mandarin is inaccurate because directionality should not be determined by syntactic structure.

D. It is impossible for speakers of these tone languages to ignore syntactic structure when applying tone sandhi.

PRACTICE PASSAGE 10

Vascular smooth muscle cells are a major component of the artery wall and are responsible for regulation of blood vessel diameter and blood flow. Upon phenotypic transition, vascular smooth muscle cells acquire the synthetic phenotype and gain the ability to migrate and remodel supporting extracellular matrix (ECM), present within all tissues and organs as a cellular scaffold. Cells connect to underlying ECM through dynamic protein complexes, focal adhesions. Phenotypic transition of vascular smooth muscle cells requires reorganization of the actin cytoskeleton, including actin polymerization at the leading edge of migrating cells, turnover of focal adhesions, and formation of invasive actin protrusions called podosomes.

Normal functions of this synthetic phenotype include vascular development and tissue repair after vascular injury. However, a major factor in the progression of atherosclerotic plaques in cardiovascular disease, is the infiltration of synthetic vascular smooth muscle cells into the artery wall. This infiltration requires ECM degradation and remodeling facilitated by invasive podosomes. Infiltration occurs when vascular smooth muscle cells acquire the motile synthetic phenotype, which is triggered by extracellular stimuli and depends on the Src signaling pathway. Studies have shown that microtubules, another type of cytoskeleton, regulate ECM remodeling by promoting formation of invasive actin protrusions and podosomes.

Precise regulation of podosome dynamics in vascular smooth muscle cells is important for preventing pathogenic behavior in the artery wall. Previously, microtubules have been shown to regulate podosome dynamics and ECM remodeling in macrophages and osteoclasts. In macrophages, direct contact with microtubule tips affects podosome dynamics including their assembly, positioning, and turnover. Similarly, in osteoclasts, podosome organization was found to be microtubule-dependent. In vascular smooth muscle cells, novel interactions between microtubules and podosomes have been recently documented. Specialized microtubules promote relocation of podosomes from the cell edge to the cell center, resulting in establishment of new adhesions between cells and the ECM. The mechanism of microtubule-dependent podosome regulation warrants further investigation.

Paragraph Summaries and Central Thesis

Instructions: For each paragraph, write a one-sentence summary of its contents and also note down what its function is in the passage (e.g., example, counterargument, alternative point of view). At the bottom, write in one or two sentences what the central thesis of the passage is.

Paragraph 1:

_____

_____

_____

Paragraph 2:

_____

_____

_____

Paragraph 3:

_____

_____

_____

Paragraph 4:

_____

_____

_____

Central Thesis:

_____

_____

_____

Passage 10 Questions

Instructions: For each question, identify the question type and circle the correct answer. The answer key can be found at the end of this chapter.

Question 1: What assumption is the author making about microtubules?

Type: _____

- A. Microtubules control remodeling by promoting formation of invasive podosomes.

- B. Microtubules regulate remodeling in macrophages.

- C. Microtubules govern osteoclast podosome organization.

- D. Microtubules regulate podosome dynamics in all cell types.

Question 2: Which of the following is a not a typical property of the synthetic phenotype?

Type: _____

- A. The capacity to generate dynamic podosomes and perform turnover for relocation.

- B. The ability to perform matrix remodeling within the supporting scaffold.

- C. An invasive nature resulting in modulation of artery function.

- D. The capability to be migratory within vascular tissue.

Question 3: How would the author view the following statement: Additional research into microtubule-dependent podosome regulation may lead to a better understanding of cardiovascular disease progression.

Type: _____

- A. The author would agree that additional research is needed, but not for the reason stated.

- B. The author would agree that additional research is needed and would also agree with the reasoning stated.

C. The author would not agree that additional research is needed.

D. Based on the passage, the author would not have an opinion on whether additional research is needed.

PRACTICE PASSAGE 11

The hedgehog (Hh) family of signaling proteins acts as a secreted signal in a conserved signal transduction pathway, central in the development of many organisms. Mis-regulation of or mutations in essential pathway components often result in birth defects and lead to cancer in adults. Hh ligands function as morphogens to govern tissue patterning during development by creating concentration gradients of the signaling molecule. Interpretation of this gradient by nearby cells determines the appropriate response; a complex group of cytosolic and membrane bound proteins, as well as transcriptional regulators, transduce the Hh signal within the Hh-receiving cell.

Hh signaling was first discovered and characterized in Drosophila; however, most of the core components and regulation of Hh signal transduction are conserved, and in all organisms Hh is synthesized as a precursor. Cleavage and lipid modifications occur within various cellular organelles which dictate successful export of Hh to the cell surface. Errors in cleavage and modification affect targeting of Hh in the signaling cell and its packaging into signaling particles for establishment of long-range concentration gradients outside the cell.

In mammals, Hh signaling has evolved to require an organelle called the primary cilium, a thin directional structure that projects from the cell surface. This ciliary structure was first discovered through a genetic screen to identify genes related to embryo development; all key Hh pathway components were enriched in the primary cilia. Phenotypes caused by cilia loss of function suggest that the primary cilium plays an active role in Hh signal transduction and is more than simply a location where Hh pathway components concentrate.

Mammalian Kif7 has been shown to physically interact with Hh pathway proteins, and its activity is required for transport of such components along the primary cilia in response to signaling. Recent studies indicate that upon pathway activation, Kif7 changes its subcellular localization from enrichment at the base to an accumulation at the tip for modulation of transduction. Mice deficient in Kif7 form primary cilia with expanded zones of Hh activity and display mis-regulation of pathway transcription factors. It is clear that Hh signaling plays a crucial role in mammalian development, as the Hh pathway is required for normal development of every organ system in mammals. Gaining an understanding of Kif7's role in the regulation of Hh pathway components, and its typical interaction with Hh ligand, will provide a greater understanding of the Hh signal transduction pathway in mammals and allow for medical advancements.

Paragraph Summaries and Central Thesis

Instructions: For each paragraph, write a one-sentence summary of its contents and also note down what its function is in the passage (e.g., example, counterargument, alternative point of view). At the bottom, write in one or two sentences what the central thesis of the passage is.

Paragraph 1:

_____

_____

_____

Paragraph 2:

_____

_____

_____

Paragraph 3:

_____

_____

_____

Paragraph 4:

_____

_____

_____

Central Thesis:

_____

_____

_____

Passage 11 Questions

Instructions: For each question, identify the question type and circle the correct answer. The answer key can be found at the end of this chapter.

Question 1: Which of the following is most similar to the author's central thesis?

Type: _____

  A. Genetic screens should be explored for the determination of Kif7's role in Hh-related cancers.

  B. Kif7 leads to errors in cleavage and thus affects targeting of Hh in signaling cells.

  C. The primary cilium plays an active signaling role beyond concentrating Hh pathway components.

  D. Understanding of Kif7 can help treat human diseases associated with defects in the primary cilium.

Question 2: If it is determined that Kif7 and a Hh pathway transcription factor are direct binding partners in Drosophila, how would this impact the author's central thesis

Type: _____

  A. This new finding would prove the author's central thesis as components between Drosophila and humans are entirely conserved.

  B. This new finding would provide further evidence to support the author's central thesis as Drosophila and humans share commonalities.

  C. This new finding would weaken the author's central thesis as Drosophila and humans are only distantly related.

  D. This new Drosophila finding would discredit the author's central thesis as it directly contradicts it.

Question 3: What does the author suggest as a novel role for Kif7?

Type: _____

A. Kif7 modulates transcription factor activity in the Hh pathway.

B. Kif7 determines a cell's capacity to form primary cilium.

C. Kif7 is crucial for normal organ development in all mammals.

D. Kif7 has been found to be a core component of the conserved Hh pathway.

PRACTICE PASSAGE 12

Just as a warrior uses his sword to fight for a cause, so does an author with his ability to write. While a universal tool, varying circumstances and divergent purposes lead to unique writing styles that convey personal perspectives. Personal circumstances, style and purpose give a foundation upon which to build our appreciation of two particularly "well-armed" authors: Shakespeare and Cervantes.

Shakespeare is heralded for the timelessness of his works and his immense control of the English language. Beyond his fluidity of writing, lies his talent for communicating ideas. Although some might insist that Shakespearean comedy exaggerates real life situations to criticize extreme behaviors, this would overlook his argument that these behaviors are fundamental aspects of human nature. Each play recounts fantastic stories that revolve around forbidden desires. By ending happily, they show that human desires, though crude, are natural and inevitable; acting in the name of love is not only acceptable, but fundamentally human. Thus, Shakespeare ridicules the absurdity of Puritan doctrine and the rigidity of their ways.

Cervantes does not end his novellas with truly happy conclusions. While his characters achieve pretenses of happiness, this is only after losing an element of freedom or self-respect. Cervantes utilizes conditional, two-sided endings to conceal his critiques of society. Cervantes responds to obsessions over honor and pure bloodlines through prevalence of characters complying with demeaning actions in the name of honor. Cervantes makes the distinction between having noble characteristics and being noble. As characters give up free spirit and outspokenness upon elevation in social status, Cervantes' picturesque and coincidental endings highlight the pitfalls of honor in Spanish society.

Shakespeare and Cervantes both exploit their ability to write in order to convey their ideas and criticisms about 16th century England and Spain. Their motives and intentions are elucidated by the happy, yet incongruous, endings to their respective plays and novellas. Both authors conclude their works similarly, but use these endings differently to accentuate divergent purposes. For both these endings shed light on the purpose of the proceeding plot rather than bringing it to a comfortable close.

Paragraph Summaries and Central Thesis

Instructions: For each paragraph, write a one-sentence summary of its contents and also note down what its function is in the passage (e.g., example, counterargument, alternative point of view). At the bottom, write in one or two sentences what the central thesis of the passage is.

Paragraph 1:

_____

_____

_____

Paragraph 2:

_____

_____

_____

Paragraph 3:

_____

_____

_____

Paragraph 4:

_____

_____

_____

Central Thesis:

_____

_____

_____

Passage 12 Questions

Instructions: For each question, identify the question type and circle the correct answer. The answer key can be found at the end of this chapter.

Question 1: What is a weakness in the argument that the author makes to support their conclusion?

Type: _____

A. The author focuses on the endings of the works of both authors, but the endings examined fail to provide any sense of closure to either texts and do not constitute true literary conclusions.

B. The author compares writing to a sword used to fight for a certain cause, but the subtle nature of the messages Shakespeare and Cervantes communicate is far less forceful.

C. The author claims that Shakespeare ridicules the absurdity of Puritan doctrine yet Shakespeare was one of the greatest proponents of Puritanism in the 16th century.

D. The author states that varying circumstances and divergent purposes lead to unique writing styles, yet uses authors from different countries and circumstances and with different purposes to examine the same literary strategy.

Question 2: Which approach does the author favor?

Type: _____

A. The author identifies a general literary strategy, analyzes two examples of that strategy, then discusses the utility of that strategy at the end of the passage.

B. The author compares and contrasts the ways in which two authors utilize a literary strategy in order to assess which author used the strategy better.

C. The author conducts textual analysis of two disparate works in order to highlight common themes that correspond to the chronology of the works' publications.

D. The author mimics a particular literary strategy as a means of determining how well it achieves its goal of social criticism, as in the works of Shakespeare and Cervantes.

Question 3: Someone who agreed with the author's main point would also be likely to agree with which of the following?

Type: _____

A. Many have attributed the use of the speaking pig character Napoleon in George Orwell's novel *Animal Farm* to social critique of authoritative world leaders due to Napoleon's cruel efforts to quell an animal rebellion against their unjust human farmer. However, this is a false attribution, as not every descriptive element in literature has a symbolic equivalent in society or politics.

B. Andy Warhol's use of pop culture images like the Campbell's soup can in his art are superficially playful, but Warhol uses his art form to convey his critique of the increasing social focus on consumerism in the latter half of the twentieth century.

C. Both A and B.

D. None of the above.

PRACTICE PASSAGE 13

In Canada, there are eight classes of drugs used to manage diabetes and over 30 different formulations. However, only two types of drugs are approved for use in pediatric populations: insulin and metformin. This is alarming as the rate of diabetes in children and adolescents is steadily increasing due to a rise in obesity and is reaching epidemic proportions. Drugs previously considered to be controversial should be re-evaluated.

The TODAY Study Group acknowledges the absence of data for pharmacological management of Type 2 Diabetes in children. Off-label use is common and oftentimes the dose is similar to that of an adult. It is critical to determine the safety and efficacy of dosage while understanding if there are any changes in the pharmacodynamics and pharmacokinetics of a drug in the developing body of a child.

The treatment options for Type 2 Diabetes in the adolescents and youth study compared the efficacy of three treatment options: (1) metformin alone, (2) metformin in combination with rosiglitazone or (3) metformin in combination with a lifestyle-intervention program. Participants were between the ages of 10 to 17, who had been diagnosed less than two years from the start of the study with a body mass index (BMI) at or above the 85th percentile.

It is interesting that the TODAY Study Group would choose to include a controversial drug such as rosiglitazone. The use of rosiglitazone in Canada, the United States and Europe is contraindicated in patients with symptomatic heart failure. In Canada specifically, rosiglitazone drug use is more restricted as it is not approved as a monotherapy, not recommended in combination with two or more drugs, and not to be used if any signs of heart failure are present. At the time of the study, it was believed rosiglitazone was associated with bone loss. This brings into question why the TODAY Study Group would want to expose children, who are experiencing skeletal growth, to such a risk, especially when there are many other treatment options available for Type 2 Diabetes. This is an example of a reckless study that prioritizes profit and speed of innovation over the health of those it aims to help.

Paragraph Summaries and Central Thesis

Instructions: For each paragraph, write a one-sentence summary of its contents and also note down what its function is in the passage (e.g., example, counterargument, alternative point of view). At the bottom, write in one or two sentences what the central thesis of the passage is.

Paragraph 1:

_____

_____

_____

Paragraph 2:

_____

_____

_____

Paragraph 3:

_____

_____

_____

Paragraph 4:

_____

_____

_____

Central Thesis:

_____

_____

_____

Passage 13 Questions

Instructions: For each question, identify the question type and circle the correct answer. The answer key can be found at the end of this chapter.

Question 1: The author indicates that the study discussed in the passage is "interesting." What does the author seem to imply by referring to the study in this way?

Type: _____

  A. This is a questionably designed study that poses necessary risks to find improved treatment options for children suffering from Type 2 Diabetes.

  B. The study is a fascinating new look into Type 2 Diabetes treatment options for children.

  C. This study into additional treatment options for children with Type 2 Diabetes is alarming in nature.

  D. This is a thought-provoking study that proposes innovative uses for drugs already on the market which can accelerate achievement of better care for pediatric Type 2 Diabetes.

Question 2: Which assumption does the author make and if found to be invalid how would this affect the author's argument?

Type: _____

  A. The author assumes the designers of the study did not consider the health risks associated with rosiglitazone use. If it was found that the designers were aware of these risks, this would have no impact on the author's argument.

  B. The author assumes the designers of the study disregard that the drug rosiglitazone is controversial. If this is not the case, the author's argument would be strengthened.

  C. The author assumes the designers of the study did not account for how rosiglitazone side effects differ between children and adults. If it was found that this assumption is unsound, this would weaken the author's argument.

D. The author assumes the designers of the study do not acknowledge the absence of pharmacological data for Type 2 Diabetes in children. If this assumption is unwarranted, this would discredit the author's argument.

Question 3: The author's writing includes which paradox?

Type: _____

A. The author presents contradictory statements regarding controversial drugs as treatment options for children with Type 2 Diabetes.

B. The author presents inconsistent statements about the soundness of this new Type 2 Diabetes study.

C. The author presents clashing statements regarding the impact of pediatric Type 2 Diabetes on society.

D. The author presents contradictory statements concerning the prevalence of administering adult Type 2 Diabetes drugs in children.

PRACTICE PASSAGE 14

Different languages use different sets of sounds to convey meaning. As a result, people who speak different languages also hear speech sounds differently. For example, /l/ as in "late" and /r/ as in "rate" are sounds that are used in English, but not in Japanese. One study found that Japanese speakers have trouble distinguishing between English /l/ and /r/ because they are not listening for the most crucial property that differentiates these two sounds. In another study, people who speak tone languages (e.g., Mandarin Chinese) attend more to pitch, but people who speak a voice quality language (e.g., Gujarati) attend more to breathiness, even though the sounds they heard were identical. These studies, among many, show that language experience influences speech perception.

Much less studied is the phenomenon that speech sounds themselves also have unique properties that affect how we hear them. For example, the common acoustic property between pitch and breathiness of having a strong lower harmonic makes it such that increasing breathiness allows people to more easily perceive lower pitch and vice versa. However, pitch and vowel duration, which do not share any common acoustic properties, do not show this effect. That is, longer or shorter vowel duration does not make it easier to perceive higher or lower pitch.

In order to understand the interplay of all of these factors in how speech is perceived by human listeners, it is necessary to compare the speech perception of two different pairs of sounds across groups of speakers that have differing degrees of experience with them. If we use sound pairs pitch and breathiness and pitch and vowel duration, then English speakers, who do not distinguish any sounds based on pitch, breathiness, or vowel duration, would make ideal candidates for the group with no experience with these distinctions. On the other hand, speakers of Hani, a Sino-Tibetan language spoken in Southwest China, who do distinguish speech sounds based on all three of these properties, would be ideal for the group who do have experience.

This two-by-two design would allow us to understand the baseline condition of how speakers with no experience perceive sounds that do not share any properties, how listener experience affects the perception of sounds that do not share any properties, how listeners with no experience might be influenced by sounds that share properties, and how listeners with experience are influenced by sounds with shared properties.

Paragraph Summaries and Central Thesis

Instructions: For each paragraph, write a one-sentence summary of its contents and also note down what its function is in the passage (e.g., example, counterargument, alternative point of view). At the bottom, write in one or two sentences what the central thesis of the passage is.

Paragraph 1:

_____

_____

_____

Paragraph 2:

_____

_____

_____

Paragraph 3:

_____

_____

_____

Paragraph 4:

_____

_____

_____

Central Thesis:

_____

_____

_____

Passage 14 Questions

Instructions: For each question, identify the question type and circle the correct answer. The answer key can be found at the end of this chapter.

Question 1: Which of the following examples is most consistent with the author's description of a two-by-two design?

Type: _____

A. A study in which children take a fake student driving course, pre-teens take a fake student driving course, teens take a fake student driving course, and adults take a fake student driving course for comparison purposes.

B. A study in which a straight-A student takes classes a year above their grade level, a poor student takes classes above their grade level, and an average student takes classes both above their grade level and below their grade level for comparison purposes.

C. A study in which a math teacher learns to speak French, a social studies teacher learns to speak French, a math teacher learns to speak French and Spanish, and a social studies teacher learns to speak French and Spanish for comparison purposes.

D. A study in which someone who has never played sports learns to play basketball, a baseball player learns to play basketball, a person who has never played sports learns to play soccer and basketball, and a baseball player learns to play soccer and basketball for comparison purposes.

Question 2: What is the purpose of the author's discussion of native Japanese speaker difficulties distinguishing between the words "late" and "rate"?

Type: _____

A. The author explains this example to show how listeners with experience may misinterpret sounds with shared properties.

B. The author is introducing an example of a language in which strong lower harmonic acoustic quality influences vowel duration.

C. The author is introducing a simpler example of how language experience influences speech perception in order to then explain a more complicated example of how language experience influences speech perception.

D. The author is laying the groundwork for the argument that native Asian language speakers have a much harder time learning English than native speakers of other languages.

Question 3: Which of the following is a tone language?

Type: _____

A. Hani

B. Gujarati

C. English

D. A and B

PRACTICE PASSAGE 15

Just as chemical systems naturally proceed towards equilibrium, so do people. Characters in Shakespeare's comedies follow this same trend; they exhibit extreme characteristics, then change and reach a state of balance, but first must experience a drastic transformation. Some argue that these changes instigate the very conflicts that must then be resolved by establishing a state of balance; however, transformations in major characters serve as catalysts for a state of balance, transformations which ultimately prove the necessity of change before a state of balance can be reached.

In *The Taming of the Shrew*, Shakespeare initially presents Kate as a fickle woman, but by the end of the play she is "tamed." Although one can construe Kate's behavior at the start of the play as beastly, she possesses a degree of intelligence which undoubtedly places her above the men she meets. In nearly every encounter, Kate uses her wit to keep men at bay, leading them to see her as a "devilish spirit." Although effective, this behavior is unbalanced. When Kate meets Petruchio – a man at her level and worthy of marriage – she adopts a more subdued nature, her method of balancing married life and an intellectually stimulating relationship. This equilibrium, although complex, could not have been reached without having first transformed.

In many cases, individuals need a catalyst in order to reach a balanced state. Kate needed to change her views of man; intriguingly, her driving force comes in the form of transformation. Despite desperately needing change and stability from the start, this cannot be reached until the right impetus for such a shift occurs.

Paragraph Summaries and Central Thesis

Instructions: For each paragraph, write a one-sentence summary of its contents and also note down what its function is in the passage (e.g., example, counterargument, alternative point of view). At the bottom, write in one or two sentences what the central thesis of the passage is.

Paragraph 1:

_____

_____

_____

Paragraph 2:

_____

_____

_____

Paragraph 3:

_____

_____

_____

Paragraph 4:

_____

_____

_____

Central Thesis:

_____

_____

_____

Passage 15 Questions

Instructions: For each question, identify the question type and circle the correct answer. The answer key can be found at the end of this chapter.

Question 1: Which new situation best captures what is described within the text?

Type: _____

A. John is a pastry chef who frequently indulges in the decadent desserts he makes. As a result, John is overweight, but this never bothered him until his doctor informed him that he had developed Type 2 diabetes as a result of his unhealthy diet. Concerned, John developed a plan with his doctor to get his weight and diet under control to properly deal with his diabetes. These days, John is still a pastry chef, but only occasionally tries the desserts he makes so that he can maintain a healthy weight.

B. Jane has always loved animals, but it never stopped her from eating her favorite meat dishes every now and then. One day Jane watched a documentary about where the meat in her community came from and the poor living conditions some farms provided for the livestock used as sources of meat. Deeply disturbed, Jane vowed never to eat meat again and became a vegetarian.

C. Alex worked very hard to get into his dream university, so he spends all of his free time studying to make sure he gets the most out of his education. He has made Dean's list every semester and even won awards for his academic accomplishments. Alex's roommate, who is very social, convinces Alex to go drinking with him at a bar one Friday night. Loving the escape alcohol gives him from the stress of his studies, Alex begins to drink to excess, going out most nights of the week and only studying when he can. Alex's friends tell him he has completely transformed.

D. Cameron is an avid runner and has competed in many marathons. This past year, while running her sixth marathon, Cameron fell and broke her leg. After a long recovery and many sessions of physical therapy, Cameron's doctor gave her permission to begin running again. A month of training behind her, Cameron signs up for her first post-injury race: a 5k.

Question 2: In using the character Kate as evidence for their overall argument, what assumption does the author make?

Type: _____

A. That Petruchio is worthy of marriage with Kate.

B. That Kate using her wit to keep men at bay is effective.

C. That Kate must change her views of man.

D. That Kate's more subdued married life balanced with her intellectual life constitutes equilibrium.

Question 3: For what purpose is this passage likely written?

Type: _____

A. To inform the reader that Shakespeare's character Kate needed to achieve more balance in her life to be happy.

B. To persuade the reader that Shakespeare featured real human patterns of development in the characters of his plays.

C. To entertain the reader with interesting commentary on the ways in which Shakespeare created his celebrated characters.

D. To persuade the reader that people tend to seek equilibrium in life and in literature.

PRACTICE PASSAGE 16

Structural violence is a concept that relates the way society is organized to an inherent and violent inequality, which advantages some people at the extreme expense of others. Implicitly related to power, it upholds contemporary hegemonic rhetoric while displacing, disenfranchising, and disempowering a subset of society - often those already marginalized or impoverished. Asylum-seekers worldwide have faced and still face an astounding level of structural violence and a host of offensives against human dignity. An exploration of the types of structural violence is integral to a deeper understanding of the constraints that asylum-seekers face.

Structural violence not only creates the need for one to leave their home country, but also creates instability during the journey. This violence can be broken down into four subsections: economic violence, political violence, gender violence, and symbolic violence; all of which act at various levels and temporalities and often in tandem with other forms of violence.

Economic violence refers to the relative and extreme impoverishment of some parts of the world in order to let other areas prosper. Beginning with colonization, and continuing to today's global corporate machines, huge swaths of the African continent have been appropriated and experimented with, often leaving them destitute and depraved. This often goes hand in hand with political violence, the systems of governance that place people into vulnerable conditions. In this case, the externalization of security measures that aim to keep asylum seekers out. Gender Violence is the violence that women and children face due to their subordinate positions in almost all societies. Violence in general and sexual violence in particular has become unavoidable. Symbolic Violence is the most invisible form as it is embodied in everyday interactions and is reproduced by the masses. It represents the normalization of words and actions and undermines freewill.

In addition to physical ramifications of violence, asylum-seekers also face enhanced mental health issues as they live in constant fear. Structural violence is a form of social amnesia that further relegates asylum-seekers to inhabit the symbolic world of the 'other.' This puts the rest of society at ease, as their own lives remain safe. These forms of violence are intertwined with concepts of morality and are often perpetrated in the name of humanitarianism.

Paragraph Summaries and Central Thesis

Instructions: For each paragraph, write a one-sentence summary of its contents and also note down what its function is in the passage (e.g., example, counterargument, alternative point of view). At the bottom, write in one or two sentences what the central thesis of the passage is.

Paragraph 1:

_____

_____

_____

Paragraph 2:

_____

_____

_____

Paragraph 3:

_____

_____

_____

Paragraph 4:

_____

_____

_____

Central Thesis:

_____

_____

_____

Passage 16 Questions

Instructions: For each question, identify the question type and circle the correct answer. The answer key can be found at the end of this chapter.

Question 1: Which of the following is not an example of hegemonic rhetoric that would support the author's thesis on structural violence?

Type: _____

A. Companies explaining how their globalization benefits impoverished countries by establishing cheap labor factories within their borders.

B. European explorers documenting that they helped the primitive people of the Gold Coast by taking over their territory to bring them into the modern age.

C. The assertion that the current social order is not preordained as women in positions of power should not be the exception.

D. The idea that illegal immigrants participate in their own oppression because they believe that they deserve less than native residents.

Question 2: In the first sentence of the passage, the author uses the word "extreme." What intentions does this word choice reveal?

Type: _____

A. This reveals the author's intentions to appeal to the reader's ethics and sway their opinion in support of their argument.

B. This hyperbole reveals that the author is inflating their claims and thus the arguments within the passage are less convincing.

C. This reveals the author's intentions to appeal to the reader's intellect in forming an opinion on the topic of extreme cases of marginalized individualized in society.

D. This word choice is irrelevant to the author's intentions.

Question 3: Which claim is least supported by the passage?

Type: _____

A. Structural violence affects people in varied and multifaceted ways.

B. Structural violence must be examined to incite barriers for the marginalized.

C. Structural violence is often imperceptible and its volatility undermines autonomy.

D. Structural violence acts temporally and is often disseminated under the guise of human welfare.

PRACTICE PASSAGE 17

Dry skin, medically known as xerosis, is a prevalent condition caused by reduced water retention due to an impaired lipid barrier. It presents as white patches, flakes and cracks accompanied by itchiness and irritation. Xerosis is a common condition; however, severe dry skin can lead to the onset of other conditions such as atopic dermatitis and eczema. The skin care industry offers a wide range of products to treat xerosis.

To evaluate effectiveness of moisturizers based on unique formulation, it is necessary to understand skin anatomy. The body's first line of defense, it acts as a two-way barrier preventing entry of foreign compounds while maintaining hydration by reducing transepidermal water loss. Moisturizers act on the stratum corneum, a selectively-permeable layer of corneocytes and intercellular lipid membrane which contains natural humectants that absorb small amounts of water to maintain elasticity and hydration. In healthy skin, the stratum corneum regularly undergoes desquamation. These processes function harmoniously to maintain normal barrier function and hydration.

Pathophysiologically, there are several causes of dry skin which impact the aforementioned harmonious processes in the stratum corneum. New moisturizer formulations to treat xerosis are constantly being designed and tested to keep consumer products relevant. A recent publication describes a new emulsion formulation containing key ingredients such as panthenol, designed for daily use. The market success of this product lies heavily on the study's production of effective results. Several authors on the paper are employees of the manufacturer's division of Dermatology. The authors claim a "new" panthenol-containing emollient even though the manufacturer itself developed the first topical panthenol formulation over 70 years ago. Analysis of the product composition is required to determine study validity and product claims.

Every skin care product makes a promise to its consumer, but most formulations are about 80% similar in composition. What distinguishes the moisturizer in question from other products on the market is the incorporation of unique skin conditioning agents like panthenol. Moisturizers must contain fundamental ingredients in order to carry out their proposed function. This leaves little room for innovation and brings to question what advantages one moisturizer has over another. It is often difficult to distinguish the advantages of a product from the disadvantages; almost all benefits are associated with a shortcoming. Consumer demands are constantly evolving and the quest for the ideal moisturizer is never complete.

Paragraph Summaries and Central Thesis

Instructions: For each paragraph, write a one-sentence summary of its contents and also note down what its function is in the passage (e.g., example, counterargument, alternative point of view). At the bottom, write in one or two sentences what the central thesis of the passage is.

Paragraph 1:

_____

_____

_____

Paragraph 2:

_____

_____

_____

Paragraph 3:

_____

_____

_____

Paragraph 4:

_____

_____

_____

Central Thesis:

_____

_____

_____

Passage 17 Questions

Instructions: For each question, identify the question type and circle the correct answer. The answer key can be found at the end of this chapter.

Question 1: Which of the following passage statements most closely indicates the author's main argument?

Type: _____

 A. Xerosis is a prevalent condition caused by reduced water retention due to an impaired lipid barrier.

 B. To evaluate effectiveness of moisturizers based on unique formulation, it is necessary to understand skin anatomy.

 C. Analysis of the product composition is required to determine study validity and product claims.

 D. Consumer demands are constantly evolving and the quest for the ideal moisturizer is never complete.

Question 2: Suppose novel ideas in this industry are presented once every century. What impact would this have on the definition of "new" proposed by the author?

Type: _____

 A. This would strengthen the author's definition.

 B. This would neither support nor weaken the author's definition.

 C. This would be consistent with the author's definition, but would not strengthen it.

 D. This would be in conflict with the author's definition.

Question 3: What assumption is the author making about the new panthenol-containing emollient?

Type: _____

 A. The author assumes that because several authors on the paper are manufacturer employees the study on this new emollient may be unsound.

B. The author assumes that skin anatomy is not critical in determining the efficacy of a new product.

C. The author assumes that most new products are vastly different from their predecessors and thus must be heavily examined for efficacy and safety.

D. The author assumes that advantages come with the infinite capacity for moisturizer innovations.

PRACTICE PASSAGE 18

In Robert Louis Stevenson's novella, The Strange Case of Dr. Jekyll and Mr. Hyde, Stevenson unravels the story of Dr. Jekyll and Mr. Hyde with the predominant concept of duality present throughout the entirety of the text. In separating the personalities of Dr. Jekyll and Mr. Hyde into two figures, Stevenson explores not only their duality in character, but also offers other underlying factors of separation external to these two personalities.

Stevenson prefigures the concept of doubling in reference to other famous duos. Interestingly, he predicates these doubling figures in relation to religion and mythology, by referring to the brothers Cain and Abel, for example. Inevitably, these allusions hold symbolism in terms of notions of duality, but also consciousness and the determinacy of good and evil within pairs. While both Cain and Abel are made in the image and likeness of God, the parable demonstrates that even if two brothers share the same fate, there is room for divergence and deviance away from the good.

The duality between Dr. Jekyll and Mr. Hyde parallels and ventures into these binary notions of good and evil. In this scientific creation of Mr. Hyde – invoked and provoked through chemical potions by Dr. Jekyll – the duality of good and evil is tinted with this implied deviance from religion. There are devilish implications of Jekyll's transformation, in the same regard that he is viewed as inherently sinister in nature. In the text, Dr, Jekyll reports his own findings of his dual persona:

> With every day, and from both sides of my intelligence, the moral and the intellectual, I thus drew steadily nearer to that truth, by whose partial discovery I have been doomed to such a dreadful shipwreck: that man is not truly one, but truly two (Stevenson 108).

Dr. Jekyll expresses his human moral dilemma – this alternation between good and evil; thought and action; truth and damnation. In exploring a moralistic notion of duality, the narrative becomes a story not only about the ways in which Dr. Jekyll and Mr. Hyde are oppositional, but also how their dualism exists within one person. As Dr. Jekyll inhabits Mr. Hyde, he embodies the degeneration of man as a conceptual symbolism for his degeneration and deviance away from oppositional forces of duality.

Paragraph Summaries and Central Thesis

Instructions: For each paragraph, write a one-sentence summary of its contents and also note down what its function is in the passage (e.g., example, counterargument, alternative point of view). At the bottom, write in one or two sentences what the central thesis of the passage is.

Paragraph 1:

_____

_____

_____

Paragraph 2:

_____

_____

_____

Paragraph 3:

_____

_____

_____

Paragraph 4:

_____

_____

_____

Central Thesis:

_____

_____

_____

Passage 18 Questions

Instructions: For each question, identify the question type and circle the correct answer. The answer key can be found at the end of this chapter.

Question 1: Which is not presented as an example of dualism within a person?

Type: _____

A. The duality of impulsive actions and measured thoughtfulness.

B. The duality of religion and mythology within the human nature.

C. The duality of good-natured intentions and deviant evil thoughts.

D. The duality of the human mind which includes morals and intellect.

Question 2: How would the author likely view the idea of mind-body dualism, or the idea that the mind and body are distinct and separable?

Type: _____

A. The dualistic approach to the mind and body is one that is correctly oppositional.

B. The binary notion of the mind and body is substantiated by the many underlying factors which necessitate their separation.

C. The idea of mind-body separation is flawed in that it does not consider the natural dualism that exists within a person's mind.

D. Mind-body dualism is symbolic of the degeneration of humanity.

Question 3: The author includes an excerpt from Stevenson's novella in which Dr. Jekyll states that he is "doomed to such a dreadful shipwreck." What is the author's intention in incorporating such language into the passage?

Type: _____

- A. To argue that duality is the truth of human nature, one that is unavoidable.

- B. To inform the reader that duality creates innate opposition within a person that results in deviance and immorality.

- C. To provide evidence for the claim that the many parts of one's personality doom one to a life of evil.

- D. To argue that duality within one's character is inherently sinister in nature and presents a moral dilemma.

PRACTICE PASSAGE 19

Type 1 diabetes (T1D) is a chronic autoimmune condition in which the pancreas produces little or no insulin, a hormone needed for the utilization of glucose as a cellular energy source. Many factors, including genetics, may contribute to T1D and despite active research there is no cure. Current treatments focus on managing glucose levels in the blood with insulin, as well as diet and lifestyle changes to minimize complications.

Within the islet region of the pancreas, beta cells produce, store, and release insulin directly into the bloodstream. In T1D, the immune system attacks beta cells within islet clusters of the pancreas leading to mis-regulation of blood-glucose levels. Although insulin injections can be life-saving for those with T1D, injection of insulin does not fully mimic endogenous insulin secreted by a healthy pancreas.

Pancreas and islet cell transplantations have emerged as promising treatments for T1D patients; however, a shortage of human organ donors and complications associated with transplantations limit this avenue. A promising new research initiative explores the generation of beta cells in vitro for implantation into T1D patients to restore normal functioning of the pancreas, thereby overcoming insulin deficiency. Many imperative issues must be addressed before securing a clinically feasible therapy for diabetes.

When engineering synthetic microenvironments for beta cells, PEG hydrogels are often considered advantageous due to their tunable and biocompatible properties. Close proximity between cells is correlated with their survival. Biomimetic hydrogels can be utilized for enhanced survival and function of beta cells in vitro. Functionalization of PEG hydrogels to mimic aspects of cell-cell communication is predicted to increase the survival and function of beta cells for transplantation. When quantified, survival of beta cells and functional ability in PEG hydrogels depended largely on the initial cell density at encapsulation. Upon addition of EphAc-Fc and ephrinA5-Fc to the hydrogel environment, the function and survival of encapsulated beta cells significantly increased; although addition is beneficial to survival and function, insulin secretion achieved in these synthetic hydrogels did not reach native levels. Future experiments should entail defining the minimal set of functional molecules necessary to reproduce the natural environment of beta cells in the human body.

Paragraph Summaries and Central Thesis

Instructions: For each paragraph, write a one-sentence summary of its contents and also note down what its function is in the passage (e.g., example, counterargument, alternative point of view). At the bottom, write in one or two sentences what the central thesis of the passage is.

Paragraph 1:

_____

_____

_____

Paragraph 2:

_____

_____

_____

Paragraph 3:

_____

_____

_____

Paragraph 4:

_____

_____

_____

Central Thesis:

_____

_____

_____

Passage 19 Questions

Instructions: For each question, identify the question type and circle the correct answer. The answer key can be found at the end of this chapter.

Question 1: A researcher that has similar views to the author would likely also agree with which of the following assertions?

Type: _____

A. The chronic nature of T1D warrants an increase in the speed at which we are researching better therapies.

B. Although there is no cure for T1D, current treatments do a reasonable job of managing daily symptoms to allow for a naturally healthy pancreas.

C. Insulin secretion achieved in synthetic hydrogels is near native levels and, thus, this technology is ready for human trials.

D. Pancreas transplantations represent promising, boundless new avenues for T1D patients and are therefore comparable to biomimetic hydrogels.

Question 2: The author refers to the issues surrounding clinically feasible T1D therapy as "imperative." What is the author's intent in employing this word choice?

Type: _____

A. The author aims to stress the importance of finding a cure for T1D.

B. The author hopes to reiterate that the issues related to elucidating T1D therapy are ones that warrant attention.

C. The author aims to accentuate the shortcomings of current T1D research.

D. The author's goal is to relate these imperative issues back to the theme of urgency earlier established surrounding such a chronic illness.

Question 3: What is the relationship between the ideas in the second paragraph and the last paragraph?

Type: _____

A. First the author makes a case for treatment that mimics natural insulin production, then the author outlines new findings that promise to provide such a therapy.

B. First the author recommends novel insulin treatments, then the author argues that high density hydrogels are the best approach.

C. First the author proposes islet cell transplantation, then the author contradicts this by supporting hydrogels instead.

D. First the author advises treatment that replicates natural insulin production, then the author proposes that additional research is needed to accomplish this goal.

PRACTICE PASSAGE 20

In Oscar Wilde's *The Picture of Dorian Gray*, the author's exploration of aestheticism is made evident within the degeneration of the painting of Dorian Gray. As Dorian Gray ages and obstructs himself from societal influence, his own reflection in the painting continues to wither, while his external beauty remains intact. In examining the external implications of beauty and aestheticism, Wilde places these two subjects in opposition with morality and immorality to explore the degeneration of both the mind and the body.

There is an inextricable link between beauty and immorality that Dorian faces within his confrontation with the likeness of his own degrading and degenerating image: "there were opiates for remorse, drugs that could lull the moral sense to sleep. But here was a visible symbol of the degradation of sin. Here was an ever-present sign of the ruin men brought upon their souls" (Wilde 74). Through this excerpt, Dorian expresses how willingly he succumbs to vices.

In reflection of Dorian's persona within society, expectations of his cold personality present his suffering in insufferable silence and render him detached from receiving pity and the sympathy of those around him. Even Allan Campbell, whose close friendship with Dorian ends poorly and in disdain, reminds Dorian of his alienated status within his own community. While blackmailed into helping Dorian, Allan states: "Your life? Good heavens! What a life that is! You have gone from corruption to corruption, and now you have culminated in crime." (Wilde 162). In this judgement of right and wrong, Dorian's request of Allan's aid would absolve him from persecution. However, it would fully allow for further disintegration of his morality. Wilde divulges in the complexities of sympathy and remorse, but at the cost of judgment over such elements of terror.

Ultimately, Dorian stabs the portrait and his body returns back to "normal"; he is granted his morality back but remains corrupted by the degeneration of his soul. Using the painting as a framework of understanding the internal, Dorian seeks to dismantle and undo all his misgivings and misdeeds. The terror that arises implicates gothic mysticism in the unexplainable and uncanniness of Dorian's house staff finding him lying dead on the ground. It is only through their perception that his image is revealed. This largely renders Dorian's self-centered narration unreliable and perhaps even delusional in nature.

Paragraph Summaries and Central Thesis

Instructions: For each paragraph, write a one-sentence summary of its contents and also note down what its function is in the passage (e.g., example, counterargument, alternative point of view). At the bottom, write in one or two sentences what the central thesis of the passage is.

Paragraph 1:

_____

_____

_____

Paragraph 2:

_____

_____

_____

Paragraph 3:

_____

_____

_____

Paragraph 4:

_____

_____

_____

Central Thesis:

_____

_____

_____

Passage 20 Questions

Instructions: For each question, identify the question type and circle the correct answer. The answer key can be found at the end of this chapter.

Question 1: Which of the following would the author be most likely to agree with?

Type: _____

A. Beauty is power.

B. Beauty is fleeting.

C. Beauty is as beauty does.

D. Beauty is in the eye of the beholder.

Question 2: The passage suggests that:

Type: _____

A. The portrait of Dorian Gray represents his moral status.

B. The portrait of Dorian Gray betrays his innermost thoughts and feelings.

C. The portrait of Dorian Gray is connected to Dorian Gray's mortality.

D. The portrait of Dorian Gray represents the ruin of man.

Question 3: Based on the passage, Dorian Gray dies because:

Type: _____

A. His remorse for his past overcomes him.

B. His fascination with gothic ideas manifests itself through his physical death.

C. His portrait is destroyed.

D. His immoral acts have destroyed him.

PRACTICE PASSAGE 21

Lipid accumulation is a defining characteristic of atherosclerotic lesions. A contributing component in artery wall plaque formation is the development and accumulation of macrophage foam cells. Macrophages are natural scavengers and absorb LDL through endocytosis; once inside the cell, LDL is metabolized to produce free cholesterol, which can then be released and taken up by cholesterol acceptors or stored as cholesterol ester within lipid droplets. A foam cell results when a macrophage internalizes large amounts of cholesterol through dysfunctional lipid flux. Accumulation of foam cells in the artery wall leads to occlusion of the artery and life-threatening consequences upon plaque rupture.

Net flux maintains cholesterol homeostasis in all cell types; differences between influx and efflux can result in net accumulation of cholesterol in macrophages. Previous studies have quantified efflux and have identified many pathways for release including diffusion, ABC transporters, and scavenger receptors; however, bidirectional cholesterol movement has not yet been studied because the reverse pathway is harder to quantify.

A recent study attempted to measure bidirectional flux and, in doing so, aimed to elucidate how the pre-existing cholesterol content of a cell and various blood components influence bidirectional flux. Investigators utilized macrophage cell lines prepared from mice which revealed that this cell type when enriched in cholesterol behaved differently than macrophages with normal cholesterol levels. Subsequent to cholesterol enrichment, macrophages exhibited increased expression of ABC transporters and reduced expression of a subset of scavenger receptors.

An investigation by a competitor research team revealed that incubation of cholesterol enriched cells in medium containing HDL resulted in a significant reduction of cellular cholesterol mass and a net efflux of cholesterol. Cholesterol-normal cells exposed to the same medium showed only small changes. Net increase in total cholesterol mass positively correlated with LDL concentrations and net loss negatively correlated with HDL levels. While these studies expand our understanding of the relationship between cholesterol mass, cholesterol efflux, and the macrophage environment, further experiments will be needed to determine connections to foam cell development and if these findings can be replicated in an atherosclerosis disease model.

Paragraph Summaries and Central Thesis

Instructions: For each paragraph, write a one-sentence summary of its contents and also note down what its function is in the passage (e.g., example, counterargument, alternative point of view). At the bottom, write in one or two sentences what the central thesis of the passage is.

Paragraph 1:

_____

_____

_____

Paragraph 2:

_____

_____

_____

Paragraph 3:

_____

_____

_____

Paragraph 4:

_____

_____

_____

Central Thesis:

_____

_____

_____

Passage 21 Questions

Instructions: For each question, identify the question type and circle the correct answer. The answer key can be found at the end of this chapter.

Question 1: What is meant by the "reverse pathway" in the second paragraph?

Type: _____

  A. The reverse pathway refers to bidirectional movement of cholesterol in macrophages.

  B. The reverse pathway refers to the release of macrophages from the artery wall, which helps to prevent blockages.

  C. The reverse pathway refers to influx of cholesterol in the formation of foam cells.

  D. The reverse pathway refers to discharge of cholesterol through macrophage endocytosis leading to the formation of foam cells.

Question 2: If a third research team found that normal macrophages expressed transporters and receptors at reduced levels, how would this affect the first research team's conclusions?

Type: _____

  A. This evidence would weaken their conclusion that cholesterol enriched macrophages behave differently than non-enriched cells.

  B. This evidence would be consistent with their conclusion that cholesterol enriched macrophages behave differently than non-enriched cells.

  C. This evidence would wholly contradict their conclusion that cholesterol enriched macrophages behave differently than non-enriched cells.

  D. This evidence would be surprising, but would strengthen their conclusion that cholesterol enriched macrophages behave differently than non-enriched cells.

Question 3: Why does the author present data from two competing research teams?

Type: _____

A. The author presents data from competing research teams to expose the flaws in research methodology used by the first team.

B. In presenting data from competing research teams, the author proposes that the second team has uncovered more substantial findings relating to cholesterol flux.

C. Presenting competing hypothesis highlights the need for improved collaboration in research to allow the ultimate goal of replicating these findings in disease models.

D. The author presents data from competing research teams to corroborate the fact that consistent progress has been made across the field.

PRACTICE PASSAGE 22

In Nancy Armstrong's article on "Why a Good Man is Hard to Find in Victorian Fiction", Armstrong indirectly turns the discussion of subjectivity onto the subject of female subjectivity in Jane Eyre, particularly in looking at female characters such as Bertha Mason. In Armstrong's discursive analysis on "femaleness" and "femininity", the subjectivity of female hysteria and madness arises from analysis of these characters in the novel, particularly in relation to their social disposition within the Victorian era.

Locked away for years, Bertha Mason's character is immediately characterized as "other" in a wildly insane and animalistic depiction of not only her living conditions, but also her lack of humanness. She "grovels" and walks "on all fours", as if she has succumbed to her own deterioration, void of all human contact, and shunned away from civilization. The room is accounted for as windowless, and in the foreground lies a burning fire. The allusions made to fire, in relation to Bertha Mason's characterization, tie in with the burning sensation of being driven to madness itself.

The importance of characterizing Bertha as a mad woman relays more about the social infrastructure of her disposition than about her character herself. Notably, Bertha Mason's story is mediated through Mr. Rochester's account of their marriage: "I found her nature wholly alien to mine, her tastes obnoxious to me, her cast of mind common, low, narrow, and singularly incapable of being led to anything higher, expanded to anything larger" (374). This evocation of "natural" behavior reiterates Armstrong's outlined suggestions of what constitutes a "bad subject", in that there are power dynamics at play in outlining the opposing binaries of "savage" versus "man". Mr. Rochester implies for himself superior social status, and superior intellectual and emotional credibility, not to mention power over her in confining and imprisoning her body. Thus, in projecting madness upon Bertha Mason's character as a bad subject, Mr. Rochester relinquishes any sense of madness attributed to his own character.

While Bertha's unruly and aggressive characterization provides acceptable grounds for questioning her soundness as a stable character, it is Mr. Rochester's imprisonment of her character that yields significant questioning regarding the gendered implications of subjectivity in madness and hysteria. Mr. Rochester's actions of imprisoning Bertha Mason justifiably measure equal grounds for "savage-like" behavior, but it is his superior social status that makes his decisions to imprison her socially acceptable.

Using Bertha Mason's character as a catalyst for what is arguably the climax of Jane's story, one can discuss Armstrong's psychoanalytic discussion of female subjectivity, while at the same time analyze the gendered framework of what constitutes the role of the wife in the house itself. One could also turn to depictions of spaces within the house in order to frame discussions of madness and hysteria in relation to the containment and self-management of the female subject within the Victorian household.

Paragraph Summaries and Central Thesis

Instructions: For each paragraph, write a one-sentence summary of its contents and also note down what its function is in the passage (e.g., example, counterargument, alternative point of view). At the bottom, write in one or two sentences what the central thesis of the passage is.

Paragraph 1:

_____

_____

_____

Paragraph 2:

_____

_____

_____

Paragraph 3:

_____

_____

_____

Paragraph 4:

_____

_____

_____

Paragraph 5:

_____

_____

_____

Central Thesis:

_____

_____

_____

Passage 22 Questions

Instructions: For each question, identify the question type and circle the correct answer. The answer key can be found at the end of this chapter.

Question 1: Which of the following most accurately captures the author's main point?

Type: _____

A. The animalistic nature that Jane Eyre's character Bertha Mason exhibits reveals the ways in which Victorian women's subjectivity was presented through the male characters' perspective.

B. The examination of female hysteria and madness in Jane Eyre's characters, such as Bertha Mason, reflects the social disposition of women in Victorian times.

C. The ways that femininity manifested itself in Victorian times is best encapsulated in Jane Eyre's character Bertha Mason.

D. The introduction of Nancy Armstrong's idea of female subjectivity reveals the flaws in logic that make Jane Eyre's presentation of femininity unreliable.

Question 2: Which of the following quotes is presented as evidence of the author's position?

Type: _____

A. The importance of characterizing Bertha as a mad woman relays more about the social infrastructure of her disposition, than about her character herself.

B. While Bertha's unruly and aggressive characterization provides acceptable grounds for questioning her soundness as a stable character, it is Mr. Rochester's imprisonment of her character that yields significant questioning regarding the gendered implications of subjectivity in madness and hysteria.

C. Mr. Rochester's actions of imprisoning Bertha Mason justifiably measure equal grounds for "savage-like" behavior, but it is his superior social status that makes his decisions to imprison her socially acceptable.

D. All of the above.

Question 3: Someone who agreed with the author's main point would also be likely to agree with which of the following?

Type: _____

A. The simplicity of the runaway slave character Jim Runaway in Tom Sawyer's *The Adventures of Huckleberry Finn* actually reveals the simplicity of behaving morally during that era, embodied by the lack of ownership of Jim as a slave.

B. The ultimate death of Romeo and Juliet in Shakespeare's "Romeo and Juliet" demonstrates that while love between different classes may be romantic, it is socially doomed.

C. Both A and B.

D. None of the above.

PRACTICE PASSAGE 23

Proper organization of the microtubule network is essential for many cellular processes including maintenance of Golgi organization and cell polarity. Traditionally, the centrosome is considered the major microtubule organizing center (MTOC) of the cell; however, recently, the Golgi has been described as an additional, centrosome-independent, MTOC.

The centrosome is well established as the principle MTOC from which symmetric microtubule networks are established. However, centrosome-independent organizing centers have distinct cellular functions including formation of asymmetric networks. It comes as no surprise that the Golgi MTOC establishes asymmetric microtubule networks because this organelle is intrinsically asymmetric. Because the centrosome and Golgi are often located in close proximity, it can be difficult to study microtubule nucleation at these independent sites during steady state.

New techniques are required for the study of overlapping MTOCs. A novel technique, ice recovery, has recently been published which allows investigators to evaluate nucleation potential. Normally obscured by the dense microtubule network present at steady state conditions, this technique allows clear visualization of distinct MTOCs and observation of newly nucleated microtubules at these locations. When cells are subjected to ice treatment, the entire microtubule network is disassembled; subsequent recovery allows for regrowth. With obstruction solved, individual MTOCs and microtubule sub-populations can be examined.

Ice recovery is a simple yet invaluable tool for the discovery and functional characterization of novel non-centrosomal MTOCs. Additionally, this inexpensive method does not require the use of microtubule drugs, such as nocodazole, which can have off-target effects within the cell. However, currently this method requires advanced imaging systems and tedious manual analysis of colocalization between MTOCs and newly nucleated microtubules; development of analysis software will be beneficial to researchers hoping to utilize this technique.

Paragraph Summaries and Central Thesis

Instructions: For each paragraph, write a one-sentence summary of its contents and also note down what its function is in the passage (e.g., example, counterargument, alternative point of view). At the bottom, write in one or two sentences what the central thesis of the passage is.

Paragraph 1:

_____

_____

_____

Paragraph 2:

_____

_____

_____

Paragraph 3:

_____

_____

_____

Paragraph 4:

_____

_____

_____

Central Thesis:

_____

_____

_____

Passage 23 Questions

Instructions: For each question, identify the question type and circle the correct answer. The answer key can be found at the end of this chapter.

Question 1: How does the author treat the idea of using nocodazole as an alternative to their proposed method?

Type: _____

  A. The author is open to this idea, as it is less expensive than other methods and has also proven to be irreplaceable.

  B. The author is opposed to this idea because it is only useful in analyzing centrosome-dependent microtubule organizing centers.

  C. The author supports this idea and introduces it in the conclusion paragraph as a major counterpoint to the novel method presented earlier.

  D. The author looks upon this unfavorably as it can add unknown variability to an investigator's analysis.

Question 2: If a new, high-priced analytical program was developed for the efficient examination of microtubule nucleation, how would this affect the author's claims about the practicality of ice recovery?

Type: _____

  A. It weakens the author's claims.

  B. It strengthens the author's claims.

  C. It neither strengthens nor weakens the author's claims.

  D. It strengthens some claims, but weakens others.

Question 3: According to the author, under what circumstances would this novel technique not be useful or necessary?

Type: _____

  A. This approach would not be useful to examine nucleation radiating from non-traditional points of origin at steady state.

B. This approach would not be necessary to examine points of overlapping nucleation from asymmetric organizing centers.

C. This technique would not be necessary to examine microtubules in cell regions that are sparsely packed.

D. This novel method would not be useful if investigators are aiming for a sophisticated, in-depth analysis of cellular dynamics.

PRACTICE PASSAGE 24

When Roger Federer smashes a tennis racket, or when Rafael Nadal yells at a tennis umpire and contests a score, viewers are entertained by the sport. However, Serena Williams is often penalized for expressing emotion and singled out for bad sportsmanship for similar behavior. Behind this insinuation of bad sportsmanship lies a largely invisible but pressing issue; one that is made increasingly visible by the emotions internalized and displayed by athletes within the game: the underlying implications of gendering and racialization.

In 2009 at the US Open, spectators in the audience and Williams' esteemed tennis champion colleagues were met with immediate shock as every serve she made was immediately foot-faulted by the game's line judge. Williams' expletives and enraged speech following in protest led to penalties that not only resulted in her loss of the match, but also accosted her in fines, plus a two-year probationary period by the Grand Slam committee. In a historically white space, Williams is presented as an anomaly, where judges deem her emotional outbursts and behavior as inherently competitive and contentious, thus continuously harboring judgement and scrutiny over her capabilities as a professional athlete. As such, it is not just her athleticism or sportsmanship being monitored, but her composure as well.

In the 2018 French Open, Williams was criticized for sporting an all-black "catsuit" on the court and was ultimately banned from wearing the one-piece during matches. Not only does this ban highlight the ways in which Williams is dressed and addressed on the court, this fixation on her attire accompanies critique of her femininity in comparison with the bodies of predominantly white individuals surrounding her. In the span of her career, Williams has withstood critique from others that have cited her appearance as less womanly that those she plays against. For Williams, her femininity intersects with experiences of marginality, expressed in racial tension, both on and off the court.

It is no secret that professional sports have not provided a level playing field for racialized athletes, as made evident in the ongoing surveillance of Serena Williams' body within the sports industry. We must discuss how racialization unfolds by attending to the policing of Williams' display of emotions on the court. Culturally, Williams exemplifies someone who emboldens and empowers individuals, both on and off the court. While she operates within a system that is historically a male-dominated, white space, she successfully serves back against critique surrounding her behavior and her body as she demonstrates her athletic capabilities in a way that actively challenges the overpowering structures of the industry she plays within.

Paragraph Summaries and Central Thesis

Instructions: For each paragraph, write a one-sentence summary of its contents and also note down what its function is in the passage (e.g., example, counterargument, alternative point of view). At the bottom, write in one or two sentences what the central thesis of the passage is.

Paragraph 1:

_____

_____

_____

Paragraph 2:

_____

_____

_____

Paragraph 3:

_____

_____

_____

Paragraph 4:

_____

_____

_____

Central Thesis:

_____

_____

_____

Passage 24 Questions

Instructions: For each question, identify the question type and circle the correct answer. The answer key can be found at the end of this chapter.

Question 1: The author uses an amalgamation of opinion and fact within the passage. Which of the following statements from the passage least exposes the author's feelings surrounding this topic?

Type: _____

    A. At the US Open, there was immediate shock as every serve Serena made was immediately foot-faulted.

    B. Serena's enraged protests have led to penalties so crippling that she lost matches.

    C. Professional sports have not provided a level playing field for all athletes.

    D. Serena is an example of someone who empowers individuals by using her athletic capabilities to actively challenge her industry.

Question 2: Someone who agreed with the author's main point would likely disagree with which of the following?

Type: _____

    A. Male athletes in traditionally female-dominated sports are viewed as anomalies and thus face additional societal scrutiny.

    B. A recent rise in actions disproportionately against marginalized women are a result of racial tension but do not have aspects of gendering.

    C. The effects of gendering on society are increasingly visible as more people fight for the use of non-binary language.

    D. Performing at the top of any industry, regardless of your personal identifiers, can challenge power structures for the betterment of our society.

Question 3: Which of the following best captures the main goal of the passage?

Type: _____

A. The goal of the passage is to provide the basis for discussion of the implications of gendering and racialization within historically male-dominated, white sports.

B. The goal of the passage is to make a case for the emotional displays of female athletes that some view as unprofessional.

C. The goal of this passage is to perpetuate gendering via the scrutiny that athletes face over appropriate attire for tennis matches.

D. The goal of the passage is to promote a level playing field for all racialized athletes through policing of emotions on the court.

PRACTICE PASSAGE 25

Transcription factors are DNA-binding proteins that regulate gene expression at the step of transcription by binding to a specific DNA sequence. Transcriptional regulation in eukaryotic organisms is complex, with several transcription factors acting in concert. Inhibitors bind transcription factors to regulate gene expression and are essential during mammalian development, but are largely inactive in adult differentiated tissues. Recent studies indicate inhibitors are abundant in stem cells contributing to stemness and the transition to cancer stem cells.

The idea of a cancer stem cell was first introduced in the late 1990s and has since been the focus of intense research. Cancer stem cells possess traits similar to traditional stem cells, the capacity to differentiate into any cell type; however, they are tumorigenic and generate tumors through self-renewal and differentiation. With conventional cancer therapy, despite tumor shrinkage, cancer stem cells clearly persist and cause relapse giving rise to new tumors revealing that subpopulations have the ability to drive the progression of cancer.

It is common for inhibitors to be short lived and to undergo rapid ubiquitylation and subsequent degradation. Due to an unknown mechanism, inhibitors can be long-lived in certain contexts. A recent study identified a deubiquitylating enzyme that confers stability to inhibitors in proliferating cells. Transcription was elevated in human osteosarcoma biopsies, a result confirmed in several cancer cell lines. Implantation of cells overexpressing inhibitors produced aggressive tumors in mice models. Targeting this pathway is the next step in cancer stem cell treatment, but first researchers will need to elucidate how inhibitors are up-regulated in tumors and why this only occurs in a subset of tumors.

Paragraph Summaries and Central Thesis

Instructions: For each paragraph, write a one-sentence summary of its contents and also note down what its function is in the passage (e.g., example, counterargument, alternative point of view). At the bottom, write in one or two sentences what the central thesis of the passage is.

Paragraph 1:

_____

_____

_____

Paragraph 2:

_____

_____

_____

Paragraph 3:

_____

_____

_____

Central Thesis:

_____

_____

_____

Passage 25 Questions

Instructions: For each question, identify the question type and circle the correct answer. The answer key can be found at the end of this chapter.

Question 1: What does the author suggest about conventional chemotherapy?

Type: _____

A. The author suggest that conventional therapies are efficient at reducing tumor size as well as in targeting what are now known to be cancer stem cells.

B. The author suggest that conventional therapies are useful for shrinking tumor mass, but do not tackle undifferentiated cells.

C. The author suggest that conventional therapies are unproductive in regards to diminishing tumor size, although they are effectual in targeting undifferentiated cells.

D. The author suggest that conventional therapies are efficient at shrinking tumor mass, but can improve in reducing the number of differentiating cells within a tumor.

Question 2: The author starts the passage by discussing transcription factors, but ends the passage discussing inhibitor stability. Why does the author organize the passage in this way?

Type: _____

A. The author organizes the passage in this way to begin with a general introduction of the topic before going into specific examples of flaws in this research direction.

B. The author starts by providing one argument, then provides a counterargument which reveals her own viewpoint.

C. The author organizes the passage in this way to begin with a general introduction of the topic before going into more specific examples of future research endeavors.

D. The author starts by in a more specific manner to set the tone of the passage, then takes a step back to provide more general knowledge needed to understand the claims presented.

Question 3: The Hierarchical Model proposes that tumors are hierarchically organized with distinct cancer stem cells at the apex of a tumor. How would the author view this model?

Type: _____

A. The author would agree with the Hierarchical Model.

B. The author would disagree with the Hierarchical Model.

C. The author would neither agree nor disagree with the Hierarchical Model.

D. The author would agree with some aspects of the Hierarchical Model, but not completely support it.

PRACTICE PASSAGE 26

Friedrich Schiller is often mistakenly regarded as a utopian or even abstract thinker. He has earned a reputation as a poet and playwright, but is seen as too much of a Romantic to participate in the discussions on moral philosophy and politics. Schiller's first published play, "The Robbers" disperses any misconceptions one might have about Schiller's frivolity. The complex characters of the play overrule the simplicity of the plot and expose Schiller's intricate insights into human psychology and character analysis.

Karl, the hero of the play, is a great paradox for Schiller. Considering Schiller's reservations about the Enlightenment project, or rather, what the drive for absolute freedom can lead to, it is important to consider Karl's complete lack of self-reflection when he is faced with adversity or obstacles. On the one hand, Karl seeks to be completely free, yet, when he is faced with a difficult, undesirable situation, he does not exercise the power of his reason; instead he is overwhelmed by his sensuousness. He gives into his passionate nature and thus becomes its prisoner. So, in a way, Karl's failure to look up to reason has a great relationship to his understanding of freedom.

Schiller is very clear that if one is simply dominated by passions the soul cannot hope for harmony and beauty. Karl is the perfect embodiment of Schiller's fear of the senses. Karl's contemplations of his misdeeds and regret come only after a decision by him has been made. He has such power, such will to assert his own self into the world that he never stops to think what sort of stance he is taking. His spontaneous, and not at all well-formed idea of justice not only offends what most deem to be the moral standards for any human being, but turns Karl into a revolting monster. With each crime Karl loses more of his humanity.

In the final scene of the play, Karl decides to give himself into the authorities to free himself from the robbers after he kills Amalia. In the last moments of the play Karl seeks to reconcile his own inner world with the world of the law. Finally realizing the excess of his binding will, he longs to repair the relationship he had with the outside world and succumbs to the established order.

Schiller never abandons the project of Karl's character. "On Grace and Dignity" echoes "The Robbers" and continues the discussion of ultimate freedom and beauty of character. One could argue that Schiller believed in the greatness of the soul, which Karl clearly possesses. The taming of excesses and proper orientation of the soul become Schiller's life-long project. It is no wonder then that although the audience is not upset by Karl's arrest, throughout the play we all root for his conversion back to humanity.

Paragraph Summaries and Central Thesis

Instructions: For each paragraph, write a one-sentence summary of its contents and also note down what its function is in the passage (e.g., example, counterargument, alternative point of view). At the bottom, write in one or two sentences what the central thesis of the passage is.

Paragraph 1:

_____

_____

_____

Paragraph 2:

_____

_____

_____

Paragraph 3:

_____

_____

_____

Paragraph 4:

_____

_____

_____

Paragraph 5:

_____

_____

_____

Central Thesis:

_____

_____

_____

Passage 26 Questions

Instructions: For each question, identify the question type and circle the correct answer. The answer key can be found at the end of this chapter.

Question 1: If it were known that Karl always reasoned through every decision he made prior to taking action, how would this affect the conclusion reached by the author?

Type: _____

 A. Karl could be deemed to be purely rational and without adherence to the drives of his passions.

 B. Karl could be deemed to simply have faulty reasoning as opposed to being ruled by his passions.

 C. Since the passage still examines sensuousness and Enlightenment era reasoning, the author's conclusion would not change.

 D. Karl could be deemed to have achieved true freedom by determining his own sense of what is moral and immoral.

Question 2: Which of the following best represents the author's conclusion?

Type: _____

 A. The passage analyzes the character Karl to reveal that Schiller's idea of utopia is actually moral frivolity and thus should not be something to which humans aspire.

 B. The passage shows how Schiller uses the character Karl to show that morality and reason are inextricably linked.

 C. The passage shows how Schiller uses the character Karl to explore how passion always trumps reason when humans are faced with adversity.

 D. The passage analyzes the character Karl to demonstrate the ways in which Schiller examines how romantic sensuousness can prohibit freedom.

Question 3: Which of the following statements from the passage is an opinion and not a fact?

Type: _____

    A. It is no wonder then that although the audience is not upset by Karl's arrest, throughout the play we all root for his conversion back to humanity.

    B. In the final scene of the play, Karl decides to give himself into the authorities to free himself from the robbers after he kills Amalia.

    C. He [Schiller] has earned a reputation as a poet and playwright, but is seen as too much of a Romantic to participate in the discussions on moral philosophy and politics.

    D. Karl's contemplations of his misdeeds and regret come only after a decision by him has been made.

PRACTICE PASSAGE 27

With the high prevalence of dementia and an aging population in Canada, an increasing number of families are providing home care for an elder in the family who has some degree of dementia. While the presence of kinship and the familiarity of the homecare environment has been shown to facilitate the caregiving process and delay unfavorable health outcomes such as death or institutionalization, caregiving for People with Dimentia (PWD) remains a highly stressful experience for these family caregivers. It may contribute to negative mental health, an increased risk of mortality and serious illness, and have devastating and long term effects on the physical, social, emotional and financial status of family caregivers of PWD. Additionally, caregiver burden had also been associated with an earlier institutionalization of the care recipient, resulting in a decrease in the quality of life for these individuals.

Unfortunately, while much is known about caregiving burden and its consequences on both the caregivers and care recipients, there is a paucity of information on the sex and gender differences that may be present between male and female family caregivers of persons with dementia. The limited literature on sex and gender influences on caregiving burden has found differences in wellbeing, psychosocial and overall health status between male and female caregivers. Additionally, differences were also observed in relation to subjective measures of health and wellbeing, with female caregivers reporting a greater perception of ill health and lower levels of quality of life than male caregivers.

Despite the fact that several studies have attempted to incorporate a sex and gender perspective in the field of caregiving burden, there has been no study conducted to identify and collect all the sex and gender distinctions in caregiving burden described in the literature. Given that more than half of family caregivers are female; these differences are paramount for evaluating and planning our healthcare systems to better meet the needs of this population. This also has implications for healthcare practitioners and researchers, who would be better able to accurately and appropriately develop interventions and technologies to better address the specific challenges and burden experienced by male and female family caregivers of persons with dementia.

The lack of information in this area calls for a systematic review of the literature with the main objective to describe the sex and gender distinctions in caregiving burden experienced by family caregivers of persons with dementia. Secondarily, this systematic review should identify differences in the prevalence of caregiving burden between male and female family caregivers of PWD, identify and synthesize the sex and gender differences in the forms of caregiving burden experienced by family caregivers of PWD, and identify and synthesize the sex and gender differences in the impact of caregiving burden experienced by family caregivers of PWD.

Paragraph Summaries and Central Thesis

Instructions: For each paragraph, write a one-sentence summary of its contents and also note down what its function is in the passage (e.g., example, counterargument, alternative point of view). At the bottom, write in one or two sentences what the central thesis of the passage is.

Paragraph 1:

_____

_____

_____

Paragraph 2:

_____

_____

_____

Paragraph 3:

_____

_____

_____

Paragraph 4:

_____

_____

_____

Central Thesis:

_____

_____

_____

Passage 27 Questions

Instructions: For each question, identify the question type and circle the correct answer. The answer key can be found at the end of this chapter.

Question 1: Which of the following best defines the author's use of "paucity" in paragraph 2?

Type: _____

    A. Depth or profoundness of detail.

    B. Abundance in terms of availability or accessibility.

    C. Bias or factual unreliability.

    D. Scarcity in terms of availability or accessibility.

Question 2: Which of the following is presented as evidence of the author's position?

Type: _____

    A. Family caregivers for PWD experience significant stress that may culminate in detrimental impacts to their overall mental health.

    B. There has been no study conducted to identify and collect all the sex and gender distinctions in caregiving burden described in the literature.

    C. Care recipients contributing to the caregiver burden also tend to have been institutionalized previously, leading to a lower quality of life.

    D. Due to the growing number of PWD in Canada, many PWD require home care.

Question 3: If it were known that female caregivers received higher pay than male caregivers, how would this affect the conclusion reached by the author?

Type: _____

    A. This would make the author's conclusion unnecessary because female caregivers would be adequately compensated for the difficulties they have to endure.

B. This would not affect the conclusion reached by the author because there still no consideration for gender in publications about caregiving.

C. This would not affect the conclusion reached by the author because the author argues for assessing the gender differences in experience of the caregiver burden.

D. This would make the author's conclusion more urgent because equal pay for both female and male caregivers is necessary to address the lack of caregivers for PWD.

PRACTICE PASSAGE 28

Gene therapy, the introduction of foreign DNA to targeted cells, is a powerful therapeutic tool that has the potential to effectively treat a wide range of inherited genetic conditions such as cystic fibrosis and hemophilia, as well as acquired genetic disorders including cancer and Parkinson's disease, by acting at the source of the problem – the genetic code. This approach is different from conventional drug-based mechanisms, which may treat the symptoms, but not the underlying genetic problem.

However, the introduction of foreign DNA to cells is incredibly challenging. Gene therapy requires the design of effective delivery systems to transport DNA to targeted cells. To facilitate this transfection process, vectors are designed and manipulated. Viral vectors have predominantly been used to traffic DNA because of their innate ability to invade cells and deliver foreign genes for therapeutic use. This property enables viral vectors to achieve high levels of transfection. Applications are limited due to their high toxicity and immunogenicity. Compared to viral vectors, non-viral vectors (NVV) are far less immunogenic and less toxic, thereby viewed as a safer alternative method to gene delivery.

NVV are developed by cationic lipids, polymers, or surfactants which self-assemble with DNA to form polyelectrolyte complexes called lipoplexes or polyplexes. Non-viral gene therapy is attractive because there are no constraints on the maximum size of the therapeutic gene to be delivered, and there is greater control over their molecular composition which allows for simplified production. However, in spite of their advantages, NVV are less efficient at delivering DNA because NVV must overcome numerous physiological barriers, in particular entry into the cell and endosomal escape. Critical improvements to their efficiency and stability can be made by: rationally designing components to effectively protect against degradation and promote cell internalization, and understanding the molecular mechanisms involved in the endosomal escape stage of transfection. Much work needs to be done to solidify gene therapy as a valid tool for the treatment of genetic conditions, but which avenue should we take?

Paragraph Summaries and Central Thesis

Instructions: For each paragraph, write a one-sentence summary of its contents and also note down what its function is in the passage (e.g., example, counterargument, alternative point of view). At the bottom, write in one or two sentences what the central thesis of the passage is.

Paragraph 1:

_____

_____

_____

Paragraph 2:

_____

_____

_____

Paragraph 3:

_____

_____

_____

Central Thesis:

_____

_____

_____

Passage 28 Questions

Instructions: For each question, identify the question type and circle the correct answer. The answer key can be found at the end of this chapter.

Question 1: Imagine that a scientific paper is published that elucidates the mechanism of endosomal escape, how would this affect the author's stance?

Type: _____

A. This publication would weaken the author's argument.

B. This publication would significantly strengthen the author's stance.

C. This publication weakens some of the author's claims, but strengthens their stance overall.

D. This publication neither strengthens nor weakens the author's position.

Question 2: The author ends the passage with a question. What does this reveal about the author's position?

Type: _____

A. This question shows the reader that the author believes viral vectors are the best way forward and the question is used to convince the reader to believe the same.

B. This question reveals that the author is undecided in which method of gene therapy is most auspicious as there are advantages to each technique.

C. This question exposes that the author believes non-viral gene therapy is the best way forward, but that the scientific community has yet to reach a consensus.

D. This question divulges that the author is undecided in which method of gene therapy is most promising as they both can be toxic to patients if used incorrectly.

Question 3: How does the author view the therapeutic use of viral vectors?

Type: _____

A. The author views the use of viral vectors as the soundest option for novel gene therapy that can help improve the lives of patients.

B. The author views the use of viral vectors as a necessary risk to allow for the development of improved gene therapy tools.

C. The author views the use of viral vectors as an outdated method for gene therapy, one with avoidable hazards.

D. The author views the use of viral vectors as toxic and therefore unethical to use for gene therapy in patients.

PRACTICE PASSAGE 29

When we speak, sound is generated by the vibrating vocal cords in the larynx and funneled through the ever-changing vocal tract between that source and the lips to form different speech sounds. In the source-filter theory of speech production, the source of the sound and the filter that shapes it are independent. The source controls the pitch of the voice and can be manipulated regardless of the position of the tongue and lips. We can also vary the shape of the vocal tract while maintaining the same pitch.

In the pitch range that characterizes normal speech, this decoupling is possible because the frequencies are low enough that all the different speech sounds that distinguish the meanings of words can be captured by the shape of the mouth. However, the theory sees its limit when applied to extraordinarily high pitch ranges, such as those used by a soprano when singing. In these ranges, acoustic information is so barren that even large changes in vocal tract shape are not able to produce different speech sounds. Moreover, when sopranos change their pitch, a fundamental component of singing, the shape of the vocal tract can dampen what little acoustic information is produced at the voice source.

Skilled sopranos thus use a technique called formant tracking to ensure their voices can be heard when singing in the higher pitch ranges. With each change in pitch that changes the acoustics of the source, sopranos change the shape of their mouths to match and amplify that sound. This is best exemplified at the height of the Queen of the Night aria from Mozart's The Magic Flute when the soprano must produce an "ah" vowel on different notes. A close up of her face reveals that she is in fact changing her lip position and even tongue position to match her pitch, despite her producing the same vowel.

Paragraph Summaries and Central Thesis

Instructions: For each paragraph, write a one-sentence summary of its contents and also note down what its function is in the passage (e.g., example, counterargument, alternative point of view). At the bottom, write in one or two sentences what the central thesis of the passage is.

Paragraph 1:

_____

_____

_____

Paragraph 2:

_____

_____

_____

Paragraph 3:

_____

_____

_____

Central Thesis:

_____

_____

_____

Passage 29 Questions

Instructions: For each question, identify the question type and circle the correct answer. The answer key can be found at the end of this chapter.

Question 1: What is the purpose of the author explaining the source-filter theory of speech production?

Type: _____

A. The author explains the source-filter theory of speech production to best be able to instruct how to sing the Queen of the Night aria.

B. The author explains the source-filter theory of speech production to show how the source of the sound a singer produces is filtered through the singer's airway.

C. The author explains the source-filter theory of speech production to contextualize how sound is actually manipulated at very high pitches.

D. The author explains the source-filter theory of speech production to show how soprano singers use it to change the pitch of the sounds they produce.

Question 2: Why do some skilled sopranos feel the need to use the formant tracking technique?

Type: _____

A. The formant tracking technique best produces the "ah" sound used by soprano singers.

B. The lack of acoustic information at high pitches means that simple vocal tract shape changes will not adequately alter and project the sound produced.

C. The change of the vocal tract form is necessary in order to change the pitch of the sound produced.

D. The formant tracking technique is actually a stylistic choice, not a need of soprano singers.

Question 3: Imagine that the source-filter theory of speech production had no limits. How would this affect the author's message?

Type: _____

A. There would be no need to discuss the use of formant tracking to produce or amplify a particular sound when singing.

B. There would be no need to examine the phonetics of singing apart from the phonetics of regular speech.

C. The author's message would not change.

D. A and B.

PRACTICE PASSAGE 30

The most widely accepted purpose of medicine is to heal, thus the end of a medical education is to serve as a healer. Even the word "physician" suggests the purpose of healing. Physician is a relatively modern word; the Greek word that is often translated as physician is "iatre" from the root iatros, as in psychiatry or geriatric. Iatros is more accurately translated as healer. At its root, medicine is a discipline intended to heal and medical education is the formative process shaping students into healers.

The act of healing is neither confined to the medical specialties nor is it solely the work of physicians. Theology, too, is a discipline of healing. This is certainly true for Christian theology, which has consistently affirmed the importance of health, albeit while acknowledging the complex relationship between health and other goods of human life. The Greek root for salvation, "sozo", can be translated as health, salvation, or wholeness. If salvation is taken as the primary good of Christian theology, then health, too, is a significant good. And yet, notable Christians have surrendered for greater purposes. Jesus' surrendering of bodily health in his crucifixion, and the many martyrs of Christian traditions, attest to the willingness of Christians to lay down their lives for faith and God. Over the centuries, Christian traditions have both celebrated and marginalized the human body.

The seemingly ambiguous regard that Christian traditions have had for the body and bodily health suggests a more complex understanding, one in which health extends beyond bodily integrity. The role of theology in healing incorporates medicine's concern for bodily health but includes other aspects of health as well. Healing is a bodily, spiritual, and religious process. The bodily aspects are clearly represented within Christian traditions in the many miracles of Jesus restoring bodily health yet Jesus' miracles suggest additional forms of healing. The frequent contact Jesus makes with the outcasts of society suggests a social component to healing. The invitations Jesus extends to follow him imply an aspect of purpose. In studying the stories of Jesus, Christian theologians investigate the wide spectrum of healing, which includes, but is not limited to, bodily health.

Paragraph Summaries and Central Thesis

Instructions: For each paragraph, write a one-sentence summary of its contents and also note down what its function is in the passage (e.g., example, counterargument, alternative point of view). At the bottom, write in one or two sentences what the central thesis of the passage is.

Paragraph 1:

_____

_____

_____

Paragraph 2:

_____

_____

_____

Paragraph 3:

_____

_____

_____

Central Thesis:

_____

_____

_____

Passage 30 Questions

Instructions: For each question, identify the question type and circle the correct answer. The answer key can be found at the end of this chapter.

Question 1: Which of the following strategies does the author use to show the similarities between the disciplines of medicine and theology?

Type: _____

A. The author shows that through bodily healing, physicians are capable of achieving spiritual healing from the weight that is lifted when the ill recover.

B. The author examines the ways in which medical physicians actually display characteristics that are praised within Christian traditions in order to show that medicine and theology are the same.

C. The author compares the bodily healing that physicians accomplish through various methods of modern medicine to the various forms of spiritual healing that Jesus accomplished with his followers.

D. The author uses the Greek roots of discipline-specific words to establish the purpose of each discipline and then explores logical connections between healing and the discipline-specific words' Greek roots to highlight similarities between the two disciplines.

Question 2: Which of the following is NOT presented as evidence of the author's point?

Type: _____

A. Over the centuries, Christian traditions have both celebrated and marginalized the human body.

B. Christian traditions understand health in a complex way that includes and extends beyond the physical body.

C. Christian theology involves healing and recognizes that health is highly important.

  D. Christian theologians often analyze bodily and spiritual healing in Jesus' history.

Question 3: If it were known that Jesus did not perform miracles restoring bodily health, how would this affect the conclusion reached by the author?

Type: _____

  A. The author would have to prove that spiritual healing is more important for people than physical healing.

  B. The author would have to justify that bodily health and spiritual health are equivalent in order to conclude that both medicine and Christian theology involve the same kind of healing.

  C. The author would have to justify the deaths of Christian martyrs who were willing to lay down their lives as a sort of medical healing.

  D. All of the above.

PRACTICE PASSAGE 31

Homo sapiens may be easily identified as bipedal, warm-blooded, vertebrate, pollical, sexually-reproducing social mammals, but persons are not so readily captured. As strong as our tendency is to analyze, dissect, and inspect to find some generalized truth, persons are infinitely complex and impossible to capture in a single classification. Persons cannot be generalized, because each person is uniquely storied by the many narratives, traditions, events, and communities that have formed them. That the purpose of education is to teach may seem obvious, but this fact sets the stage for the argument that to fulfill their purpose, teachers must be attentive to the uniquely storied persons in their classroom.

The irreducibility of human life makes the tasks of teaching both interesting and difficult. To teach, educators must pay close attention to the student before them. They must appreciate his or her complexity to effectively understand their learning style and perspectives. Of course, to completely understand an infinitely complex person is impossible as we cannot ever know another person's trials and tribulations completely. The task of the educator, then, is to gain enough understanding to teach what they can.

Complexity leads to disagreement and frustration when helping others. Students, in their particularities, are sometimes difficult to understand and often even more difficult to sympathize with. Our inability to know another person fully can make their behaviors inexplicable and frustrating. "Why won't this student do what I tell them to?" is a common refrain among educators. "Why won't they change their behavior?" or "why are they so difficult?" are other common expressions. Some teachers have even gone so far as to declare challenging students "hateful," as they provoke such strong feelings of disapproval.

Educators use models and guidelines to help manage the complexity of students, but eventually are forced to acknowledge the impenetrable complexity of the person sitting in front of them. It has been said that "it is easy to love people; it is much harder to love a person." People are easy to love because they are amorphous and far-away. It is easy to say, "I love humanity" or "I love all human beings." But what about the person sitting in my classroom?

Paragraph Summaries and Central Thesis

Instructions: For each paragraph, write a one-sentence summary of its contents and also note down what its function is in the passage (e.g., example, counterargument, alternative point of view). At the bottom, write in one or two sentences what the central thesis of the passage is.

Paragraph 1:

_____

_____

_____

Paragraph 2:

_____

_____

_____

Paragraph 3:

_____

_____

_____

Paragraph 4:

_____

_____

_____

Central Thesis:

_____

_____

_____

Passage 31 Questions

Instructions: For each question, identify the question type and circle the correct answer. The answer key can be found at the end of this chapter.

Question 1: Which of the following statements by the author is NOT an opinion?

Type: _____

   A. Complexity leads to disagreement and frustration when helping others.

   B. The irreducibility of human life makes the tasks of teaching both interesting and difficult.

   C. [Teachers] must appreciate [the student's] complexity to effectively understand their learning style and perspectives.

   D. Homo sapiens may be easily identified as bipedal, warm-blooded, vertebrate, pollical, sexually-reproducing social mammals...

Question 2: Someone who agreed with the author's main point would also be likely to agree with which of the following?

Type: _____

   A. Teachers must make every effort to have students reach a consensus on the instruction style they prefer.

   B. Standardized tests do not adequately measure how intelligent students are because there are many different types of intelligence that vary among individuals.

   C. Educators should not be concerned with the overall progress of their class; they should be concerned with individual students' progress.

   D. Students are often disobedient in the classroom because they are struggling to make their complex background stories fit in the mold of modern education.

Question 3: Who is the author's intended audience in this passage?

Type: _____

    A. Education administrators

    B. Teachers

    C. Students

    D. The general public

PRACTICE PASSAGE 32

What does it mean to give attention? Examining the origins of the word reveals that attention is the act of stretching to another person, place, object, or time. To stretch to something implies effort and closing a gap. To truly understand its meaning, attention must be examined in the context of human suffering. Gillian Rose provides this context in her memoir *Love's Work* where she offers a powerful description of attention and its importance in caring for others. Attention is the work of love; it is the purest expression of love.

Rose argues that to love is to enter another person's experience; that love is attention to suffering. To attend to suffering is to attend to another person's life. It is to acknowledge their existence with all its complexity and difficulty. Suffering is universally experienced by all people. To deny another's suffering is a result of one's own unresolved suffering. Denial and unexamined suffering are two of the main reasons for unhappiness. The meaning of love is inseparable from its importance. For Rose, to love someone, or to give attention to them, provides sustenance for existence. Without attention, including the experience of suffering, a person cannot live fully. Without love, we cannot live abundantly.

Rose's claim appears counterintuitive; it seems more prudent to pay attention to ourselves rather than others. When we encounter someone that is suffering, it is less difficult, less costly, and less risky to pass them by. However, according to Rose, this diminishes both our opportunity and capacity to love. Every time we turn away from suffering, we stunt our ability to attend to others. When we turn toward suffering and open ourselves to others' lives, we foster our ability to attend to and love others. Rose recognizes the difficulty of love's work. Nevertheless, she continues to attend to the suffering of others, demonstrating the meaning of attention.

Paragraph Summaries and Central Thesis

Instructions: For each paragraph, write a one-sentence summary of its contents and also note down what its function is in the passage (e.g., example, counterargument, alternative point of view). At the bottom, write in one or two sentences what the central thesis of the passage is.

Paragraph 1:

_____

_____

_____

Paragraph 2:

_____

_____

_____

Paragraph 3:

_____

_____

_____

Central Thesis:

_____

_____

_____

Passage 32 Questions

Instructions: For each question, identify the question type and circle the correct answer. The answer key can be found at the end of this chapter.

Question 1: A person who agrees with the author's main point would be most likely to:

Type: _____

A. Ignore a homeless person asking for money because homelessness is a structural problem and requires a public policy solution to adequately address the issue.

B. Ignore a homeless person asking for money because they may not actually be suffering. The complexity of factors leading to someone being homeless includes actions that were the fault of the person living on the streets.

C. Respond to a homeless person asking for money, taking the time to talk to them about what they have been through that led them to live on the streets.

D. Respond to a homeless person asking for money, giving them cash to heal their suffering .

Question 2: Which of these claims is least congruent with the claim that the author is making?

Type: _____

A. We are best able to attend to and love others when we open up to the struggles and needs of others.

B. Attention is best understood in circumstances of human suffering.

C. Love is giving consideration to the suffering another person experiences.

D. It is wiser to pay attention to one's own suffering before trying to attend to the suffering of others.

Question 3: What does Rose do when challenging us to expand our horizons and devote our whole attention to those suffering in our midst?

Type: _____

    A. Rose shows that the suffering of others is always more important than our own suffering.

    B. Rose shows that the truest definition of attention is love's work.

    C. Rose shows that suffering requires either love or attention to diminish.

    D. Rose shows that human suffering, while a normal phenomenon, prohibits us from loving others.

PRACTICE PASSAGE 33

We must constructively criticize norms and assumptions to more appropriately situate medicine within the broader context of human life. Modern medicine has a long history marked by socioeconomic circumstances, political pressures, individual decisions, and many other factors. These historical elements are worth attending to in the process of evaluating and reforming current medical practices and healthcare systems. Theology, as a study of narratives, a repository of authority, and a historical discipline, provides helpful insights in this endeavor.

One particularly well-developed line of inquiry into theology's care for the practice of medicine focuses on the significant changes medicine underwent during the 18th century Enlightenment period. Theologians from diverse traditions have pointed to the Enlightenment as a turning point in medical epistemology, particularly regarding the medical understanding of the human body and its health. The combination of an instrumental approach to nature and the moral imperative to relieve the condition of man caused the relief of suffering to become the highest social priority.

Our modern conception was influenced by several Enlightenment thinkers who promoted a view of human nature that led to a mechanistic understanding of the human body. Descartes' contribution to the mechanistic model of human nature was to deny the possibility of discovering ends or purposes for human beings. He argued that to find purpose in human life required subjectivity and such ends would be unverifiable and unreliable. The outcome produced was a view of the human body that would persist for many centuries. The body as a machine is a well-established metaphor in medicine today, despite efforts to develop a more holistic understanding.

Paragraph Summaries and Central Thesis

Instructions: For each paragraph, write a one-sentence summary of its contents and also note down what its function is in the passage (e.g., example, counterargument, alternative point of view). At the bottom, write in one or two sentences what the central thesis of the passage is.

Paragraph 1:

_____

_____

_____

Paragraph 2:

_____

_____

_____

Paragraph 3:

_____

_____

_____

Central Thesis:

_____

_____

_____

Passage 33 Questions

Instructions: For each question, identify the question type and circle the correct answer. The answer key can be found at the end of this chapter.

Question 1: The author uses the word "epistemology" in paragraph two to mean:

Type: _____

A. System of knowledge acquisition and verification.

B. Division of religious and secular interpretations.

C. Regulation or guideline of practice.

D. Hierarchical anatomical structure.

Question 2: Which of the following could be considered the best evidence that "the body as a machine" is a well-established metaphor in medicine?

Type: _____

A. There are systems in our bodies that each have dedicated tasks, like the digestive system.

B. The fact that food can be considered fuel for our bodies.

C. Although initially cruder than models used today, the use of prosthetic limbs for amputees.

D. Commonly-made statements like "getting a tune-up" to describe a yearly physical exam.

Question 3: Someone who agreed with the author's main point would also be likely to agree with which of the following?

Type: _____

A. To best understand legal principles, we must assess the use of all statutes in all levels of the judicial system.

B. To best understand education systems today, we must examine the role that Greek philosophy played in the formation of widely adopted teaching methods like the Socratic method.

C. To best understand modern warfare, we must examine the use of crude weaponry in early tribal conflicts.

D. To best understand how art reflects real life, we must first define what constitutes a piece of art and which artistic disciplines can be deemed legitimate.

PRACTICE PASSAGE 34

The intracellular communication between membrane receptors on the exterior surface of cells is mediated by a limited number of signaling pathways. The ERK1/2 linear signal transduction pathway transmits mitogenic signals prompting cell division while the p38 signaling cascade is mitogen activated and transmits stress signals. P38 is involved in many cellular responses including cell cycle regulation, development, and anoikis - a form of programmed cell death that occurs when anchorage-dependent cells detach from underlying supports.

Stress-activated p38 can induce cell death, and its inhibition facilitates mammary tumorigenesis. It is known that inactivation of this tumor suppressor leads to mammary tumors in experiments with mice. Human breast cancer patients often have mutations in genes leading to mis-regulation of p38. The timing and location of p38 signaling necessary to prevent mammary tumor formation is unknown. Hypotheses indicate that p38-dependent inhibition of ERK1/2 signaling may limit accumulation of luminal cells by activating anoikis during morphogenesis.

Early breast cancer lesions are characterized by loss of acinar organization and filling of the luminal space. The molecular mechanisms responsible for creation of the luminal space are not well defined and it is not known how oncogenes, genes with the potential to cause cancer, induce filling. Kinases activate p38 via phosphate group transfer. In stressed cells, levels of phosphorylated p38 were increased as well as proteins upstream and downstream of p38. Cells undergoing morphogenesis in the absence of p38 formed acini filled with luminal cells. Importantly, it was found that multiple cell types treated with a p38 inhibitor had decreased luminal apoptosis.

Paragraph Summaries and Central Thesis

Instructions: For each paragraph, write a one-sentence summary of its contents and also note down what its function is in the passage (e.g., example, counterargument, alternative point of view). At the bottom, write in one or two sentences what the central thesis of the passage is.

Paragraph 1:

_____

_____

_____

Paragraph 2:

_____

_____

_____

Paragraph 3:

_____

_____

_____

Central Thesis:

_____

_____

_____

Passage 34 Questions

Instructions: For each question, identify the question type and circle the correct answer. The answer key can be found at the end of this chapter.

Question 1: As a part of the conclusion, the author notes an important finding. What does this finding suggest about p38?

Type: _____

A. This suggests that p38 regulates lumen formation during mammary morphogenesis.

B. This suggest that p38 does not play a role in the formation of abnormal mammary tissue.

C. This suggests that kinases, rather than p38, regulate lumen formation during mammary tumorigenesis.

D. This suggests that periods of low stress promote p38-dependent anoikis.

Question 2: If it was found that mouse cells undergoing morphogenesis in the absence of p38 formed irregular acini, but human cells did not, how would this impact the author's stance?

Type: _____

A. This new data would strengthen the author's stance regarding p38's role in mammary tissue lumen formation.

B. This new data would weaken the author's stance regarding p38's role in mammary tissue lumen formation.

C. This new data would negate the author's stance regarding p38's role in mammary tissue lumen formation.

D. This new data would not impact the author's stance regarding p38's role in mammary tissue lumen formation.

Question 3: As the topic of mammary tumorigenesis is introduced, why does the author mention that there are a "limited number of signaling pathways"?

Type: _____

A. The author mentions limited pathways to undermine the significance of this topic.

B. The author mentions limited pathways to underscore the importance of understanding these pathways and their involvement in tumorigenesis.

C. The author mentions limited pathways support the claim that more research is needed in uncovering additional pathways.

D. The author mentions limited pathways to highlight the work that has already been done to pinpoint the cause of tumorigenesis.

PRACTICE PASSAGE 35

An unequal system results in many migrants falling through the cracks rather than getting the care they require. Scholar Miriam Ticktin, wrote about the arbitrary inequality of the Refugees Appeals Commission in France. She explained how a judge in the commission granted refugee status to some deserving asylum seekers, but not to others who were seemingly equally as deserving. Ticktin came to learn that most decisions were made on the basis of emotion. The judge prioritized women and homosexuals for asylum. Others with equally tragic narratives did not get chosen to stay in France. This legitimation narrative is less about fact and more about feeling.

The idea of "moral economy of care" exposes the dichotomy of our perceptions between the deserving legitimate "refugee" and the seemingly undeserving "economic migrant" or "illegal immigrant". As Ticktin established, the "legitimate" must have an element that yields a moral narrative. It is not always the rule of law or search for the truth that applies, but rather a person's inclination. Generally the type of migrant most accepted, sought after even, are the highly skilled; what is preferred is living intellect in the form of a human mind.

Ahmad, a young Senegalese asylum seeker who spoke at an international border and migration conference in Spain, gave the audience a parting message: "If you think we are coming to make money", he said, "this is not the case. What we are after is a life - a better life, that is all." What Ahmad faces in Europe is this "moral economy of care," analyzed from political-legal, service, and clinical dimensions, which he does not fit. He is neither fleeing civil war, nor is he highly skilled, nor does he represent what Ticktin calls the "suffering body" that grants our compassion. "Moral economy of care" has no place for people like Ahmad, who are fleeing a slow death rather than a speeding bullet.

Paragraph Summaries and Central Thesis

Instructions: For each paragraph, write a one-sentence summary of its contents and also note down what its function is in the passage (e.g., example, counterargument, alternative point of view). At the bottom, write in one or two sentences what the central thesis of the passage is.

Paragraph 1:

_____

_____

_____

Paragraph 2:

_____

_____

_____

Paragraph 3:

_____

_____

_____

Central Thesis:

_____

_____

_____

Passage 35 Questions

Instructions: For each question, identify the question type and circle the correct answer. The answer key can be found at the end of this chapter.

Question 1: What assumption is the author making about illegal immigrants?

Type: _____

   A. The author assumes that the rule of law always applies when determining refugee status.

   B. The author makes the assumption that their narrative is not equally tragic.

   C. The author assumes that their stories do not evoke the necessary feeling.

   D. The author assumes that these individuals are highly skilled.

Question 2: Which approach does the author favor?

Type: _____

   A. A non-arbitrary system formed on the basis of emotion.

   B. Dichotomy within the system to help those that are suffering most immediately.

   C. A system that analyzes the utility of individuals seeking to enter a country.

   D. An objective system for those who are deserving.

Question 3: Which of the following examples would refute the author's idea that the legitimate must have an element of moral narrative?

Type: _____

   A. Refugee status was granted to a homosexual individual seeking asylum from a life of brutal torture in their home country.

B. A sick individual suffering from late-stage cancer was allowed to stay in France to seek medical care that was superior to what he could receive in his impoverished home country.

C. Refugee status was granted to a woman seeking escape from a life of persecution for her religious beliefs.

D. Refugee status was granted to a woman that illegitimately entered the country to perform a highly skilled job in academia.

PRACTICE PASSAGE 36

The value of human life is unquantifiable and invaluable. It is astonishing that some would discredit this value by suggesting euthanasia as a valid means to end one's life. Euthanasia is the act of intentionally ending a life to relieve suffering. Many purport that euthanasia can be done in an ethical way that painlessly kills a patient suffering from an uncurable condition, an incredibly painful disease, or for those in a permanent coma. In most countries this unfathomable approach to patient care is illegal, and rightfully so.

How is it that in Switzerland intentionally helping another person to kill themselves, otherwise known as assisted suicide, is legal? This is not a criminal act under Swiss law if altruistically motivated. The only law that prohibits assisted suicide is when it is performed with selfish motives. It is questionable that this country condones assisted suicide when performed by non-physicians. In Switzerland, suicide is viewed as possibly rational, and legal assisted suicide need not involve a physician nor a terminally ill patient. Why allow non-physicians to perform this immoral act when it remains illegal for physicians to do so? What is the difference in criminality?

Opponents argue that killing patients violates a physician's professionalism and duty to do no harm. Consulting the Swiss Academy of Medical Sciences proves to be of no help in settling this matter. The Academy ambiguously states in its ethical recommendations that assisted suicide is not a part of physician activity. Even if understood to discourage physicians, legally physicians have the same discretion as any citizen as long as their motives are altruistic. Proponents prefer the term "physician-assisted death" or "physician aid in dying" as these patients want to live, but realize that they are in fact facing death. In practice, many physicians are opposed to assisted suicide and euthanasia and hospitals have barred these acts from their premises. This is a step in the right direction as we wait for the Swiss legal system to come to its senses.

Paragraph Summaries and Central Thesis

Instructions: For each paragraph, write a one-sentence summary of its contents and also note down what its function is in the passage (e.g., example, counterargument, alternative point of view). At the bottom, write in one or two sentences what the central thesis of the passage is.

Paragraph 1:

_____

_____

_____

Paragraph 2:

_____

_____

_____

Paragraph 3:

_____

_____

_____

Central Thesis:

_____

_____

_____

Passage 36 Questions

Instructions: For each question, identify the question type and circle the correct answer. The answer key can be found at the end of this chapter.

Question 1: If new evidence revealed that terminally ill patients in favor of physician-assisted death viewed their inevitable death as an undignified one, how would this impact the author's view that this practice goes against a physician's duty to do no harm?

Type: _____

   A. This new evidence would weaken the author's argument that this practice goes against a physician's responsibility to do no harm.

   B. This new evidence would bolster the author's argument that this practice is in opposition to a physician's duty to do no harm.

   C. This new evidence would completely disrepute the ethical concerns that form the basis of the author's argument against physician-assisted death.

   D. This new evidence neither strengthens nor weakens the author's position on physician-assisted death.

Question 2: Which of the following does the author not present as a comparison between euthanasia and assisted suicide?

Type: _____

   A. The author sees euthanasia as ending life to mitigate suffering and assisted suicide as a more general ending of life.

   B. The author sees euthanasia as immoral and assisted suicide as a possibly reasonable end to one's life.

   C. The author sees euthanasia as nonsensical and assisted suicide as appalling.

   D. The author sees euthanasia as a threat to integrity while assisted suicide is presented as criminal.

Question 3: What is the relationship between the ideas presented in the first paragraph and those found in the third paragraph?

Type: _____

A. The first paragraph presents the author's view of euthanasia as inscrutable, while the third paragraph identifies assisted suicide as a reasonable alternative.

B. The first paragraph presents euthanasia as incomprehensible, while the third paragraph proposes the author's argument that physician aid-in-dying is an integral part of a citizen's duty.

C. The first paragraph establishes that the author is intrigued by the varied approaches to euthanasia globally, while the third paragraph presents major flaws in criminalizing euthanasia.

D. The first paragraph establishes that the author is aghast by the prospect of euthanasia, while the third paragraph makes a call to action.

PRACTICE PASSAGE 37

The human mind creates order, patterns, and groups out of chaos. One such example is the categorization of people into generational cohorts. These groupings are defined by the birth year of their constituents not by their age as is a common misconception. Regardless of age, you will always belong to the same generation you were born into. Millennials have dominated recent discussions, but what is Generation X and what ideals do they represent?

A now wide-spread idea that can be contributed to Generation X is the idea of work-life balance. What sets Generation X apart from earlier cohorts? Born between 1964 and 1980, they naturally question authority and comprise a workforce that is more independent. Whereas the Baby Boomer Generation, born between 1946 and 1964, placed higher priority on work over personal life. The Silent Generation, born prior to 1946, is considered among the most loyal of workers. Generation X does not want to repeat the workaholic lifestyle of their predecessors but rather aims for a balanced life.

Current trends consider work-life integration, rather than work-life balance. The latter views each component as separate and two parts to be balanced; work is one part of an employee's experience that must not take away too much from a person's outside life and vice versa. Work-life integration evolved this idea to accommodate continually shifting generational experiences. This idea proposes finding a career that supports one's lifestyle, or life outside of work; seek a job that fits your lifestyle rather than molding your life to the constraints of your job.

Which idea is the way forward? The answer lies in understanding the gap between the concepts of work-life balance and integration. University of California, Berkeley is a proponent of work-life integration because the alternative evokes binary opposition between work and life. This antagonism leaves many unfulfilled as they try to fill a variety of roles. Companies must create a healthy work culture that integrates what people want out of life.

Paragraph Summaries and Central Thesis

Instructions: For each paragraph, write a one-sentence summary of its contents and also note down what its function is in the passage (e.g., example, counterargument, alternative point of view). At the bottom, write in one or two sentences what the central thesis of the passage is.

Paragraph 1:

_____

_____

_____

Paragraph 2:

_____

_____

_____

Paragraph 3:

_____

_____

_____

Paragraph 4:

_____

_____

_____

Central Thesis:

_____

_____

_____

Passage 37 Questions

Instructions: For each question, identify the question type and circle the correct answer. The answer key can be found at the end of this chapter.

Question 1: The author states that integration evolves the idea of balance. What does the author intend with the word choice "evolve?"

Type: _____

A. The author intends to show that integration now represents an entirely new concept when compared to balance.

B. The author intends to establish that the idea of integration is antagonistic to the traditional idea of balance.

C. The author intends to imply that the idea of balance has changed and surpassed the idea of integration.

D. The author intends to show that integration represents a more modern take on the older concept of balance.

Question 2: Futurist Jacob Morgan suggested that a progression towards work-life integration is indicative of the way we now do business as it is nearly impossible to avoid work and life merging. How would the author view this idea?

Type: _____

A. The author would view this as further evidence that companies must shift to accommodate what people want out of life.

B. The author would view this as a counterpoint to the idea of continually shifting generational experiences and would thus disagree with Morgan's stance.

C. The author would view this as confirmation of the unhealthy opposition that companies create between work and other aspects of life.

D. The author would view this as another example of the human mind's tendency to look for patterns amongst chaos and would thus agree with Morgan's ideas.

Question 3: Which of the following passage statements is most necessary to establish the claim the author is making?

Type: _____

   A. The now wide-spread idea of work-life balance can be contributed to Generation X.

   B. Generation X does not want to repeat the workaholic lifestyle of their predecessors but rather obtain a more balanced life.

   C. The alternative evokes binary opposition between work and life, an antagonism that leaves many unsatisfied.

   D. Work is one part of an employee's experience that must not take away from a person's outside life.

PRACTICE PASSAGE 38

Following the critiques of the Liberal peace agenda, state-building in fragile states or post-conflict regions has proven to be problematic. State-building exerts Western hegemony by powerful donors. Intervention in these so-called fragile states attempts to democratize through Western ideals, but often fails miserably. In examining the American mission titled "Operation Iraqi Freedom," this initiative was unsuccessful, a costly failure, and one that arguably resulted in greater violence. It is important to note key areas in which state-building is limited and that its main premise is nation driven, prioritizing the security of the West over other regions.

Western nations play a critical role in aiding countries in post conflict regions. Nations that intervene are prevalent in the development of security. Intervention is often enforced by the West through a liberal agenda. The concept of liberal peace emerged from the end of the Cold War, and was a response to anything that threatened international peace and security. What terminology is used when employing frameworks for international security and peace? To better understand the liberal agenda commonly enforced by Western nations, we must first examine the concept of failed states.

The term became prevalent in the 1990s and has become critical for international peace and security. The term is highly debated, further complicating the concept of state-building. Examination of the qualities that failed states exhibit may cause one to support intervention. Failed states are often dangerous, plagued by warring factions, and have deep-seated intercommunal enmity. Collapse of government only increases vulnerability to violence and uprising of rebel regimes that leave innocent civilians in the midst of the crossfire.

However, we must recognize the limitations of the notion of failing. This causes us to wrongly generalize solutions for stronger states in which state-building becomes necessary for peace. On the contrary, one can argue that state-building jeopardizes peace as there is no consensus on what success entails. It is critical that we neglect misguided terminology and navigate away from current strategies as they inflict greater harm. Moving forward, it would be best to employ fewer measures than more.

Paragraph Summaries and Central Thesis

Instructions: For each paragraph, write a one-sentence summary of its contents and also note down what its function is in the passage (e.g., example, counterargument, alternative point of view). At the bottom, write in one or two sentences what the central thesis of the passage is.

Paragraph 1:

_____

_____

_____

Paragraph 2:

_____

_____

_____

Paragraph 3:

_____

_____

_____

Paragraph 4:

_____

_____

_____

Central Thesis:

_____

_____

_____

Passage 38 Questions

Instructions: For each question, identify the question type and circle the correct answer. The answer key can be found at the end of this chapter.

Question 1: How would the author view the statement that use of the terminology "failed states" can cause further oppression of struggling nations?

Type: _____

- A. The author would agree with this statement.

- B. The author would disagree with this statement.

- C. The author would not have an opinion on this statement.

- D. Based on the information in the passage, it cannot be determined how the author would view this statement.

Question 2: What does the author view as the relationship between terminology and success?

Type: _____

- A. The author views neglecting accurate terminology as a means to cull success.

- B. The author views inaccurate terminology as a roadblock to success.

- C. The author views generalizing terminology as a means to achieve greater success.

- D. The author views employing intricate terminology as a framework for success.

Question 3: Which statement best expresses why the author feels that state-building is problematic?

Type: _____

- A. While Western nations recognize their own limitations, they play a too great role in aiding countries in post conflict regions and thus are overstepping under the guise of promoting international peace.

B. Intervention of Western nations into failed states is unethical and perpetuates deep-seated intercommunal enmity thus sabotaging the peace they aim to defend.

C. Western nations wield their own ideals rather than placing the needs of delicate nations first, thus jeopardizing the peace they aim to protect.

D. Western nations minimize violence for innocent civilians in fragile states, but these initiatives are too costly and thus unsustainable.

PRACTICE PASSAGE 39

Roxanne Lynn Doty's "Desert Tracts: Statecraft in Remote Places" examines the boundaries in narrative writing and that of state borders. When analyzing the piece, it becomes apparent that Doty is still shedding away her scholarly traditions, and honing in on the "other" voice; a critical role of a writer, and as she suggests, one often neglected in academia. Her voice attempts to bring awareness but silences leave the reader to assume along the way. Her honesty is refreshing and her positioning strategically plays along the boundaries figuratively and quite literally.

The silences in Doty's approach are subtle but still exist between her words. As a reader, one can only see glimpses of Doty's reasoning or purpose in tackling anti-immigration in America. We are not fully aware as to why she cares about the hopeful souls trying to cross an unforgiving desert illegally from Mexico into America. She does not fully explore reasoning, presuming the readers should know. Although assumptions can be made, it is not fair to generalize, and unfortunately Doty's lack of direction resorts the reader to such generalizations. The reader would benefit from an explanation about why these souls are hopeful and what governs America's special position as one for which so many would risk their lives.

When broadening one's observations, questions arise surrounding the motive behind the text. Is Doty forcing readers to buy into America's patriotism or is she simply interpreting statistics? Doty is quick to inform of America's alarming and growing concern towards illegal immigration; this concern is presented as a distant issue that does not directly affect her but "others." One is left patiently waiting for an answer which becomes vague and irrelevant. Doty reinstates her concept of "othering," which she attempts to vanquish from reality by bringing it to the forefront of international relations. Doty addresses that traditional attempts often neglect certain people which reinforces this cycle of "othering." These hopefuls are invisible.

While using an angry undertone that even mocks neglectful international relations, Doty does not find it necessary to disclose why she cares. The tensions that fuel her passion offer no clarity, no starting point or a finish line, mirroring the journey of the people crossing the border. Perhaps Doty as an outsider to this border crossing phenomenon is so far removed that she cannot find the words to explain it. As a reader, one must make uncertain assumptions; silences echo the distance that Doty feels towards hopefuls and towards the traditional discourse of international relations.

Paragraph Summaries and Central Thesis

Instructions: For each paragraph, write a one-sentence summary of its contents and also note down what its function is in the passage (e.g., example, counterargument, alternative point of view). At the bottom, write in one or two sentences what the central thesis of the passage is.

Paragraph 1:

_____

_____

_____

Paragraph 2:

_____

_____

_____

Paragraph 3:

_____

_____

_____

Paragraph 4:

_____

_____

_____

Central Thesis:

_____

_____

_____

Passage 39 Questions

Instructions: For each question, identify the question type and circle the correct answer. The answer key can be found at the end of this chapter.

Question 1: What does the author's tone communicate regarding her stance on Doty's writing?

Type: _____

   A. The author appreciates Doty's refreshing perspective, but finds her detached delivery less than convincing.

   B. The author disagrees with Doty's perspective as she offers no clarity on the issue.

   C. The author agrees with Doty's concerns and celebrates her unconventional, distant writing technique.

   D. The author values Doty's inspirational perspective which prompts the reader to come to their own conclusions.

Question 2: The author muses on why Doty writes the way that she does. What assumption about Doty's approach is not evident within the passage?

Type: _____

   A. The author assumes that Doty aims to write in a way that breaks away from conventional academia to find a new voice.

   B. The author assumes that Doty is strategic in her use of silences to dispute anti-immigration, mirroring the journey of immigrants.

   C. The author assumes that Doty thinks her readers are knowledgeable on the topic of immigration and its associated concerns.

   D. The author assumes that Doty, although an outsider herself, wants her readers to buy into patriotism and the hope of the America Dream.

Question 3: If it was found that Doty did not intend to express what the author refers to as an "angry undertone," how would this affect the author's opinion?

Type: _____

   A. This would improve the author's opinion of Doty's skills as a writer.

   B. This would reduce the author's opinion of Doty's skills as a writer.

   C. This would neither increase nor decrease the author's opinion of Doty's skills as a writer.

   D. This would discredit the author's opinion of Doty's skills as a writer.

PRACTICE PASSAGE 40

Society's construction of females' participation in crime has been perceived within a narrow scope. Victimization within prison is increasingly prevalent among today's correctional facilities, in which many sexual assaults go unreported. As examined through the hegemonic and feminist perspective, prison is also constructed to manifest traditional roles of masculinity and femininity. The masculine structure of prison has generated gender barriers. The rights of female inmates have been neglected within the criminal justice system, harboring oppression, victimization, and ultimately, gender inequality. We must examine the detrimental factors that impact female inmates within the prison culture.

The gendered nature of crime is defined by masculinity and is exerted by men. Men are perceived to be aggressive and tough, while women are passive and weak. Both men and women "do gender" in accordance to the masculine and feminine roles assigned within society. Crime is often used to exert a masculine identity. Criminality among females seems inconceivable since it does not comply with the traditional gender role of femininity. Women are underrepresented and overtly penalized for deviating.

Prisons were always established as a form of punishment, whereby criminals were captured and confined. However, due to the lack of prisons for women, female inmates experienced confinement within maximum facilities. Female offenders were originally housed in male corrections but in separate units. Prisons have since changed and transformed, housing minor offenders separately from hard criminals. With the development of female prisons, incarceration for women has risen. Female crime began to surface, but was given little attention.

Overtime, the criminological compass began to shift and investigative research developed. Media has played a role in steering research towards particular issues, often sensationalizing regardless of crime rates. Public fear becomes exaggerated, while offences committed by women are decreasing. Media exaggeration is a reaction towards the notion that female criminals deviate from the traditional role of women. A feministic standpoint of the traditional female role within corrections further corroborates the argument that women are neglected within the criminal justice system. Female inmates have redefined the "typical offender" and challenged the patriarchal structure of prisons. Further awareness, accountability and effective developments are essential and regulation must be mandated to render justice within prisons.

Paragraph Summaries and Central Thesis

Instructions: For each paragraph, write a one-sentence summary of its contents and also note down what its function is in the passage (e.g., example, counterargument, alternative point of view). At the bottom, write in one or two sentences what the central thesis of the passage is.

Paragraph 1:

_____

_____

_____

Paragraph 2:

_____

_____

_____

Paragraph 3:

_____

_____

_____

Paragraph 4:

_____

_____

_____

Central Thesis:

_____

_____

_____

Passage 40 Questions

Instructions: For each question, identify the question type and circle the correct answer. The answer key can be found at the end of this chapter.

Question 1: Many activists refute the discriminatory practices within prisons, claiming they may violate human rights. How would the author view the stance of these activist?

Type: _____

A. The author would agree that discriminatory practices within prisons are unjust, but would not go as far to say that this is a human rights violation.

B. The author would agree that discriminatory practices within prisons are unacceptable, but would be firmer in her stance that this is a human rights violation.

C. The author would not agree that practices within prisons are discriminatory and thus would not be concerned about human rights violations.

D. The author would request additional information before deciding if practices within prisons must be reformed to quell possible human rights violations.

Question 2: What is a weakness in the argument that the author makes to support their conclusion?

Type: _____

A. The author presents research on the unjust treatment of females within the prison system, but provides little information regarding male treatment. This weakens the author's argument as it appears biased and one-sided.

B. The author suggests a connection between skewed media and perpetuation of traditional gender roles, but this claim is weakened by the author's statement that female inmates challenge male-dominated structures.

C. The author states that women are victimized within prison, but does not provide examples of such maltreatment. This weakens the author's argument as it appears undeveloped.

D. The author proposes that criminality among females should be considered more broadly, but does not explain why this narrow viewpoint is harmful. This weakness in the author's argument and makes it less compelling.

Question 3: What does the author mean by "do gender" as it is used in the second paragraph?

Type: _____

A. The author means that males and females conduct inconceivable roles within prisons, ones that are distinct from those in the remainder of society.

B. The author means that males and females perpetuate roles throughout society that were originally established by the media.

C. The author means that males and females carry out typical roles in society regardless of the environment in which they find themselves.

D. The author means that males inflict certain roles upon females to create gendered crime within society which is perpetuated in correctional facilities.

Wow, that was a lot of passages! Give yourself a pat on the back if you've just completed all 40 of them. You should now feel very comfortable with reading different passages, identifying the author's central thesis, and navigating tricky questions about the passages, all in a timely manner.

However, your practice does not end here! Recall from *Chapter V: BeMo's Top Strategies & 7 Steps to ACE Any CARS Passage* that you must practice with AAMC's passages, which most closely approximate the difficulty of the passages you will encounter on the actual MCAT. You should, of course, still apply the same strategies you've been learning here to those passages, but this next step will ensure that you are prepared for the official test. Of course, at regular intervals before your test date, you should also be completing full-length practice tests using AAMC's materials so that you can check whether you are consistently improving.

If at any point during your practice, you feel that you have hit an impasse, we're here to help! BeMo experts are happy to assist you with your CARS preparation, no matter what stage you find yourself at. Whether you have just started and are already overwhelmed, or you have been making good progress but just need that additional push to continue your upward trajectory, we are happy to provide you with timely, expert feedback. We'll identify your strengths and areas of weakness so that you can clear the hurtles that stand in your way of success on this challenging section of the MCAT.

If you are serious about acing your interview and getting into your dream program, go to BeMoCARS.com to learn more now. We look forward to working with you!

ANSWER KEY

Passage 1

    Question 1   *Answer:* B, Reasoning Within the Text

    Question 2   *Answer:* A, Reasoning Beyond the Text

    Question 3   *Answer:* D, Foundations of Comprehension

Passage 2

    Question 1   *Answer:* A, Foundations of Comprehension

    Question 2   *Answer:* A, Reasoning Beyond the Text

    Question 3   *Answer:* D, Reasoning Within the Text

Passage 3

    Question 1   *Answer:* A, Reasoning Beyond the Text

    Question 2   *Answer:* D, Reasoning Within the Text

    Question 3   *Answer:* B, Foundations of Comprehension

Passage 4

    Question 1   *Answer:* C, Reasoning Beyond the Text

    Question 2   *Answer:* D, Reasoning Within the Text

    Question 3   *Answer:* B, Foundations of Comprehension

Passage 5

    Question 1   *Answer:* B, Reasoning Within the Text

    Question 2   *Answer:* B, Reasoning Beyond the Text

    Question 3   *Answer:* D, Foundations of Comprehension

Passage 6

    Question 1   *Answer:* A, Reasoning Within the Text

    Question 2   *Answer:* B, Reasoning Beyond the Text

    Question 3   *Answer:* C, Foundations of Comprehension

Passage 7

> **Question 1** *Answer:* C, Reasoning Beyond the Text
>
> **Question 2** *Answer:* D, Foundations of Comprehension
>
> **Question 3** *Answer:* A, Reasoning Within the Text

Passage 8

> **Question 1** *Answer:* A, Foundations of Comprehension
>
> **Question 2** *Answer:* C, Reasoning Beyond the Text
>
> **Question 3** *Answer:* C, Reasoning Within the Text

Passage 9

> **Question 1** *Answer:* B, Foundations of Comprehension
>
> **Question 2** *Answer:* D, Reasoning Beyond the Text
>
> **Question 3** *Answer:* A, Reasoning Within the Text

Passage 10

> **Question 1** *Answer:* D, Reasoning Within the Text
>
> **Question 2** *Answer:* C, Foundations of Comprehension
>
> **Question 3** *Answer:* B, Reasoning Beyond the Text

Passage 11

> **Question 1** *Answer:* D, Foundations of Comprehension
>
> **Question 2** *Answer:* B, Reasoning Beyond the Text
>
> **Question 3** *Answer:* A, Reasoning Within the Text

Passage 12

> **Question 1** *Answer:* D, Reasoning Within the Text
>
> **Question 2** *Answer:* A, Foundations of Comprehension
>
> **Question 3** *Answer:* B, Reasoning Beyond the Text

Passage 13

> **Question 1**   *Answer:* C, Foundations of Comprehension
> **Question 2**   *Answer:* C, Reasoning Beyond the Text
> **Question 3**   *Answer:* A, Reasoning Within the Text

Passage 14

> **Question 1**   *Answer:* D, Reasoning Beyond the Text
> **Question 2**   *Answer:* C, Reasoning Within the Text
> **Question 3**   *Answer:* A, Foundations of Comprehension

Passage 15

> **Question 1**   *Answer:* A, Reasoning Beyond the Text
> **Question 2**   *Answer:* C, Reasoning Within the Text
> **Question 3**   *Answer:* B, Foundations of Comprehension

Passage 16

> **Question 1**   *Answer:* C, Reasoning Beyond the Text
> **Question 2**   *Answer:* A, Reasoning Within the Text
> **Question 3**   *Answer:* B, Foundations of Comprehension

Passage 17

> **Question 1**   *Answer:* C, Foundations of Comprehension
> **Question 2**   *Answer:* D, Reasoning Beyond the Text
> **Question 3**   *Answer:* A, Reasoning Within the Text

Passage 18

> **Question 1**   *Answer:* B, Reasoning Within the Text
> **Question 2**   *Answer:* C, Reasoning Beyond the Text
> **Question 3**   *Answer:* A, Foundations of Comprehension

Passage 19

> **Question 1**   *Answer:* A, Reasoning Beyond the Text
>
> **Question 2**   *Answer:* B, Foundations of Comprehension
>
> **Question 3**   *Answer:* D, Reasoning Within the Text

Passage 20

> **Question 1**   *Answer:* C, Reasoning Beyond the Text
>
> **Question 2**   *Answer:* A, Foundations of Comprehension
>
> **Question 3**   *Answer:* D, Reasoning Within the Text

Passage 21

> **Question 1**   *Answer:* C, Foundations of Comprehension
>
> **Question 2**   *Answer:* B, Reasoning Beyond the Text
>
> **Question 3**   *Answer:* D, Reasoning Within the Text

Passage 22

> **Question 1**   *Answer:* B, Foundations of Comprehension Text
>
> **Question 2**   *Answer:* D, Reasoning Within the Text
>
> **Question 3**   *Answer:* A, Reasoning Beyond the

Passage 23

> **Question 1**   *Answer:* D, Reasoning Within the Text
>
> **Question 2**   *Answer:* D, Reasoning Beyond the Text
>
> **Question 3**   *Answer:* C, Foundations of Comprehension

Passage 24

> **Question 1**   *Answer:* C, Reasoning Within the Text
>
> **Question 2**   *Answer:* B, Reasoning Beyond the Text
>
> **Question 3**   *Answer:* A, Foundations of Comprehension

Passage 25

Question 1   *Answer:* B, Foundations of Comprehension

Question 2   *Answer:* C, Reasoning Within the Text

Question 3   *Answer:* A, Reasoning Beyond the Text

Passage 26

Question 1   *Answer:* B, Reasoning Beyond the Text

Question 2   *Answer:* D, Foundations of Comprehension

Question 3   *Answer:* A, Reasoning Within the Text

Passage 27

Question 1   *Answer:* D, Foundations of Comprehension

Question 2   *Answer:* B, Reasoning Within the Text

Question 3   *Answer:* C, Reasoning Beyond the Text

Passage 28

Question 1   *Answer:* D, Reasoning Beyond the Text

Question 2   *Answer:* B, Reasoning Within the Text

Question 3   *Answer:* C, Foundations of Comprehension

Passage 29

Question 1   *Answer:* C, Reasoning Within the Text

Question 2   *Answer:* B, Foundations of Comprehension

Question 3   *Answer:* D, Reasoning Beyond the Text

Passage 30

Question 1   *Answer:* D, Foundations of Comprehension

Question 2   *Answer:* A, Reasoning Within the Text

Question 3   *Answer:* B, Reasoning Beyond the Text

Passage 31

Question 1   *Answer:* D, Reasoning Within the Text

Question 2   *Answer:* B, Reasoning Beyond the Text

Question 3   *Answer:* B, Foundations of Comprehension

Passage 32

Question 1   *Answer:* C, Reasoning Beyond the Text

Question 2   *Answer:* D, Reasoning Within the Text

Question 3   *Answer:* B, Foundations of Comprehension

Passage 33

Question 1   *Answer:* A, Foundations of Comprehension

Question 2   *Answer:* D, Reasoning Within the Text

Question 3   *Answer:* B, Reasoning Beyond the Text

Passage 34

Question 1   *Answer:* A, Reasoning Within the Text

Question 2   *Answer:* B, Reasoning Beyond the Text

Question 3   *Answer:* B, Foundations of Comprehension

Passage 35

Question 1   *Answer:* C, Reasoning Within the Text

Question 2   *Answer:* D, Foundations of Comprehension

Question 3   *Answer:* D, Reasoning Beyond the Text

Passage 36

Question 1   *Answer:* A, Reasoning Beyond the Text

Question 2   *Answer:* B, Foundations of Comprehension

Question 3   *Answer:* D, Reasoning Within the Text

Passage 37

Question 1 *Answer:* D, Foundations of Comprehension

Question 2 *Answer:* A, Reasoning Beyond the Text

Question 3 *Answer:* C, Reasoning Within the Text

Passage 38

Question 1 *Answer:* A, Reasoning Beyond the Text

Question 2 *Answer:* B, Reasoning Within the Text

Question 3 *Answer:* C, Foundations of Comprehension

Passage 39

Question 1 *Answer:* A, Foundations of Comprehension

Question 2 *Answer:* D, Reasoning Within the Text

Question 3 *Answer:* B, Reasoning Beyond the Text

Passage 40

Question 1 *Answer:* B, Reasoning Beyond the Text

Question 2 *Answer:* A, Reasoning Within the Text

Question 3 *Answer:* C, Foundations of Comprehension

CHAPTER IX

The Final Secret of Successful Applicants

We hope you enjoyed the book. We certainly have enjoyed teaching you what we know. As promised, we held nothing back and included everything we teach to our students in our CARS prep programs found at BeMoCARS.com. We are confident that practicing with our strategies will take you a long way, but there is one missing piece of the puzzle we were not able to include in this book: expert feedback. In our experience, applicants improve the most when they take advantage of our realistic CARS passages and get personal feedback from one of our experts.

Here is how our CARS preparation programs work in 3 simple steps:

Step 1: We pick the best experts for you. Our consultants work remotely, so we are not limited to a small talent pool in a narrow geographical location, and we can look for the best experts anywhere in the world. We screen dozens of M.D. and Ph.D. applicants every month. The multi-step application process is rigorous and involves a functional test, an online assessment, and an online panel interview with our senior team, including our CEO, Dr. Behrouz Moemeni. Only 5% of all applicants get hired, which means we are as selective with our candidates as many medical schools are with theirs. After new applicants are hired, they receive extensive training from our lead trainers, after which they continue to be monitored for six months before they become permanent members of our team. Our core team is thus composed of highly qualified, fully committed individuals who are there to support you through your application journey.

Step 2: Join us for a CARS prep session and learn our proven strategies directly from one of our experts. Our experts will not only show you how to prepare in advance, manage your stress, approach each passage and question, they will also tailor the feedback to your unique needs by identifying your strengths and weaknesses. We are committed to teaching you skills that last a lifetime, not cheap tricks just to get around the MCAT.

Step 3: Let us help you monitor your progress. We track your accuracy and time management on realistic CARS passages. This numeric scoring method gives us quantitative data so we can evaluate each student's performance objectively, rather than subjectively based on our fleeting impressions. You can continue to practice and receive feedback from our admissions experts until they are confident that you are 100% ready to ace the MCAT CARS. Yes, that's right! Some of our programs include unlimited sessions with expert feedback!

Furthermore, all of our programs are backed by a 100% Satisfaction Guarantee™ and some even include our Get In Or Your Money Back® guarantee.

These are all the reasons why we are trusted by applicants who do not want to leave their success up to chance. If you are serious about acing the MCAT CARS, go to BeMoCARS.com to learn more now. We look forward to working with you!

CHAPTER X

Bonus Resources

Congratulations, you have made it to the end—almost. Thank you for trusting BeMo to guide you through your MCAT CARS journey. We have prepared some additional FREE resources to help you become more prepared for the CARS and the rest of the MCAT and more confident on test day.

Specific CARS Resources:

MCAT CARS Strategy from a 99th Percentile Scorer

https://bemoacademicconsulting.com/blog/mcat-cars-strategy

THE BEST MCAT CARS Practice by a 528 Scorer
Including sample passages, analysis and answers.

https://bemoacademicconsulting.com/blog/sample-mcat-cars-question-and-answer

Ace the Critical Analysis and Reasoning Section of the MCAT in Three Steps

https://bemoacademicconsulting.com/blog/ace-critical-analysis-and-reasoning-section-of-mcat

General MCAT Resources:

MCAT Study Schedule: The Best Schedule
6-Month, 3-Month, 1-Month, and 1-Week Study Schedule!

https://bemoacademicconsulting.com/blog/mcat-study-schedule

How Hard is the MCAT? - The Truth

https://bemoacademicconsulting.com/blog/how-hard-is-the-mcat

How Long is the MCAT: The Detailed Breakdown

https://bemoacademicconsulting.com/blog/how-long-is-the-mcat

MCAT Diagnostic Test: Do I Take It?

https://bemoacademicconsulting.com/blog/mcat-diagnostic-test

MCAT Tutor: Do I Really Need One?

https://bemoacademicconsulting.com/blog/mcat-tutor

Manufactured by Amazon.ca
Bolton, ON

24716396R00216